BARRACKS, BIVOUACS AND BATTLES

LECTOR HOUSE PUBLIC DOMAIN WORKS

BARRACKS, BIVOUACS AND BATTLES

ARCHIBALD FORBES

ISBN: 978-93-90198-75-7

Published: 1891

LECTOR HOUSE LLP
E-MAIL: lectorpublishing@gmail.com

BARRACKS BIVOUACS AND BATTLES

BY

ARCHIBALD FORBES, LL.D.

1891

All the pieces in this little volume are reprints. I have to express my obligations to the proprietors and editors of the periodicals to which they were originally contributed, for the permission to reproduce them.

A. F.

CONTENTS

HOW "THE CRAYTURE" GOT ON THE STRENGTH

Mick Sullivan was a private soldier in G troop, 30th Light Dragoons, of some six years' service. Since the day old Sergeant Denny Lee 'listed him in Charles Street, just outside the Cheshire Cheese, close by where the Council door of the India Office now is, Mick had never been anything else than a private soldier, and never hoped or needed hope to be anything else if he served out his full twenty-four years, for he could neither read nor write, and his regimental defaulter sheet was much fuller of "marks" than the most lavish barrack-room pudding is of raisins. Nevertheless the Queen had a very good bargain in honest Mick, although that was scarcely the opinion of the adjutant, who was a "jumped-up" youngster, and had not been in the Crimea with the regiment. The grizzled captain of G troop, who was a non-purchase man, and had been soldiering for well on to twenty years, understood and appreciated Mick better. Captain Coleman knew that he had come limping up out of that crazy gallop along "the valley of death" with a sword red from hilt to point, a lance-thrust through the calf of his leg, and a wounded comrade on his back. He had heard Mick's gay laugh and cheery jest during that dreary time in the hollow inland from Varna, when cholera was decimating the troop, and the hearts of brave men were in their boots. He remembered how Mick was the life and soul of the gaunt sorry squad inside the flimsy tent on the bleak slope of Kadikoi during that terrible Crimean winter, when men were turning their toes up to the daisies by sections, and when the living crawled about half frozen, half sodden. Mick's old chestnut mare (G 11) was the only horse of the troop that survived the winter, kept alive by her owner's patient and unremitting care: if it was true, as fellows swore who found her cruelly rough—she was known by the name of the "Dislocator," given to her by a much-chafed recruit, whose anatomy her trot had wholly disorganised—if it was true that in that hard winter she had frozen quite hard, and had never since come properly thawed, it was to Mick's credit that she was still saving the country the price of a remount. There was no smarter man or cleaner soldier in all the corps than the harum-scarum Tipperary man; he had a brogue that you could cut with a knife; and there was nothing he would not do for whisky but shirk his turn of duty and hear his regiment belittled without promptly engaging in single combat with the disparager of the "Ould Strawboots."

Mick did a good deal of punishment drill at varying intervals, and his hair was occasionally abnormally short as a result of that species of infliction known as "seven days' cells." He had seldom any other crime than "absent without leave," and he had never been tried by court-martial, although more than once he had had a very narrow squeak, especially once when he was brought into barracks by a picket after a three days' absence, with a newspaper round his shoulders instead of stable jacket and shirt. No doubt he had drunk those articles of attire, but the plea that they had been stolen saved him from the charge of making away with "regimental necessaries," which is a court-martial offence. The 30th Light, just home from the Crimea, were quartered at York; and Mick, after two or three escapades which were the pardonable result of his popularity as one of the heroes of the Light Cavalry charge, had settled down into unwonted steadiness. He went out alone every evening, and at length his chum took him to task for his unsociality, and threatened to "cut the loaf."

"Arrah now," was Mick's indignant reply, "it's a silly spalpeen ye are to go for to think such a thing. Sure if it hadn't been a great saycret intirely, ye'd have known all about it long ago. I've been coortin', ye divil! Sure an' she's the purtiest crayture that iver ye clapt yer two eyes upon, aye, an' a prudent girl too. So that's the saycret, chum; an' now come on up to the canteen, an' bedad we'll drink luck an' joy to the wooin'!"

Over their pot of beer Mick told his comrade the simple story of his love. His sweetheart, it seemed, was the daughter of a small shopkeeper in the outskirts of the city, and, as Mick was most emphatic in claiming, a young woman of quite exemplary character. Thus far, then, everything was satisfactory; but the obvious rock ahead was the all but certainty that Mick would be refused leave to marry. He had not exactly the character entitling him to such a privilege, and the troop already had its full complement of married people. But if the commanding officer should say him nay, then "Sure," Mick doughtily protested, "I'll marry the darlint widout lave; in spite of the colonel, an' the gineral, and the commander-in-chief himself, bedad!"

Next morning Mick formed up to the adjutant and asked permission to see the colonel. The adjutant, after the manner of his kind, tried to extract from him for what purpose the request was made, but Mick was old soldier enough to know how far an adjutant's ill word carries, and resolutely declined to divulge his intent. After the commanding officer had disposed of what are called at the police-courts the "charges of the night," Mick was marched into the presence by the regimental sergeant-major; and as he stood there at rigid attention, the nature of his business was demanded in the curt hard tone which the colonel with a proper sense of the fitness of things uses when addressing the private soldier.

"Plase yer honour, sor, I want to get—to get married," blurted Mick, for the moment in some confusion now that the crisis had come.

"And, plase yer honour, Mr. Sullivan," retorted the chief with sour pleasantry, "I'll see you d—d first!"

"Och, sor, an' how can ye be so cruel at all, at all?" pleaded Mick, who had recovered from his confusion, and thought a touch of the blarney might come in useful.

"Why, what the deuce do you want with a wife?" asked the colonel angrily.

"Sure, sor, an' pwhat does any man want wid a wife?"

The regimental sergeant-major grinned behind his hand, the adjutant burst into a splutter of laughter at the back of the colonel's chair, and that stern officer himself found his gravity severely strained. But he was firm in his refusal to grant the indulgence, and Mick went forth from the presence in a very doleful frame of mind.

At "watch-setting" the same night Mr. Sullivan was reported absent, nor did he come into barracks in the course of the night. The regimental sergeant-major was a very old bird, and straightway communicated to the adjutant his ideas as to the nature of Mick's little game. Then the pair concerted a scheme whereby they might baulk him at the very moment when his cup of bliss should be at his lips. At nine in the morning about a dozen corporals and as many files of men paraded outside the orderly-room door. To each of the likeliest religious edifices licensed for the celebration of marriages a corporal and a file were told off, with instructions to watch outside, and intercept Sullivan if he should appear in the capacity of a bridegroom. Clever as was the device, it came very near failing. The picket charged with the duty of watching an obscure suburban chapel, regarding it as extremely improbable that such a place would be selected, betook themselves to the taproom of an adjacent public-house, where they chanced on some good company, and had soon all but forgotten the duty to which they had been detailed. It was, however, suddenly recalled to them. A native who dropped in for a pint of half-and-half, casually observed that "a sojer were bein' spliced across the road." The moment was a critical one, but the corporal rose to the occasion. Hastily leading out his men, he stationed them at the door, while he himself entered, and stealing up to the marriage party unobserved, clapped his hand on Sullivan's shoulder just as the latter was fumbling for the ring. The bride shrieked, the priest talked about sacrilege, and the bride's mother made a gallant assault on the corporal with her umbrella; but the non-commissioned officer was firm, and Mick, whose sense of discipline was very strong, merely remarked, "Be jabers, corporal, an' in another minute ye would have been too late!"

He was summarily marched off into barracks, looking rather rueful at being thus torn from the very horns of the altar. Next morning he paid another visit to the orderly-room, this time as a prisoner, when the commanding officer, radiant at the seeming success of the plot to baulk Mr. Sullivan's matrimonial intentions, let him off with fourteen days' pack drill. Having done that punishment, he was again free to go out of barracks, but only in the evening, so that he could not get married unless by special license, a luxury to which a private dragoon's pay does not run. Nevertheless he cherished his design, and presently the old adage, "Where there's a will there's a way," had yet another confirmation.

One fine morning the regiment rode out in "watering order." About a mile outside the town, poor Mick was suddenly taken very ill. So serious appeared his condition that the troop sergeant-major directed him to ride straight back into barracks, giving him strict orders to go to hospital the moment he arrived. Presently, Mick's horse, indeed, cantered through the barrack gate, but there was no rider on its back. The sentry gave the alarm, and the guard, imagining Mick to have been thrown, made a search for him along the road outside; but they did not find him, for the reason that at the time he was being thus searched for he was being married. The ceremony was this time accomplished without interruption; but the hymeneal festivities were rudely broken in upon by a picket from the barracks, who tore the bridegroom ruthlessly from the arms of the bride, and escorted him to durance in the guard-room.

Mick had seven days' cells for this escapade, and when he next saw his bride, he had not a hair on his head a quarter of an inch long, the provost-sergeant's shears having gone very close to the scalp. He had a wife, it was true; but matrimonial felicity seemed a far-off dream. Mick had married without leave, and there was no place in barracks for his little wife. Indeed, in further punishment of Mick, her name was "put upon the gate," which means that the sentry was charged to prohibit her entrance. Mick could get no leave; so he could enjoy the society of his spouse only between evening stables and watch-setting; and on the whole he might just as well have been single—indeed better, if the wife's welfare be taken into consideration. Only neither husband nor wife was of this opinion, and hoped cheerily for better things.

But worse, not better, was to befall the pair. That cruellest of all blows which can befall the couple married without leave, suddenly struck them; the regiment was ordered on foreign service. It was to march to the south of England, give over its horses at Canterbury, Christchurch, and elsewhere, and then embark at Southampton for India.

Next to a campaign, the brightest joy in the life of the cavalry soldier is going on "the line of march," from one home station to another. For him it is a glorious interlude to the dull restrained monotony of his barrack-room life, and the weary routine of mounted and dismounted drill. "Boots and saddles" sounds early on the line of march. The troopers from their scattered billets concentrate in front of the principal hotel of the town where the detachment quarters for the night, and form up in the street or the market-place, while as yet the shutters are fast on the front of the earliest-opening shop. The officers emerge from the hotel, mount, and inspect the parade; the order "Threes right!" is given, and the day's march has begun. The morning sun flashes on the sword-scabbards and accoutrements, as the quiet street echoes to the clink of the horse-hoofs on the cobblestones. Presently the town is left behind, and the detachment is out into the country. There had been a shower as the sun rose—the "pride of the morning" the soldiers call the sprinkle—just sufficient to lay the dust, and evoke from every growing thing its sweetest scent. The fresh crisp morning air is laden with perfume; the wild rose, the jessamine, the eglantine, and the "morning glory" entwine themselves about the gnarled thorn of the hedgerows, and send their tangled feelers straggling up the ivy-clad trunks of the great elms and oaks, through whose foliage the sunbeams are shooting. From the valley rises a feathery haze broken into gossamer-like patches of diverse hues; and here and there the blue smoke of some early-lit cottage fire ascends in a languid straightness through the still atmosphere. The hind yoking his plough in the adjacent field chants a rude ditty, while his driver is blowing his first cloud, the scent of which comes sluggishly drifting across the road with that peculiarly fresh odour only belonging to tobacco-smoke in the early morning. As the rise is crowned, a fair and fertile expanse of country lies stretched out below—shaggy woods and cornfields, and red-roofed homesteads, and long reaches of still water, and the square tower of the venerable church showing over the foliage that overhangs the hamlet and the graveyard. Then the command "Trot!" is passed along from the front, and away go the troopers bumping merrily, their accoutrements jingling and clanking, their horses feeling the bit lightly, tossing their heads, arching their necks, and stepping out gallantly, in token that they too take delight in being on the road. Three miles of a steady trot; then a five minutes' halt to tighten girths and "look round" equipments; then up into the saddle again. The word comes back along the files, "Singers to the front!" whereupon every fellow who has, or thinks he has, a voice, presses forward till the two front ranks are some six abreast across the road. Now the premier vocalist—self-constituted or acclaimed—strikes up a solo whose principal attribute is unlimited chorus; and so to the lusty strain the detachment marches through the next village, bringing all the natives to their doors, and attracting much attention and commendation, especially from the fair sex. The day's march half over, there is a longer halt; and the kindly officers send on a corporal to the little wayside beerhouse just ahead, whence he speedily returns, accompanied by the landlord, stepping carefully between a couple of pailsful of foaming beer. Each man receives his pint, the officers' "treat"; and then, all hands in the highest spirits, the journey is resumed; trot and walk alternate, the men riding "at ease," until the verge is reached of the town in which the detachment is to be billeted for the night. Then "Attention!" is called, swords are drawn, the files close up, and the little array marches right gallantly through the streets to the principal hotel. Here the "billeting sergeant," who is always a day's march ahead, distributes the billets, each for a couple of troopers, and chums are allowed to share the same billet. A willing urchin shows the way to the Wheatsheaf, whose hearty landlord forthwith comes out with a frank welcome, and a brown jug in hand. Horses cleaned and bedded down, accoutrements freed from the soil of the road, dinner—and a right good dinner—is served, the troopers sitting down to table with their host and hostess. The worthy Boniface and his genial spouse have none of your cockney contempt for the soldier, but consider him not only their equal, but a welcome guest; and the soldier, if he is worth his salt, does his best to conduct himself so as not to tarnish the credit of his cloth.

Than Mick Sullivan no soldier of the gay 30th Light Dragoons was wont to enjoy himself more on the line of march. But now the honest Irishman was silent and depressed. He was a married man. That of itself did not sadden him; he did not repent his act, rash as it had been. But he had married without leave, and his little wife was entitled to no privileges—she was not "on the strength." Mick had prayed her to remain at home with her father, for he could not afford her travelling expenses, and even if he could, he knew, and he had to tell her, that they must part at the port of embarkation. But "the Crayture," as Mick called her, was resolute to go thus far. Poll Tudor and Bess Bowles, accredited spouses, "married women on the strength," took train at Government expense, and knew their berths on the troopship were assured. But for "the Crayture" there was no railway warrant, far less any berth aboard. March for march, with weary feet and swelling heart, the poor little woman made with the detachment, tramping the long miles between York and Southampton. Mostly the kind souls where Mick was billeted gave her bite and sup and her bed; now and then the hayloft was her portion. Ah me! in the old days such woful journeys were often made; I believe that nowadays the canteen fund helps on their way soldiers' wives married without leave.

The troopship, with her steam up, was lying alongside the jetty in Southampton Dock, and troop by troop as they quitted the train, the men of the 30th Light were being marched aboard. Mick had bidden "the Crayture" farewell, and had drowned his grief in drink; as they marched toward the jetty, his chum reproached him on account of his unsoldierly condition.

"Arrah now," wailed Mick piteously, "sure, an' if it wor yersilf lavin' the darlint av a young wife behind ye, glad an' fain ye would be to take a dhrap to deaden yer sorrow. Whin I sed good-bye to the Crayture this mornin' I thought she'd have died outright wid the sobs from the heart av her. Och, chum, the purty, beautiful crayture that I love so, an' that loves me, an' me lavin' her to the hard wurrld! Be gorra, an' there she stands!"

Sure enough, standing there in the crowd, weeping as if she would break her heart, was Mick's poor little wife.

"Hould me carabine, chum, just for a moment, till I be givin' her just wan last kiss!" pleaded the poor fellow, and with a sudden spring he was out of the ranks unobserved, and hidden in the crowd that opened to receive him. His chum tramped on, but he reached the main-deck of the troopship still carrying two carbines, for as yet Mick had not re-appeared.

The comrade's anxious eyes searched the crowded jetty in vain. But they scanned a scene of singular pathos. The grizzled old quarter-master was wiping his shaggy eyelashes furtively as he turned away from the children he was leaving behind. There were poor wretches of wives who had been married without leave, as "the Crayture" had been—some with babes in their arms, weeping hopelessly as they thought of the thousands of miles that were to part them from the men of their hearts. And there were weeping women there also who had not even the sorrowful consolation of being entitled to call themselves wives; and boys were cheering, and the band was playing "The Girl I left behind me," and non-commissioned officers were swearing, and some half-drunk recruit-soldiers were singing a dirty ditty, and heart-strings were being torn, and the work of embarkation was steadily and relentlessly progressing.

The embarkation completed, the shore-goers having been cleared out of the ship and the gangway drawn, there was a muster on deck, and the roll of each troop was called. In G troop one man was missing, and that man was Mick Sullivan. The muster had barely broken off, when a wild shout from the jetty was heard. There stood Mick very limp and staggery, "the Crayture" clinging convulsively round his neck, and he hailing the ship over her shoulder. Behind the forlorn couple was a sympathising crowd of females sobbing in unmelodious concert, with here and there a wilder screech of woe from the throat of some tender-hearted country-woman of Mr. Sullivan. After some delay, Mick was brought on to the upper deck of the trooper, where he stood before the lieutenant of his troop in an attitude meant to represent the rigidity of military attention, contrasting vividly with his tear-stained face, his inability to refrain from a frequent hiccough, and an obvious difficulty in overcoming the propensity of his knee-joints to serve their owner treacherously.

"Well, Sullivan," said the young officer, with an affectation of sternness which under the circumstances was most praiseworthy, "what do you mean by this conduct?"

"Plase, sor, an' beg yer parrdon, sor, but I didn't mane only to fall out just for wan last worrd. It wasn't the dhrink at all, at all, sor; it's the grief that kilt me intirely. Ah, sure, sor," added Mick insinuatingly, "it's yersilf, yer honour, that is lavin', maybe, a purty crayture wapin' for yer handsome face!"

The touch of nature made the officer kind. "Get out of sight at once, you rascal," said he, turning away to hide rather a sad smile, "and take care the colonel don't set eyes on you, else you'll find yourself in irons in double-quick time."

"Thank ye, sor; it's a good heart ye have," said Mick over his shoulder, as his chum hustled him toward the hatchway. "The Crayture" was on the pier-head waving her poor little dud of a white handkerchief, as the troopship, gathering way, steamed down Southampton Water, and the strains of "The Girl I left behind me" came back fainter and more faint on the light wind.

Bangalore, up country in the Madras Presidency, was the allotted station of the 30th Light. The regiment had barely settled down in the upland cantonment, when tidings came south of the mutiny of Bengal native troops on the parade-ground of Berhampore. Every mail brought news from the north more and more disquieting, and in the third week of May the devilry of Meerut was recounted in the gasping terseness of a telegram. The regiment hoped in vain for a summons to Bengal, but there was no other cavalry corps in all the Madras Presidency, and the authorities could not know but that the Madras native army might at any moment flame out into mutiny. In the early days of June a sergeant's party of the 30th Light was sent down from Bangalore to Madras to perform some exceptional orderly duty, and to this party belonged Mick Sullivan and his chum. A week later Sir Patrick Grant, the Madras Commander-in-Chief, was summoned by telegraph to Calcutta, to assume the direction of military operations in Bengal, consequent on poor General Anson's sudden death. The *Fire Queen* anchored in the roads with Havelock aboard, fresh from his successes in Persia, and it was arranged that the two old soldiers should hurry up to Calcutta without an hour's delay. Grant wanted a soldier-clerk to write for him on the voyage, and a soldier-servant warranted proof against sea-sickness to look after his chargers aboard ship. There was no time for ceremony, and Mick's chum, who was a well-educated man, was laid hold of as the amanuensis, while Mick himself was shipped as the general's temporary groom. The services of the pair ceased when Calcutta was reached, and they were attached to the Fort William garrison, pending the opportunity to ship them back to Madras. But the two men, burning for active service, determined to make a bold effort to escape relegation to the dull inactivity of Bangalore. Watching their chance, they addressed their petition to Sir Patrick, as he sat in the verandah of his quarters in the fort "Quite irregular," exclaimed the veteran Highlander, "but I like your spirit, men! Let me see; I'll arrange matters with your regiment. You want to be in the thick of it at once, eh? Well, you must turn infantrymen; the Ross-shire Buffs are out at Chinsurah, and will have the route to-morrow. You can reach them in a few hours, and I'll give you a *chit* to Colonel Hamilton which will make it all right for you. One of you is a Highlander born, and as for you, Sullivan, if you talk Erse to the fellows of the 78th, they won't know it from Argyllshire Gaelic."

Three hours later the comrades had ceased for the time to be Light Dragoons, and were acting members of the Grenadier Company of the Ross-shire Buffs. Hart, the regimental sergeant-major, had presented them to Colonel Hamilton, who duly honoured Sir Patrick's *chit*, and had sent them over to the orderly-room tent, where they found the adjutant, that gallant soldier now alas! dead, whom later his country knew as Sir Herbert Macpherson, V.C.

"What is your name, my man?" asked Macpherson of Sullivan.

"Michael Donald Mactavish Sullivan, sor," responded Mick, with a face as solemn as a mute's at a funeral.

"What countryman are you?"

"An Argyllshire Tipperary man, sor," replied Mick, without the twinkle of an eyelash.

"How came you by your two middle names? They are surely not common in Tipperary?"

"Och, yer honour, I was christened by thim two afther me grandmother, an' she was, I belave, a pure-bred Scotchman. It is in dutiful mimory of her, rest her sowl, that I want for to jine the Ross-shire Buffs."

"Well," replied Mr. Macpherson imperturbably, "your dutiful aspiration shall be gratified."

The chum answered the formal questions regarding himself, and then the regimental sergeant-major was directed to take the pair to the quarter-master sergeant, to receive the clothing and accoutrements of infantrymen.

Quarter-master Sergeant Tulloch, "Muckle Tulloch," as he was called in the regiment because of his abnormal bulk, was, although a Scot, a man of humour; and it occurred to him that the new Irish Ross-shire Buff might furnish some amusement. Highland regiments do not wear the kilt on Indian service; indeed the tartans are not brought out from home. But there happened by some odd chance to be a Highland uniform among the quarter-master's stores; and this Tulloch solemnly made over to Mick Sullivan, instructing him to attire himself in it at once, that its fit might be ascertained. The store had been temporarily established in the unoccupied house of a wealthy native, and Sullivan went into one of the empty rooms to don the unaccustomed garments. Tulloch and the sergeant-major, as well as Mick's chum, stood listening to Mick fervently d—ing the "quare blankets," as he struggled with the difficulties presented by kilt and plaid. At length it seemed as if he had accomplished the task somehow, and he was heard to stride to the farther end of the long bare apartment. The partly-open door revealed Mr. Sullivan, drawn up to his full height in front of a large panel-mirror. He certainly presented an extraordinary aspect. For one thing, the kilt, which had been made for a short man, was very much too short for Mick, and a yard or two of naked leg protruded from below it. Then he had fastened on the sporran behind instead of in front, and it hung down in the former region like a horse's tail. The plaid was put on something in the fashion of a comforter, and his lower extremities were encased in his long cavalry Wellington boots, from the heels of which the spurs stuck out fiercely. He had struck an attitude, and was soliloquising—

"Be the holy, Michael Donald Mactavish Sullivan, an' it's yersilf is the purty spictacle intirely! Troth, an' it would puzzle that dacent woman your mother to idintify the fruit of her womb in this disguise. Sure an' it's a beautiful dress, an' the hoighth av free vintilation! Supposin' I was sittin' down on an ant-hill? Och, musha, an' pwhat would Tipperary think if she wor to see me this day? Faix," he went on, after a long scrutinising gaze, "it's mesilf is doubtful whether I'm pwhat ye would call dacent; but the divil a ha'p'orth care I," with a sudden burst of reassurance, "sure, if I'm ondacent, that's the Quane's look-out, may the hivins be her bed!"

At this the listeners could not refrain from a burst of laughter, which brought Mick's soliloquy to an abrupt conclusion. He became a little angry when he found he had been sold, and was not to have the kilt after all his trouble; but presently found consolation in the ant-hill view of the subject, and accepted his woollen doublet and dungaree trousers with a bland condescension. Next day the 78th began to move up country to the Allahabad concentration, and a few weeks later Havelock led out into the country of bloodthirsty mutiny that scant devoted vanguard of the British force which was to reconquer India.

Spite of cruel heat, sunstrokes, cholera, and the exhaustion of long marches, the little column pressed on blithely, for the stimulus of hope was in the hearts of the men. But that hope was killed just when its fulfilment was all but accomplished. To the soldiers, spent with the fighting of the day, as they lay within but one short march of Cawnpore, came in the dead of night the woful tidings of the massacre of the company of women and children, the forlorn remnant of the Cawnpore garrison whom the Nana Sahib had spared from the butchery of the Slaughter Ghaut. Next morning Havelock's little army camped on the Cawnpore *maidan*, and Mick and his chum, accompanied by big Jock Gibson, one of the 78th pipers, with his pipes under his arm, set out in a search for the scene of the tragedy. Directed by whispering and terrified natives, they reached the Bibi Ghur, the bungalow in which the women and children had been confined, and in which they had been slain. With burning eyes and set faces, the men looked in on the ghastly and the woful tokens of the devilry that had been enacted inside those four low walls—the puddles of blood, the scraps of clothing, the broken ornaments, the leaves of bibles, the children's shoes—ah, what need to catalogue the pitiful relics! Then they followed the blood-trail to the brink of the awful well, filled and heaped with the hacked and battered dead. Sullivan lifted up his voice and wept aloud. His comrade, of dourer nature, gazed on the spectacle with swelling throat. Big

Jock Gibson sank down on the ground, sobbing as he had never done since the day his mother said him farewell, and gave him her Gaelic blessing in the market-place of Tain. As he sobbed, his fingers were fumbling mechanically for the mouthpiece of his pipes. Presently he slipped it absently into his mouth. As the wind whistles through the bare boughs of the trees in winter, so came, in fitful soughs, the first wayward notes from out weeping Jock's drone and chanter. At length he mastered the physical signs of his woe, or rather, it might have been, he transferred his emotion from his heart into his pipes; and as the other two left him, he was sitting there, over the great grave, pouring forth a wild shrill dirge—a pibroch and a coronach in one.

An hour later, to a group of comrades gathered in a little tope in front of the tents, Mick Sullivan was trying, in broken words, to tell of what he had seen. He was abruptly interrupted by Jock Gibson, who strode into the midst of the circle, his face white and drawn, his pipes silent now, carried under his arm.

"Comrades," began Jock, in a strange far-away voice, "I hae seen a sicht that has curdlet my bluid. The soles o' my brogues are wat wi' the gore o' women an' bairns; I saw whaur their corpses lay whummled ane abune anither, strippit and gashed, till the well was fu' ow'r its lip. Men, I can speak nae mair o' that awesome sicht; but I hae broucht awa' a token that I fand—see!"

And Jock pulled from out his breast a long heavy tress of golden hair cut clean through, as if with a slash of a sharp sword that had missed the head. As he held it out, it hung limp and straight in a sunbeam that fell upon it through the leaves of the mango-trees. The rough soldiers bared their heads in the presence of it.

Old Hamish Macnab, the Kintail man, the patriarch of the regiment, stepped forward—

"Gie me that, Jock Gibson!"

Jock handed Macnab the token from the place of the slaughter.

"Stan' roun' me, men!" commanded Macnab.

The Highlanders closed about him silently, impressed by the solemnity of his tone.

Then Macnab bade them to join hands round him. When they had done so, he lifted up his voice, and spoke with measured solemnity, his eyes blazing and the blood all in his old worn face—

"By the mithers that bore ye, by yer young sisters and brithers at hame in the clachan an' the glen, by yer ain wives an' weans some o' ye, swear by this token that henceforth ye show nae ruth to the race that has done this accursed deed of bluid!"

Sternly, from deep down in every throat, came the hoarse answer, "We swear!" Then Macnab parted out the tress into as many locks as there were men in the circle, distributing to each a lock. He coiled up the lock he had kept for himself, and opening his doublet, placed it on his heart. His comrades silently imitated him.

All the world knows the marvellous story of Havelock's relief of Lucknow;

against what odds the little column he commanded so gallantly fought its way from Cawnpore over the intervening forty miles; with what heroism and what losses it battled its way through the intricacies and obstacles of the native city; till at length, Havelock and Outram riding at its head, it marched along the street of death till the Bailey-guard gate of the Residency was reached, and greetings and cheers reached the war-worn relievers from the far-spent garrison which had all but abandoned hope of relief. Before the advance from Cawnpore began, Mick Sullivan and his chum, remaining still nominally attached to the Highland regiment, had joined the little force of irregular cavalry which Havelock had gathered from the infantrymen who could ride, while he waited at Cawnpore for reinforcements. As scouts, on reconnaissance duty, in pursuits and in sheer hard fighting, this little cohort of mounted men had its full share of adventure and danger, and the Light Dragoon comrades had great delight in being once again back in the saddle.

When the main column had pressed on into the Residency, the wounded of the fighting in the suburbs and native town had been left behind in the Motee Mahal along with the rearguard. On the morning after the entrance, a detachment of volunteers sallied out to escort into the Residency the doolies in which the wounded still lay inadequately cared for. The return journey from the first was much molested by hostile fire, many of the native bearers bolting, and leaving the doolies to be carried by the escorting Europeans. The guide became bewildered, and the head of the procession of doolies deviated from the proper route into a square which proved a perfect death-trap, and has passed into history as "Doolie Square." The handful of escorting soldiers, of whom Mick's comrade was one, fought desperately to protect the poor wounded lying helpless in the doolies; but the rebels drove them back by sheer weight, and massacred a large proportion of the hapless inmates. Too late to save these, the fire of the escort cleared the square, and fortunately no more doolies entered the fatal *cul-de-sac*. Suddenly the little party holding their ground there became aware of a great commotion in the street, just outside the archway which formed the entrance to the square. Pistol-shots were heard, and loud shouts in Hindustanee mingled with something that sounded like a British oath. A sally was at once made. Darting out of the square through the archway, the sallying party fought their way through the swarm of Sepoys outside to where a single European swaying a cavalry sabre, his back against the wall, and covering a wounded boy-officer who lay at his feet, was keeping at bay, now with a dexterous parry, anon with a swift sweeping cut, and again with a lightning thrust, the throng of howling miscreants who pressed around him. The foremost man of the sallying party, cutting down a Pandy who turned on him, sprang to the side of the man with the dripping sabre in his hand.

"Look if the lad's alive," were the first words of Mick Sullivan, for he was the man with the sabre.

Mick's chum, for he it was who had headed the rescuers, stooped down, and found the young officer alive and conscious. He told Mick so.

"Thin hould me up, acushla, for it's kilt intirely I am," and poor Mick threw his arm over his chum's shoulder, and the gallant fellow's head fell on his breast.

The Pandies were massing again, so the little party, carrying Mick and the officer, struggled back again into their feeble refuge inside the square. The youngster was seen to first, and then Dr. Home proceeded to investigate Mick's condition.

"Och an' sure, docthor jewel, ye may save yersilf the trouble. I'm kilt all over—as full of wownds as Donnybrook is of drunk men at noightfall. I've got me discharge from the sarvice, an' that widout a pinsion. There's niver a praiste in an odd corner av the mansion, is there, chum?"

The chum told him the place was not a likely one for priests.

"I'd fain have confissed before I die, an' had a word wid a praiste, but sure they can't expict a man on active sarvice to go out av the wurrld as reg'lar as if he were turnin' his toes up in his bed. Chum," continued the poor fellow, his voice becoming weaker as the blood trickled from him into a hollow of the earthen floor, "chum, dear, give us a hould av yer hand. Ye mind that poor young crayture av a wife of mine I left wapin' fur me on the quay av Southampton. There's some goold and jools in the dimmickin' bag in me belt, an' if ye could send them to her, ye would be doin' yer old chum a kindness."

The chum promised in a word—his heart was too full for more. Mick lay back silent for a little, gasping in his growing exhaustion. But suddenly he raised himself again on his elbow, and in a heightened voice continued—

"An', chum, if ever ye see the 30th Light again, tell them, will ye, that Mick Sullivan died wid a sword in his hand"—he had never quitted the grip of the bloody sabre—"an' wid spurs on his heels. I take ye all to witness, men, that I die a dhragoon, an' not a swaddy! Divil a word have I to say against the Ross-shire Buffs, chaps—divil a word; but I'm a dhragoon to the last dhrap av me blood! Ah me!"—here honest Mick's voice broke for the first time—"ah me! niver more will I back horse or wield sword!"

And then he fell back, panting for breath, and it seemed as if he had spoken his last words. But the mind of the dying man was on a train of thought that would still have expression. Again he raised himself into a sitting posture, and loud and clear, as if on the parade-ground, there rang out from his lips the consecutive words of command—

"Carry swords!"

"Return swords!"

"Prepare to dismount!"

"Dismount!"

A torrent of blood gushed from his mouth, and he fell forward dead. Mick Sullivan had dismounted for ever.

* * * * *

When the great mutiny was finally stamped out, Mick Sullivan's chum got himself sent back to the 30th Light, down in the Madras Presidency. He delivered his poor comrade's dying message to the regiment, and told the tale of his heroic death; and how Outram had publicly announced that, had he survived, he would have recommended Mick for the Victoria Cross. From colonel to band-boy, the 30th Light was deeply moved by the recital. The regiment subscribed to a man to place a memorial-stone over Mick's grave in the cemetery inside the Lucknow Residency, where he had been laid among the heroes of the siege. The quarter-master took temporary charge of the "goold and jools" which were Mick's legacy to "the Crayture," and the colonel himself wrote home instructions that every effort should be made to find the little woman and have her cared for.

* * * * *

One morning, about a month later, the colonel and his wife were taking their early canter on the Bangalore *maidan*. As they crossed the high road from down country, they noticed, tramping through the deep dust, a white woman with a child in her arms. She dragged herself wearily; the pale fagged face, and the wistful upward look at them as she trudged by, moved the good heart of the colonel's wife.

"Speak to her," she said to her husband; "she is a stranger, and forlorn."

"Where are you bound for, my good woman?" asked the colonel; "have you come far?"

The woman set down the child, a well-grown boy, who looked about two years old, and with a long sigh of weariness replied—

"I've come from England, sir, and I am on my way to the 30th Light Dragoons to find my husband."

"That little chap is quite too heavy for you to carry. What is your name, young one?"

The urchin sprang to "attention," saluted with rigid accuracy, and gravely replied—

"Mick Tullivan, Tir!"

"Good God!" whispered the colonel's wife; "it's Sullivan's widow—it's 'the Crayture' herself. Gallop to barracks for a gharry, and while you are gone, I will tell her. God pity her!"

And the kind lady was out of the saddle, and had the boy in her arms, and her tears were raining on his face, as the colonel rode away on his errand.

When the gharry arrived "the Crayture" was sitting by the wayside, the skirt of her dress drawn over her face, her head on the shoulder of the colonel's wife, her boy gripped tight in her arms.

The Mem Sahib carried the poor thing to her own bungalow for a day or two; and then good-hearted old Bess Bowles, the trumpeter's wife of G troop, came and took her and her boy away to the room that had been prepared for her in the married quarters. Perhaps it was not exactly in accordance with strict regulations, but the colonel had put the widow woman "on the strength"—she was no longer an unrecognised waif, but had her regimental position. Her ration of bread and meat her husband's comrades of G troop contributed; the officers made a little fund that sufficed to give her soldier's pay. She earned it, for a week after she "joined," the surgeon found her in the hospital, in quiet informal possession of the ward in which lay the most serious cases; and when next year the cholera smote the regiment, the rugged old Scot pronounced her "worth her weight in gold." She has long ago been a member of the sisterhood of army nurses. I remember her out in Africa during the Zulu war, and since then she has smoothed soldiers' pillows in the Egyptian campaigns; but she is still, and will be till the day she dies, a supernumerary "on the strength" of the 30th Light. She never married again; she is an elderly woman now, and the winsomeness of the days when we knew her as "the Crayture" has gone; but the quiet faithful courage that sustained her on the weary line of march and the forlorn-hope expedition to the East, is staunch still in her honest heart. The sergeant-major of to-day of G troop in the 30th Light—I call the corps by its old familiar name still, but they are Hussars now—is a straight, clean-built young fellow, with a light heart, a bright eye, and a quaint humour. His name is Mick Sullivan, and he is the son of "the Crayture," and of the man who died in the porch of "Doolie Square."

THE FATE OF "NANA SAHIB'S ENGLISH-MAN"

One fine evening in September 1856, young Mr. Kidson entered Escobel Castle by the great front door, and was hurrying across the hall on his way to the passage leading to his own apartments, when his worthy old mother, who had seen from her parlour window her son approach the house, ran out into the hall to meet him in a state of great agitation. It was little wonder that the aspect the young man presented excited the good creature's maternal emotion. The region around his right optic was so puffed and inflamed as to give the surest promise of a black eye of the first magnitude in the course of a few hours; to say that his nose was simply "bashed" is very inadequately to describe the condition of that feature; his lower lip was split and streaming with blood; and he carried in his left hand a couple of front teeth which had been forcibly dislodged from their normal position in his upper jaw. He was bareheaded, and he carried on his clothes enough red clay to constitute him an eligible investment on the part of an enterprising brickmaker. "Guid be here, my ain laddie!" wailed the poor mother in her unmitigated Glasgow Doric, "what's come tae you? Wha has massacred my son this fearsome bloodthirsty gait?" "Oh, hang it!" was the genial youth's sole acknowledgment of the maternal grief and sympathy, as, dodging her outstretched arms, he slunk to his rooms and rang vehemently for hot water and a raw beef-steak.

Young Mr. Kidson's parents were brand-new rich Glasgow folks, who in their old age of vast wealth had recently bought the Highland estate of Escobel, in the hope to gratify Mr. Kidson senior's ambition to gain social recognition as a country gentleman and to become the founder of a family, an aspiration in which he received but feeble assistance from his simple old wife, who had a tender corner in her memory for the Guse-Dubs in which she was born. Their only son, the hero of the puffed eye and the "bashed" nose, had been ignominiously sent down from Oxford while yet a freshman. At present he was supposed to be doing a little desultory reading in view of entering the army; in reality he was spending most of his time in boozing with grooms and gamekeepers in a low shebeen. A downright bad lot, this young Mr. Kidson, of whom, in the nature of things, nothing but evil could come.

While he was skulking into the privacy of his "den," an extremely pretty girl was sobbing convulsively on the breast of a stalwart fair-haired young fellow, whose eyes were flashing wrath, whose face still had an angry flush, and the knuckles of whose right hand were cut open, the blood trickling unheeded down the weeping girl's white dress. She, Mary Fraser, was the daughter of the clergyman of the parish; the young man, by name Sholto Mackenzie, was the orphan nephew of the old laird of Kinspiel, a small hill-property on the mountain slope. The two were sweethearts, and small chance was there of their ever being anything more. For Kinspiel was strictly entailed, and the old laird, who was so ill that he might die any day, had a son who had sons of his own, and was in no position, if he had the will, to help on his dead sister's manchild. Mary Fraser and Sholto Mackenzie had trysted to meet this evening in the accustomed pine glade on the edge of the heather. The girl was there before the time. Young Mr. Kidson, listlessly smoking as he lounged on a turf bank, caught a glimpse of her dress through the trees, and promptly bore down on her. There was a slight acquaintance, and she returned his greeting, supposing that he would pass on. But he did not—on the contrary, he waxed fluent in coarse flatteries, and suddenly grasping the girl in his arms was making strenuous efforts to snatch kisses from her, undeterred by her struggles and shrieks. At this crisis Sholto Mackenzie, hearing the cries, came running up at the top of his speed. Young Mr. Kidson, fancying himself a bit as a man who could use his fists, had not the poor grace to run away. While the girl leant half fainting against a tree there was a brief pugilistic encounter between the young men, as the issue of which Mr. Kidson was disabused of a misconception, and presented the aspect which a few minutes later brought tribulation to his mother. As he carried himself and his damages off, he muttered through his pulped lips with a fierce oath that the day would come when his antagonist should rue the evening's work. Whereat the antagonist laughed contemptuously, and addressed himself to the pleasant task of calming and consoling his agitated sweetheart.

Before the grouse season closed the old laird of Kinspiel was a dead man, and there was no longer a home for Sholto Mackenzie in the quaint old crow-stepped house in the upland glen among the bracken. What career was open to the penniless young fellow? He had no interest for a cadetship, and that Indian service in which so many men of his race have earned name and fame was not for him. In those days there was no Manitoba, no ranching in Texas or Wyoming; the Cape gave no opportunities, the Argentine was not yet a resort for English youth of enterprise, and he had not money enough to take him to the Australian gold-diggings or to the sheep-runs of New Zealand. He saw no resource but to offer himself to the Queen's service in the capacity of a private soldier, in the hope that education, good conduct, and fervent zeal would bring him promotion and perhaps distinction. By the advice of a local pensioner he journeyed to London and betook himself to the metropolitan recruiting centre in Charles Street, Westminster. No Sergeants Kite now patrol that thoroughfare in quest of lawful prey; nay, the little street with its twin public-house headquarters is itself a thing of the past. About the centre of the long wooden shanty recently built for the purposes of the census, stood the old "Hampshire Hog," with its villainous *rendezvous* in the rear; nearer the Park on the opposite side, just where is now the door of the India Office, the "Cheshire Cheese" reared its frowsy front. In the days I am writing of, recruits accepted or had foisted on them the "Queen's Shilling," received a bounty, gave themselves for twenty-four years' service, and were escorted by a staff-sergeant to their respective regiments. Now there is neither Queen's shilling nor bounty, and the recruit, furnished with a travelling warrant, is his own escort to Ballincollig or Fort George. What scenes had dingy Charles Street witnessed in its day! How much sin and sorrow; too late remorse, too late forgiveness! In many a British household has Charles Street been cursed with bitter curses; yet has it not been, in a sense, the cradle of heroes? It sent to battle the men whose blood dyed the sward of the Balaclava valley; it fed the trenches of Sebastopol; it was the sieve through whose meshes passed the staunch warriors who stormed Delhi and who defended Lucknow, who bled and conquered at Sobraon and Goojerat.

Sholto Mackenzie had eaten Queen Victoria's rations for some six months, had been dismissed recruits' drill, and become a duty soldier, when the order was issued that the "30th Light," the regiment into which he had enlisted, was to go out for its turn of service in India, and of course the young soldier went with his regiment. Those were the days before big Indian troopships and the Suez Canal; reinforcements for India went out round the Cape. Sholto's troop was accompanied by two married women who were on the strength of the regiment. Nowadays the soldier's wife adorns her room in the married quarters with cheap Liberty hangings, and walks out in French boots and kid gloves. Mrs. Macgregor and Mrs. Malony lived each her married life and reared her family in a bunk in the corner of the troop-room of which she had the "looking after." Such a life seems one of sheer abomination and barbarism, does it not? Yet the arrangement had the surprising effect, in most instances, of bringing about a certain decency, self-restraint, and genuinely human feeling alike in the men and the married woman of the room. Neither Mrs. Macgregor nor Mrs. Malony had ever been abroad before; and both evinced a strong propensity to take with them copious mementoes of their native land. Mrs. Macgregor, honest woman, had manifested that concentrativeness which is a feature in the character of the nation to which, as her name indicated, she belonged. She had packed into a great piece of canvas sheeting a certain feather-bed, which, as an heirloom from her remote ancestors, she was fond of boasting of when the other matrons were fain to sew together a couple of regimental palliasse covers, and stuff the same with straw. In the capacious bosom of this family relic she had stowed a variety of minor articles, among which were a wash-hand jug of some primeval earthenware, a hoary whisky decanter—which, trust Mrs. Macgregor, was quite empty—a cradle, sundry volumes of Gaelic literature, and a small assortment of cooking utensils. Over those collected properties stood grimly watchful the tall, gaunt woman with the gray eye, the Roman nose, and the cautious taciturnity. Of another stamp was Mrs. Malony, a little, slatternly, pock-marked Irishwoman. Her normal condition was that of a nursing-mother—nobody could remember the time when Biddy Malony had not a brat hanging at that bosom of hers which she was wont partially to conceal by an old red woollen kerchief. Biddy was a merry soul, spite of many a trial and many a cross—always ready with a flash of Irish humour, just as ready as she always was for a glass of gin. She had not attempted the methodical packing of her goods and chattels, but had bundled them together anyhow in a chaotic state. Her great difficulty was her inability to perform the difficult operation of carrying her belongings "in her head," and after she had pitchforked into the baggage-van a quantity of incongruous *débris*, she was still in a bewildered way questing after a wicker bird-cage and "a few other little throifles."

Embarking along with his comrades and reaching the main deck of the troopship, Sholto found the two ladies already there—Mrs. Macgregor grimly defiant, not to say fierce, in consequence of a request just made to her by a sailor for a glass of grog; Mrs. Malony in a semi-hysterical state, having lost a shoe, a wash-tub, and, she much feared, one of the young Malonys. Matters were improved, however, when Sholto found the young bog-trotter snugly squatted in the cows' manger. The shoe was gone hopelessly, having fallen into the water when its wearer was mounting the gangway; and Mrs. Malony happily remembered that she had made a present of the missing wash-tub to a "green-grosher's lady" in the town of embarkation.

Sholto had been made lance-corporal soon after the troopship sailed, and served in that rank during the long voyage with so much credit that when the regiment reached Bangalore the colonel of the 30th Light gave him the second stripe, so that he was full corporal in less than a year after he had enlisted. During a turn of guard duty about three months after he joined at Bangalore, he happened to hear it mentioned in the guard-room that a new officer—a cornet—had arrived that day, and had been posted to the vacancy in the troop to which Sholto belonged. The new-comer's name was not stated, and beyond a cursory hope that he would turn out a good and smart officer, Corporal Mackenzie gave no further heed to the matter. Late the same night, he was relieving the sentry on the mess-house post when the merry party of officers broke up. Laughing and chatting they came out under the verandah, a little more noisy than usual, no doubt because of the customary "footing" in champagne paid by the new arrival. As they passed Sholto, a voice caught his ear—an unfamiliar voice, yet that stirred in him an angry memory; and as the officers lounged past him in the moonlight, he gazed into the group with earnest inquisitiveness. Arm and arm between two subalterns, his face inflamed with drink, his mouth full of slang, rolled the man he had thrashed among the Scottish pines. As he grinned his horse-laugh Sholto discerned the vacuum in his upper teeth which his fist had made that evening; and now this man was his officer. The eyes of the two met, and Kidson gave a sudden start and seemed about to speak, but controlling the impulse, he smiled a silent smile, the triumphant insolence of which stung Sholto bitterly. Verily his enemy was his master; and Sholto read the man's nature too truly not to be sure that he would forgo no jot of the sweet revenge of humiliation.

Very soon the orderly sergeant of the troop fell unwell, and Sholto had to take up his duty, one detail of which was to carry the order-book round to the bungalows of the troop-officers for their information. This duty entailed on Sholto the disagreeable necessity of a daily interview with Mr. Kidson. That officer took the opportunity of throwing every imaginable slight on the corporal, but was careful not to give warrant for any specific complaint. But it was very bitter to be kept standing at attention for some ten minutes at a time, orderlybook in hand, until Mr. Kidson thought fit to lay aside his book, or to desist from pulling his terrier's ears. Often the cornet was in his bedroom; and while waiting for his appearance Sholto noticed how ostentatiously careless his officer was as to his valuables—a handful of money or a gold watch and chain left lying on the table amid spurs and gloves and soda-water bottles.

The morning after an exceptionally long wait for Mr. Kidson's emergence from his bedroom, Sholto was returning from the horse lines when the regimental sergeant-major met him and ordered him to his room under arrest. In utter bewilderment he begged for some explanation, but without success. When he reached his cot, he casually noticed that his box was open and the lock damaged, but he was too disturbed to give heed to this circumstance. Presently a sergeant came and escorted him to the orderlyroom. Here he found the colonel sitting in the windsor arm-chair with the discipline book open before him, the adjutant standing behind him, and on the flank Mr. Kidson and the sergeant-major of his own troop. The colonel, if a stern, was a just man; and in a grave tone he expressed his concern that so heinous a charge should come against a young soldier of character hitherto so creditable. Sholto replied that he had not the remotest idea what the nature of the charge was. The old chief shot a keen glance at him as he spoke—

"Corporal Mackenzie, you are accused of stealing a gold watch and chain, the property of Mr. Kidson. What have you to say to this charge?"

The lad's head swam, and for a moment he thought he was going to faint. Then the blood came back to his heart and flushed up into his face as he looked the colonel straight between the eyes and answered—

"It is a wicked falsehood, sir!"

"Then of course you deny it?"

"I do, sir, if it were the last word I had to say on earth!"

"Mr. Kidson," said the old soldier in a dry business tone, "will you state what you know about this matter?"

Thus enjoined, Kidson briefly and with a certain nervous glibness stated that after Corporal Mackenzie had left his quarters on the previous afternoon, he had missed his watch and chain. That morning he had renewed the search unsuccessfully. He had previous suspicions of Corporal Mackenzie having from time to time stolen money from off his table. He had reported the matter to his troop sergeant-major, who had at once searched Corporal Mackenzie's kit, with what result the sergeant-major would himself state.

The sergeant-major for his part had only to testify that having been spoken to by Mr. Kidson on the subject of his loss, he had taken another sergeant-major with him, and searched Corporal Mackenzie's box, where he had found the missing watch and chain, which he had at once handed to the adjutant, who now held it.

The evidence was strong enough to hang a man.

"Corporal Mackenzie," said the colonel, with some concern, "the case seems very clear. What you have to say, if anything, you must say elsewhere. It is my duty to send you back for a district court-martial."

Sholto was confined in a room adjacent to the quarter-guard for a few days, when he was brought before the court-martial, which heard the evidence against the prisoner, to whom then was given the opportunity to cross-examine the witnesses. But the president would not allow interrogations tending to establish animus on Mr. Kidson's part against the prisoner, and finally poor Sholto lost his temper, and exclaimed with passion—

"Your permission to cross-examine is nothing better than a farce!"

"Perhaps," retorted the president, with a grim smile,—"perhaps you may not think the punishment which will probably befall you a farce!"

Sholto's defence was in a sentence—the assertion of his complete innocence. He had known Mr. Kidson in other days, he said, when as yet both were civilians, and they had parted in bad blood.

A member of the court demanded that Mr. Kidson should have the opportunity of contradicting this assertion, if in his power to do so; whereupon that officer emphatically swore that to his knowledge he had never seen Corporal Mackenzie in his life before he joined the 30th Light there in Bangalore. So Sholto was put back to wait for many days while the finding of the court-martial was being submitted to the Commander-in-Chief.

One evening Mick Sullivan his comrade brought him his tea as usual—the good fellow never would let the mat-boy carry his chum his meals. He stood looking at Sholto for a while with a strange concern in his honest face; and then he broke silence—

"Sholto, me lad, it's me heart is sore for you this day. Yer coort-martial will be read out to-morrow morning! Aye, and—and"—his voice sank into a whisper—"the farrier-major has got the ordhers for to rig the thriangles. It's to be flogged ye are, my poor fellow!"

Sholto sent his chum away abruptly; he could not talk, he could hardly think; all he could do was to wish himself dead and spared this unutterable shame. Death came not, but instead the morning; and with the morning came Mick with a copious dose of brandy, which he entreated his comrade to drink, for it would "stun the pain." "Every fellow," he argued, "primed himself so before a flogging, and why shouldn't he?"

But Sholto refused to fortify himself with Dutch courage; and then poor Mick produced his last evidence of affection in the shape of a leaden bullet which he had beaten flat, and which held tight between the teeth, he knew from personal experience, was a great help in enabling a fellow to resist "hollerin' out."

Presently the escort fell in and marched the prisoner to the riding-school. Sholto found there two troops of the regiment drawn up, in front of them a knot of officers, among whom he noticed Mr. Kidson, and in front of them again the colonel, with the court-martial documents in his hand. The lad's eye took in the doctor, the farriers—each with his cat—and the triangle rigged against the wall under the gallery. The sergeant of the escort ordered him to take two paces to the front, remove his cap, and stand at attention. And so he stood, outwardly calm, waiting for his sentence.

"Proceedings of a district court-martial"—the colonel began, reading in a loud voice from the scroll in his hand. To Sholto the document seemed interminable. At last the end came. "The Court, having considered the evidence brought before it, finds the prisoner, No. 420, Corporal Sholto Mackenzie, G troop, Thirtieth Light Dragoons, guilty of the said charge of theft, and does hereby sentence the said prisoner to be reduced to the rank and pay of a private dragoon"—here the colonel paused for a moment and then added—"and further to undergo the punishment of fifty lashes."

The regimental sergeant-major strode up to Sholto, with a penknife ripped the gold lace corporal stripes from the arm of his jacket, and threw them down on the tan. Then the colonel's stern cold voice uttered the word "Strip." There was a little momentary bustle, and then Sholto was half hanging, half standing, lashed by the wrists and ankles to the triangles, while the farrier-major stood measuring his distance, fingering the whip-cords of his "cat," and waiting for the word "Begin"!

Suddenly a wild shriek pealed through the great building from the gallery above the head of the man fastened up there to be flogged.

"Arrah musha, colonel dear!" followed in shrill accents—"for the love of the Holy Jasus and the blissed Vargin, hould yer hand, and spare an innocent man! I tell ye he's as innocent as the babe unborn, and it's mesilf, Bridget Malony, an honest married woman on the strength, that can pruve that same! Ochone, colonel dear, listen to me, won't yez?"

All eyes were concentrated on the little gallery. It was a sort of gazebo, built out from the wall at the height of about ten feet, and the only access to it was from outside. Bending eagerly over the rail, attired in nothing but a petticoat and a chemise, her hair streaming wildly over her shoulders, and with a round bare place like a tonsure on the crown of her head, which gave her a most extraordinary appearance, was visible Mrs. Malony. She had been struck down by a sunstroke the day Sholto was put under arrest, and had been in hospital ever since.

The general opinion was that the good woman was crazy: but Mrs. Malony knew her own mind—she had something to say, and she was determined to say it. She had just finished her wild appeal to the colonel, when she cast a hurried glance over her shoulder, and then, indifferently clad as she was, nimbly climbed over the rail, and dropped upon the tan. At that moment a couple of nurses rushed into the balcony, but they were too late. Mrs. Malony had got the "flure"; straight up to the colonel she ran on her bare feet, and broke out again into vehement speech.

"I swear to yer honner the corporal is as innocent as my little Terence, what should be at his mother's breasht this moment. He is, so help me God! There is the rapscallion uv a conspirator," she yelled, pointing a long, bare, skinny arm at Mr. Kidson; "there is his white-livered tool!"—and up went the other arm like a danger-signal pointing to the sergeant-major. "Hear me shpake, sor," cried the woman, "and sure am I ye'll belave me!"

"Nonsense," said the chief, "you are mad or drunk, woman! Here, take her away!" and he beckoned to the nurses.

But the major, a Scotsman, intervened.

"At least hear her story," he argued; "there must be some reason in all this fervour of hers. I know the woman; she is no liar."

"Well, what have you to say, Mrs. Malony?" said the colonel.

"One moment, sir!" interposed the major, and there passed a few words in an undertone between him and the colonel—then the latter spoke aloud.

"Mr. James," said he, addressing the adjutant, "take Mr. Kidson outside and remain there with him, and you, Sergeant-Major Norris, take charge of Sergeant-Major Hope. Mr. James, you will see that the two are kept apart."

And then Mrs. Malony gained her point and was allowed to tell her story. She had been "doing for" Mr. Kidson, she said, ever since he joined. The day before Sholto was put under arrest, when she was in the lumber-room of Mr. Kidson's bungalow, she overheard the plot concocted between him and the sergeant-major. Early next morning, when the regiment was out at "watering order," she had watched Sergeant-Major Hope go to Corporal Mackenzie's cot, pick the lock of his trunk, take out his holdall, and therein place Mr. Kidson's watch and chain. An hour later, when she was on her way to the bungalow of the "praste" to ask "his riverence's" advice as to what she should do, she received a sunstroke, and was insensible for several days. When she recovered consciousness she had forgotten everything that happened for a day or more before her accident until that morning, when she happened to hear the attendants gossiping amongst themselves that Corporal Mackenzie was to be flogged that day for stealing Mr. Kidson's watch and chain. Then everything flashed vividly back into her memory, and she had made her escape from the hospital and reached the scene just in time.

Mrs. Malony spoke with amazing volubility, and the telling of her story did not occupy more time than a few minutes. When she was done, and stood silent, panting and weeping, the colonel turned to the sergeant of the guard and ordered the prisoner to be unfastened and marched back to the guard-room. While Mrs. Malony had been speaking, nobody had noticed Sholto, and when they went to cut him loose, they found that he had fainted. The parade was dismissed; and the colonel, the major, and the adjutant adjourned to the orderly room. Mr. Kidson was ordered to be brought in. He met Mrs. Malony's accusation with a flat and contemptuous denial, desiring with some insolence in his tone to know whether the colonel could think it proper to take the word of a crazy Irish barrack-room slut before that of an officer and a gentleman. "That depends on circumstances, and whether I happen to accept your definitions," was the colonel's dry comment, as he formally put Mr. Kidson under arrest, and having ordered him to his quarters, called for the sergeant-major to be brought in. This man was a poor faint-hearted rascal. He was ghastly pale, and his knees trembled as he flinched under the colonel's searching eye. On cross-examination he broke down altogether, and at length, with many protestations of remorse, confessed the whole truth, and that Mr. Kidson had bribed him to co-operate in the scheme to ruin Corporal Mackenzie. This wretched accomplice was in his turn sent away into close arrest, and Mr. Kidson was re-summoned into the orderly room and informed that his sergeant-major had confessed everything.

The two field-officers were fain to avert from the regiment the horrible scandal, even at the cost of some frustration of justice. The option was given to Kidson of standing a court-martial, or of sending in the resignation of his commission within an hour and quitting the station before the day was out. Then and there the shameless blackguard wrote out the document, made an insolent sweeping salaam all round, mounted his tat, and rode off to his bungalow. As he was crossing the parade-ground he encountered Sholto Mackenzie, who had just been released by the colonel's orders, leaving the guard-room a free man and surrounded by a knot of troop-mates, conspicuous among whom was Mick Sullivan, half mad with delight. As Kidson passed the group with a baleful scowl, the trammels of discipline snapped for once, and a burst of groans and hooting made him quicken his pace, lest worse things should befall. In two hours more the disgraced man was clear of the cantonment.

In the previous article it has been told how in the early days of the great mutiny Mick Sullivan and his comrade were transmogrified from cavalrymen into members of that gallant regiment the Ross-shire Buffs—the old 78th Highlanders—and did good service in the "little fighting column" at the head of which Havelock fought his way up country from Allahabad to Cawnpore. It was on the afternoon of Havelock's first fight, the sharp action of Futtehpore, that Sholto Mackenzie and Mick Sullivan were lying down in the shade of a tree waiting for the baggage to come up. Futtehpore town had been carried by a rush, and there had been some hand-to-hand fighting in the streets—for the mutinied Sepoys dodged about among the houses and had to be driven out. There was a delay in following up the fugitives; for a waggon-load of rupees had been upset in the principal street and the temptation of the silver caused the soldiers to dally, while others straggled in search of food and drink. Meanwhile the mutineer cavalry rallied beyond the town. Palliser's Irregulars were sent forward to disperse the formation, followed by such men of our infantry as could hastily be mustered. Among those who went forward was Sholto Mackenzie. Palliser's native troopers were half-hearted and hung back when their chief charged the Sepoy horse, with the result that Palliser was dashed from his horse, and would have been cut to pieces but for the devotion of his ressaldar, who lost his own life in saving that of his leader.

"Did you notice," said Sholto to his comrade as they rested, "the squadron leader of the Pandy Cavalry that handled Palliser's fellows so roughly out yonder?"

"Bedad, an' I did not!" replied Sullivan. "Every divil av thim was uglier than the other, an' it's their own mothers should be ashamed to own the biling av thim!"

"Look here, Mick," said Sholto, "I'll take my oath I saw that dog Kidson to-day, in command of the Pandy Squadron!"

"Kidson!" ejaculated Sullivan in the wildest astonishment. "It's dhramin' ye are! Sure Kidson must be either prowlin' somewhere in Madras, or else on his road home to England!"

"I tell you I am as sure I saw him to-day as I am that I see you now. It was he who dismounted Palliser and cut down the ressaldar. I am convinced it was he and none other!"

"Well, if you're so sure as that, it's no use to conthradick ye. Plase the saints, ye may get a close chance at him soon, and then—Lord pity him!"

Mick's aspiration was fulfilled. The "close chance" came to Sholto a few days later, in the heart of the battle of Cawnpore. The Highlanders had rolled up the Sepoy flank by a bayonet charge, had shattered their centre, and captured the village on which it rested. The mutineer infantry of the left and centre were in full rout, their retreat covered by a strong body of native cavalry which showed a very determined front.

Sholto and his comrade were close together in the ranks of the Ross-shire Buffs, when the former suddenly grasped the latter's arm, and in a low earnest voice asked—

"Mick, do you see that officer in charge of the covering squadron of the Pandies?"

Sullivan gazed long and intently, and then burst out—

"By the holy poker, it's that treacherous blackguard Kidson!"

"Right, Mick, and I must get at him somehow!"

"Wid all my heart, chum, but it's aisier said than done, just now, at any rate. You must mark time, and trust to luck!"

Just then Barrow came galloping up at the head of his handful of horsemen, and besought the chief to let him go at the mutineer sowars. But Havelock shook his head, for Barrow's strength all told was but eighteen sabres. But a little later Beatson, the Adjutant-General, who, stricken with cholera and unable to sit his horse, had come up to the front on a gun-carriage, saw an opportunity after the General had ridden away, and took it on himself to give Barrow leave to attack. The flank of the grenadier company of the Highlanders, where Sholto stood, was close to Beatson's gun-carriage, in rear of which his horse was led, and a sudden thought struck the young fellow. Stepping forward with carried rifle, he told Captain Beatson that he was a cavalry soldier, and noticing the led horse, begged eagerly to be allowed to mount it and join the charge for which the volunteer cavalry were preparing.

"Up with you, my man!" said poor dying Beatson. "Here, you shall have my sword, and I don't want it back clean, remember!"

Sholto was in the saddle with a spring, and made the nineteenth man under Barrow's command; a mixed lot, but full of pluck to a man. As he formed up on the flank, there reached his ears honest Mick's cheery advice—

"Now, Sholto, me dear lad, keep yer sword-hand up and yer bridle-hand down, an' remimber ye reprisint the honour an' glory of the ould 30th Light!"

Barrow threw away his cigar, gathered up his reins, and with a shout of "Charge!" that might have given the word of command to a brigade, rammed his spurs into his horse's flank and went off at score, his little band close on his heels. Hard on the captain's flank galloped Sholto Mackenzie, a red spot on each cheek, his teeth hard set, his blazing eyes never swerving from the face of one man of that seething mass on which they were riding. "Give 'em the point, lads!" roared Barrow, as he skewered a havildar and then drove right in among them. The white-faced man with the black moustache, who was Sholto's mark, rather shirked out of the *mêlée* when he saw it was to be close quarters; but Mackenzie, looking neither to the right nor to the left, with his bridle-hand well down, and Beatson's sword in full play, drove his way at length within weapon's length of the other.

"Now, liar and perjurer!" he hissed from between his teeth, "if you are not coward as well, stand up to me and let us fight it out!"

Kidson's answer was a lurid scowl and a pistol bullet, which just grazed Sholto's temple. Lifting his horse with his bridle-hand, and striking its flanks with his spurless heels, the latter sent his sword-point straight at Kidson's throat. The thrust would have gone through and out at the further side, but that the sword-point struck some concealed protection and was shivered up to the hilt. The renegade Briton smiled a baleful smile as he brought his weapon from guard to point, as if the other was at his mercy. But this was not so; with a shout Sholto tightened the curb-rein till his horse reared straight on end, striking it as it rose with the shattered sword hilt. The maddened animal plunged forward, receiving in his chest the point of Kidson's sword; and Sholto on the instant bending forward fastened a deadly grip on the other's throat. The impetus hurled both of them to the ground, and now, down among the horses' feet, the close-locked strife swaying and churning above them, their struggle unto the death was wrought out. Kidson struggled like a madman; he bit, he kicked, he fought with an almost superhuman fury; but the resolute grip of the avenger never slackened on his throat. Sholto held on with his right hand, groping about with his left for some weapon wherewith to end the contest. At length his grasp closed on the hilt of a dropped sword;—and a moment later it was all over with the man whom the survivors of Havelock's Ironsides speak of with scorn and disgust to this day by the name of "Nana Sahib's Englishman."

THE OLD SERGEANT

The scene of my little story is a sequestered hill-parish away up among the brown moors and sullen pinewoods of northern Scotland, and the date of it is full forty years ago, when I was a boy living in the grey old manse down in the sheltered glen which was the only picturesque "bit" of all the parish whose minister my father was. It was a curiously primitive region. Its crofters and farmers lived out their lives and were laid in the old graveyard up on the hillock—hardly a soul of them having ever been twenty miles outside the parish bounds. There was a vague lingering tradition concerning a scapegrace son, long since dead and gone, of old Sandy McCulloch of the Calternach—how the daring young ne'er-do-well had actually left his native land, made his way to India—we boys used to look up the map of India in the manse atlas—had married a "begum" there, and had finally been poisoned off by that mysterious female. This tradition had engendered a fine wholesome terror of begums, and all kinds of adventures that haply might involve matrimonial connections therewith, with disastrous results to follow. So our young men stayed at home and tilled the sour cold land laboriously but contentedly. There were a few exceptions, it is true. Now and then a young fellow would take the Queen's shilling, and go out from among us on a career of soldiering. They seldom came back, for Cardwell's name had not yet been heard in the land, and short service in the army was a reform undreamed of. When a man 'listed then, it was nominally for life; actually, until his bodily vigour was so impaired that he was held no longer fit for service, and then he got a pension for the remainder of his days. But what with hard service abroad, what with cholera in Hindustan and Yellow Jack in the West Indies, what with poor fare in barracks and on noxious crowded transports, no great proportion of the soldiers of those days managed to keep alive long enough to attain the pensioned period. There was but one army-pensioner in our parish, and he is "the old sergeant" of my story.

They were grand old specimens, those veterans of a bypast era. To them the credit of their old regiment and the honour of the service were dearer than anything else in all the world. They had a great self-respect that had been instilled by the discipline they had undergone, and by the dangers they had passed through. They had a single-hearted loyalty to the Crown they had served, and a manly belief in the country which their strong arms and ready weapons had helped to save. It is no doubt all right in a military sense that there are no old soldiers among us now; but of this I am sure, that in a good many respects the country is the worse for the want of them.

There was a Sunday morning of my boyhood which I remember as if it were yesterday. The Sunday school, held in the grey old schoolroom on the edge of the wood in the centre of which stood the parish kirk, had just been dismissed. The bell had not yet begun to ring, but it was the custom of the great straggling parish to hold its grand weekly palaver, summer and winter alike, on the little wood-encircled open space around the kirk, during the half-hour before the simple Presbyterian service began. To this end, the folk who were to constitute the congregation were gathering, coming in by twos and threes along the various paths centring on the kirk. Good old Willie Duffus, the elder from the far-distant Forgie district, had climbed and descended the bleak shoulder of Muldearie, had picked his devious way across the moss, had forded the burn, and was now so close at hand that I could discern the weather-beaten fluffiness of his ancestral beaver, and the resplendent brass buttons on the mediæval blue coat which had not been new when it had been his grandfather's wedding-garment. Johnny Mills, the cripple tailor, who was wont to carry his goose and ironing-board from farmhouse to farmhouse, and to accept his food as part of his poor pay, came shambling up the dykeside from his hovel in the kailyard under the old willow-tree. With an air of rustic patronage which he could well afford, since most of the poor folk were in his books, Sandy Riach, the "merchant" of the Kirktoun, came strutting up the path from the little wooded hamlet. The farm lads, with their straw-coloured or red hair cut square in the nape of the neck, brilliant as to chest in their scarlet or blue plush vests studded with big white bone buttons, clumped kirkward in their heavy hobnailed boots, exchanging now and then a word of clumsy badinage with the lasses in their tartan shawls, and the rig-and-fur stockings and stout shoes they had put on after wading the burn down in the hollow. Old Maggie Dey, as she wended her slow way leaning on her stick, would stop now and again for a confidential whisper with a good-wife; for Maggie was the parish "howdie" —*Anglice*, midwife—and had officiated at the introduction into this vale of tears of more than half of the population of the parish. Just on the rise of the "manse-brae" I could discern my mother's bonnet as she climbed the steep knoll, with a little cohort of my younger brothers and sisters by her side, walking orderly, as beseemed the day and the occasion.

Ha! there was old Robbie Strachan nailing up a notice on the half-open church door, and now he was unfastening the bell-rope from its hook high up on the porch wall, preparatory to the statutory twenty minutes' tolling of the clangorous old bell up there on the stumpy belfry. We boys, keenly alert, were watching Robbie's every motion, rejoicing in the prospect of one of our chiefest weekly joys; for Robbie when he was in a good humour would let us have the rope and do the ringing, all save the peremptory final peals known as the "ringing in," while he conversed sedately with a knot of his cronies.

Robbie Strachan, the bellman and "kirk officer" of our parish, was a tall, gaunt old fellow, lean-faced and high-featured, straight still as a pine, although in his time he had put in forty years of hard soldiering. His regulation mutton-chop whiskers, white as snow, just reached the corners of his grim old mouth, the rest of his lined visage closely shaven. You would have known him at a glance for an old soldier, by his balanced step, his square shoulders, and his disciplined attitudes; he stood proclaimed yet more plainly by the well-brushed threadbare trews of Gordon tartan that encased his lean and wiry nether limbs. Robbie had been a sergeant in the local regiment, the gallant Ninety-Second, and in its ranks had borne the brunt of many a stubborn fray. He had worn the brogues from off his feet in Moore's disastrous retreat on Corunna, and had helped to bury that noble chief "by the struggling moonbeam's misty ray and the lantern dimly burning." He had been in the thick of the fierce bayonet struggle in the steep street of Fuentes de Oñoro, had climbed the ridge to the desperate fight of Albuera, and had taken a hand in carrying the bridge of Almarez. A wound had kept him from Salamanca, but he was in Graham's front line on the day of Vittoria, and had many a tale of the rich plunder that fell to the conquerors in that short, sharp, and decisive combat. He had heard the bullets patter on the rocks of Roncesvalles, had waded the "bloody Bidassoa" under the shadow of the lofty Rhune, and was only hindered from being in at the death in the final desperate struggle on the glacis of Toulouse, by having got a bullet in the chest as he waded up to the knees behind Picton through the marsh which Soult vainly imagined protected his front at Orthez.

Robbie was but a corporal when he went down at Orthez, but he was full sergeant on that wet June morning of the following year when "Cameron's pibroch woke the slumbering host" to range itself in "battle's magnificently stern array!" Bullets had an unpleasant habit of finding their billets in him, and he was knocked over again on the forenoon of Waterloo when hanging on to the stirrup-leather of a Scots Grey in the memorable charge of the "Union Brigade" and shouting "Scotland for ever!" in unison with the comrades of horse and foot hailing from the land of cakes. The army surgeons in their cheery manner pronounced him as full of holes as a cullender, and were for invaliding him then and there as unfit for further service; but Robbie stoutly pleaded that he would be as good a man as ever when his wounds were healed, and triumphantly made good his words. So he had put in fifteen years' subsequent soldiering, and had heard the British drum-beat all round the world, ere, some ten years before the date of my story, he had been retired with a sergeant's pension for life and something additional for wounds. He was an old man now, but he carried his years well, and was still a good man in the harvest field, or with the spade. Most of his work with that implement was done in the manse garden, and we manse boys used to spend hours in listening to his stories of his old fighting days, while he made the drills for the garden peas, or dibbled in the kail plants in the plot behind the gooseberry bushes.

An exemplary man in a general way, Sergeant Robbie had his little failings; but for which he would have been an elder of the parish instead of being but the bellman and kirk officer. He was rather quick-tempered, and when moved to wrath, he swore in a manner which conclusively proved he had been with the army in Flanders. Then again, occasionally, on pension days mostly, he would take more whisky than was good for him. When he got "fou," it was always in the light of day, and so he exposed himself. As he marched home from the little public-house down at Blackhillock, with "the malt abune the meal," his effort to appear preternaturally sober was quite a spectacle. Always stiff of attitude, he was then positively rigid: he would sway, but it was the swaying of a ramrod; when haply he fell into the ditch, there was no collapsing in a limp heap—he went down all of a length, as if there was not a joint in all his long body. But these exhibitions were comparatively infrequent, and were excused in the eyes of the parish censors because of the hole in the sergeant's head made by the Waterloo bullet.

He and his old wife, who had seen a great deal of the world from the top of a baggage-waggon, but who was a most worthy domestic soul, lived together in a cottage at the back of the wood. The couple had an only son. When the youth grew into a strapping lad, Robbie had marched him down to Gordon Castle, to take counsel concerning his boy's future, with his patron the Duke. It was in Robbie's strong arms that the Duke—then Lord March—had lain, when the surgeons probed unsuccessfully for the bullet that pierced his chest on the day of Orthez, and which His Grace carried in him to the grave. As the result of this conference, Robbie had taken his son into Aberdeen, and enlisted him in his own old corps, the Gordon Highlanders. I remember the young fellow coming home on furlough, and the sensation among the simple folk as he swaggered up to the kirk in his flowing tartans and with the ostrich-feather bonnet on his handsome head. Old Robbie was a proud man that day, for his son had the corporal's stripe already on his arm, although he had been barely three years a soldier.

If I have been over-minute in the attempt to depict Sergeant Robbie, I advance the double excuse, that he was among the prominent figures of my youth time, and that the type is now as extinct as the dodo. The old man stepped out from under the kirk wall with the bell-rope in his hand, and we boys darted forward to make our request that he would hand it over to us and let us do the ringing for him. But there was a strange stern expression in his face that gave us pause. "No the day, laddies," was all he said, as he took post at the corner of the stone dyke, and began to sway the chafed old rope. We stood silently by, in wonder at his mood. We had known him cross; but he was not cross now: in the gloomy set face and the unwonted silence there was something quite new and strange to us. And yet another strange thing, his wonted cronies held away from him this morning. There was something mysterious in the air. The people, as they gathered in the open space outside the kirk, formed little muttering knots. From these, every now and then, a person would drop out, and strolling up to the kirk door in a seemingly purposeless way, would stand there a while looking up at the notices displayed on it, and then saunter back to the group he had left, or drift into another. It was curious that, no matter wherever you looked, every one seemed to be stealing furtive glances at Sergeant Robbie, standing out there by himself swaying the bell-rope with his long lean arms. And furtive as they were, the old man was clearly conscious of those glances. His face grew harder, grimmer, and more set; yet once or twice gazing up at him in my bewilderment with a boy's curiosity, I thought I noticed a quivering of the muscles about the close-gripped lips.

The "ringing in" was finished, and the congregation had passed into the kirk. As Sergeant Robbie, carrying the big pulpit Bible, strode up the aisle in front of the minister, it seemed to me that I had never seen him carrying so high that old white head of his, with the cicatrix of the Waterloo bullet in the gnarled forehead. Every eye was on the old fellow, and he knew it, and bore himself with a quiet courage in which somehow there came to be felt an element of pathos. It was curious again how all eyes centred upon him when in his extempore prayer the minister besought "consolation for those who were in sore trouble and mourning over the falling away of one near and dear to them." Robbie stood straight and square, his face fixed — only his lean brown throat swelled for a moment as if he were resolutely forcing down a spasm of emotion. Tibbie his wife stood by his side, and when the old soldier laid his hand on her shoulder she quelled with a strong effort her rising sobs.

The simple service ended, the people streamed out through the door that Robbie had thrown open; we of the manse party were the last to emerge. It was part of Robbie's duty, as kirk officer, to "cry" to the dispersing congregation all notices placed in his hands for purposes of publicity, the duplicates of which he had previously nailed on the kirk door. The kirk officer in those primitive regions was the chief medium for giving good advertisement. As we came out Robbie was standing in the centre of a large circle, calling out in his high falsetto the particulars of a "displenish sale." "Fower good stots, three milk kye, a pair of workhorses, farm implements, household furniture," and so on.

This finished, there was a pause. Sergeant Robbie folded up the sale advertisement; as he did this his hand was trembling so that it fell to the ground. He stooped, picked the paper up and put it in the rear pocket of his coat; then from out his breast-pocket he pulled a folded blue document. He braced himself firmly, came to rigid "attention" as if he were in the presence of his commanding officer, and slowly opened out the blue paper.

"Dinna read it, Robbie!" "Dinna read it, sergeant!" came from a dozen voices in the sympathising circle around him. "It's no necessar' — ye needna, ye maunna read it," cried the senior elder, James Cameron, of the Gauldwell, with a sob in his thin old voice.

It was as if the sergeant heard no word of dissuasion. He had opened out the paper and was holding it between his hands, standing there braced at "attention" and fighting down the working in his throat that momentarily was staying his voice.

Behind him, as he thus struggled, broke out the piteous wail "Oh, my laddie, my laddie!" from the very depths of poor Tibbie's heart, followed by a burst of loud sobs.

The sergeant did not turn to his wife — boy as I was, I remember it struck me that he dared not.

"Belnabreich," he said to an old farmer standing directly in front of him, "Belnabreich, tak' her hame, tak' her awa' frae this, in the name of God!"

Old Belnabreich moved towards Tibbie, but before he reached her she got the mastery of herself again.

"Thank ye, Belnabreich," she said, "ye've a kind heart; but I'm gaun tae bide here, whaur my man is. We've come through muckle thegither, and we'll thole this disgrace thegither, and syne him an' me, bairnless noo, will tak' our sorrow hame thegither."

The water was standing in the sergeant's eyes, but the spasm was out of his throat now, and in a steady strong voice that carried far, he read out the print on the face of the blue paper. And this was what it befell him to have to read:

WHEREAS No. 1420, Corporal Peter Strachan of the 92nd Regiment, age twenty-four years, height five feet eleven inches, complexion ruddy, hair red, eyes blue, distinguishing marks none, enlisted at Aberdeen on the — — day of — — 1844, born in the Parish of Auchterturff, in the County of Banff, and resident in said parish before enlistment: DESERTED from the said regiment at Montreal, Canada, on the — — day of — — 1848: The lieges are hereby warned under pain of law against harbouring the said deserter, and are strictly enjoined to give immediate information to the nearest police officer should they become cognisant of his whereabouts, to the end that he may be apprehended and duly punished.

ALASTAIR MCPHERSON, Col., Comg.
Gordon Highlanders.

GOD SAVE THE QUEEN!

The sergeant uttered the final invocation in a loud firm tone, and a graceless callant in the background, unwitting of the tragedy of the situation, cried "Hurrah." Otherwise there reigned a dead silence, as the old man, turning to his wife, gave her his arm with a certain courtliness rare among north country husbands of the humbler classes, and conducted her out of the little throng. The pair were allowed to get out of hearing ere the little stir of comment and condolence set in—it did not last long, for most of the folk had to trudge some distance to their homes. I remember watching the lonely couple as they wended their way along the path by the side of the wood, the dumpy huddled figure in the duffle shawl leaning against the tall spare form in the quaint old blue coat that had once belonged to the Duke, and the threadbare tartan trews that were a relic of the old regimentals.

From that Sunday old Sergeant Robbie was an altered man. Never more did he cross the hill for the once cherished "crack" with his Peninsular friend the Duke. Never more could the lads entice him to a dram in the Blackhillock public-house. He duly came to his work in the manse garden, but we boys hung about him in vain for stories of his old fighting days; a great silence had fallen upon the old man. His lean figure began to lose its erectness, and soon you scarcely would have known him for a veteran soldier. There remained one link only between him and my father, the interchange of the snuff-mull. But there were no more of the genial little chats that had been wont to accompany the give-and-take. From that Sunday Robbie was a man of monosyllables, and even my mother could not penetrate his grim reserve. He became yet more laconic after he lost Tibbie, who never held her head up from the day she knew of her son's disgrace. The poor old woman faded out within a couple of years, and Robbie had no longer the consolation that comes from having sorrow shared. After her death he gave up his duties as bellman and kirk officer, and scarcely left his cottage except to attend church. When I went to say farewell to him before leaving home to go to school, I found him sitting in front of the fire, staring blankly at the smouldering peats. That was the last time I saw the old man.

A year or two later a letter from home told me that old Robbie had heard from his son. The deserter, it appeared, had made his way to Chicago, had gone into some business in that stirring place, and was making money fast. He had written home begging his parents—he had not heard of his mother's death—to come out to him in America, and had enclosed a draft for an ample sum of money to pay the charges of the voyage and journey. The stern old man would hold no terms with the son who had disgraced his parents and dishonoured his uniform. He told my father curtly that he had folded the draft in a blank sheet of paper, and sent it back by return of post.

The tough old soldier, weary of life as he was, lasted a few years longer. At length one day the parish was stirred by the news that he had been found lying dead in a ditch some three miles away from his cottage, about half-way between it and the village of Keith. And before that day was done, the parish throughout its length and breadth knew also that Robbie's son, the deserter, had been apprehended and carried off to jail by Neil Robertson, the head of the county police.

The strange details were gathered piecemeal. A niece, a girl, who had come to live with the old man in his later feebleness, told that one night late a knock had come to the cottage door. The old man had opened it himself and was confronted by his son. She had overheard their brief colloquy. The son had begged the father to forgive him, and to leave home at once with him for America; he had a conveyance close by, and they might start immediately. The stern father had bidden the son begone out of his sight. He would not let the young man pass the threshold of the cottage, and told him plainly that if he did not quit the neighbourhood without an hour's delay, he would inform against him. With that he had shut the door in his son's face, prayed with tears and groans for two hours, and then lain down in his clothes. Before daylight the son had returned to the cottage, having, he told her, spent the night in the adjacent wood, and from outside the window had adjured his father to see him, if but for a moment. The old man would speak no word, lying silent in the press-bed opposite the fire; and as the day dawned the son had gone away, calling out to his father that he would come back again at night. The old man had lain late, groaning and praying in bed; about noon he had got up, read a chapter of the Bible aloud, and taking his stick had gone forth. She had hoped he was gone to look for his son; but he never came back, and the next thing she heard was that he had been found dead. The son had returned at night, but she had "steekit" the door, and made no answer when he called.

Neil Robertson, the head of the county police, furnished the sequel of the sad story. The old sergeant had come to his house in Keith as the short day was waning, and said he had come to do his duty and formally lodge the information that Peter Strachan, a deserter from the 92nd Regiment, had been to his cottage that morning, and that he believed him to be still in its neighbourhood. Robertson, knowing the relationship, had been reluctant to take the information, but the sergeant had sternly bidden him do his duty, as he was doing his. The old man was quite exhausted, Robertson testified, and he had begged him to take some rest and had offered him refreshment. But he had declined either to rest or to eat and drink, and had gone straight away. The life had gone out of the old sergeant as he was sadly trudging homeward, having done what he held to be his duty, as a true liegeman of the Crown, in whose service he had fought and bled.

THE GENTLEMAN PRIVATE OF THE "SKIL-AMALINKS"

It was in the autumn of the year 1856 that a squadron of that gallant Light Cavalry Regiment familiarly known as the "Skilamalinks" crossed Sheffield Moor, rode down Snighill, and proceeded along the valley of the dirty Don to the old cavalry barracks in the angle made by the divagation of the upper and lower Western roads. The "Skilamalinks" had followed Cardigan in that glorious, crazy gallop up the long valley of Balaclava, and when the eventful twenty-five minutes were over, their gallant array had dwindled to a weak troop, in which there was scarcely a scatheless man and horse. The bitter winter on the Chersonese had yet further thinned the handful that had escaped the Russian cross-fire, and there was a time when the "Skilamalinks" could barely furnish for duty a weak picket. But when the cruel winter ended, reinforcements came pouring in so freely that before the battle of the Tchernaya the regiment was near its full strength. It had returned to England, dismounted, early in 1856, had spent the summer in south of Ireland quarters, engaged in reorganisation and breaking in the remounts which had been sent to it, and in the autumn it had got the route for Yorkshire, headquarters at York, with out-quarters at Sheffield, and, if I remember rightly, at Leeds. Captain Jolliffe, the senior captain of the regiment, was in command of the Sheffield squadron, and it was as a lance-corporal in that fine soldier's troop that I, No. 420, Arthur Fraser, rode into the cramped little barrack-yard at the fork of the roads. My moustache is snow-white now, and, as I walk, I limp a bit from the Cossack lance-thrust through the calf of the leg which is my souvenir of the memorable Light Cavalry charge; but when I dismounted in the Sheffield barrack-yard thirty-five years ago, there was not in Queen Victoria's army, although I say it, a more strapping young fellow than Lance-Corporal Arthur Fraser, of A troop in the "Skilamalink" Hussars.

It is many a long year since I last saw the dense smoke under whose pall Sheffield breathes hard over its grindstones, and no doubt there are many changes in the dingy, rough, cordial town. When I last soldiered there our quarters were in the fine new barracks, a mile beyond the ramshackle old structure at the fork of the roads. The young soldiers took delight in the airy spaciousness of the former, whose front looks across to the public-house famous in my day for the tenpenny ale one glass of which made a fellow garrulous, and whose flank overhangs the beautiful valley which has long since recovered from the devastation wrought by the bursting of the great dam high up in its throat; but the old soldiers still nourished pleasant memories of the cramped old quarters nearer to the heart of the town. For aught I know, those may have been demolished long ago, and the Sheffielder of to-day may know them no more; but when our out-marching squadron on its way to Norwich last rode along the lower road toward Snighill, we oldsters looked rightward at the dingy tiled roofs, and at the little windows of what had been our troop-rooms, but which were now let out to civilian inhabitants who cultivated scrawny geraniums and reluctant fuchsias in stumpy little window-boxes. And as I gazed my heart swelled and the water came into my eyes, for the scene recalled the memory of a tragic occurrence which had for years cast a gloom on my life.

Most people are aware that nowadays no inconsiderable number of young gentlemen are serving in the ranks of the army. These are mostly men with a specific aim. They are fellows who have failed to get into the service as officers either through the front door of Sandhurst, or through the easier side door of the Militia. So they enlist, work hard, and keep steady, while their connections meanwhile are exciting all the influence in their power to further their promotion to commissioned rank. But it is not so generally known that in the old purchase days there was quite a considerable leaven of gentle-manhood in the ranks, without any such specific anxiety for promotion as actuates the gentleman-ranker of to-day. The gentleman-ranker of the old days—so far back as the Peninsular War he was common enough in the army—for the most part enlisted because he had come to grief in some fashion or other. Nowadays, a fellow who has done this has many resources other than the ranks. You find him in the Australian bush, in a mining camp of the Western States, in a Florida orange garden, on a ranche in Texas, or in the "fertile belt" out beyond Winnipeg. He may be prospecting in the Transvaal or galloping after steers in the Argentine. I have shaken the hand—and a deuced greasy hand it was—of a broken baronet doing duty as cook in a New Zealand timber-cutting camp, and have had a hackman at Portage la Prairie who was the son of a noble marquis, and had himself a courtesy title. For the broken gentleman of the Crimean war time there were no such opportunities of obscurity and possible redemption. The alternatives for him were utter blackguardism or the ranks of the army. When he chose the latter he invariably went for cavalry, ignorant or regardless of the harder work devolving on that arm; and almost invariably it was a light cavalry regiment in which he enrolled himself—always under a false name. The "Skilamalinks" were a favourite corps with gentlemen recruits under a cloud. Its chief was proud of this preference, and showed kindness to the waifs of good family. In my day they were invariably posted to A troop, which Captain Jolliffe ruled so kindly and yet so firmly, and which went in the regiment by the name of "the Gentlemen's Troop." When possible the gentlemen were always quartered together in the same troop-room, and were on their honour to behave creditably and show a good example in every respect. There were twelve of us, I remember, in one of those low-roofed attics above the stables in the old cavalry barracks of Sheffield. The corporal in charge of the room was the son of a great squire and M.P.; his mother the daughter of a Scotch marquis.

My chum was a stalwart and handsome young fellow, who had joined on the same day I became a "Skilamalink." He was reticent as to his antecedents; but he had confided to me that he had held a commission in an Indian native cavalry regiment, had come a mucker over high play at Simla, could not bring himself to face his mother (who was the widow of a clergyman of small means), had thrown up his commission, come home, and had 'listed for "the Skilamalinks" at the old "Hampshire Hog" in Charles Street, Westminster, on the very day he landed. As we rode back together from out the hell of slaughter on the morning of Balaclava, Charlie Johnstone (of course a "purser's" name) had killed the Cossack who had speared me, and cut down another who was in the act of skewering me from behind. Farther up the valley I believe I saved his life when the cannon-shot that bowled over his horse broke his leg, and when, lame though I was, I managed to carry him on my back up to the cover of Brandling's battery on the Causeway Ridge. So you may believe we were friends and comrades, and had a love for each other "passing the love of woman."

My chum was not a very social person, although always on perfectly good terms with his comrades of the "gentlemen's" barrack-room. He had frequent accesses of gloom, caused, I assumed, by the sudden shipwreck he had made of a career that must have been very promising, for he was a man of strong intellect, highly accomplished, a fine linguist, and well versed in military history and the science of war. When the shadow fell upon him, he used to spend much of his time in the stable with his mare. She was rather a notable animal. Desperately wounded as she was in the retreat from the Balaclava Charge, she had pulled herself together, reached the rallying-place of the Light Brigade, and formed up on the flank of the troop to which she belonged. She had recovered from her injuries with extraordinary rapidity, and had withstood with singular fortitude the hardships and starvation of the terrible winter; and she now among all troop horses in the regiment was the only survivor of the famous Charge. The dreadful Crimean winter had left its mark upon her. Before that evil time her nature had been gentle, and her paces smooth and easy. But during the worst of it, too weak to stand, she had long lain embedded in frozen mud and snow. She had risen, indeed, out of this misery, and had regained strength and shapeliness, but ever after she was the roughest trotter in the regiment. And with the ease of her paces had gone, too, the mare's temper. She had become a vicious and dangerous savage, to approach which was unsafe for any one save only the trooper who had ridden her in the Charge, to whom she was uniformly gentle and affectionate. Johnstone would sit by her for hours at a time on the manger at her head, or on the hanging bale by her side, talking in low tones to the old jade, and she listened to him for all the world as if she understood him, which, indeed, I am sure, he more than believed that she did.

Christmas Day in the army is the great festival of the year. The preparations for its adequate celebration are commenced days in advance. I hear—but I do not know whether it is true—that the cost of the Christmas dinner is now defrayed out of the canteen fund. But in our day—at all events in the cavalry regiments—the captain of each troop took, and was proud to take, that obligation upon himself as regarded his own men. There used to be quite a little ceremony about the matter. Some ten days in advance the troop sergeant-major would go round the barrack-rooms, and make a little speech in each room. "Men," he would say, striking an attitude, "our worthy captain has commissioned me to inform you that he will have great pleasure in having the men of his troop eat their Christmas dinner at his expense, and that he will also contribute toward the celebration of the day half a gallon of stout per man, which he regards as an adequate allowance if his men, as he anxiously desires, are to keep reasonably sober, and not discredit him and themselves by getting drunk." Cheers would follow this intimation, and a sarcastic old soldier might interject the remark, "The captain don't know, Sergeant-Major, how strong A troop heads are. We could drink a gallon per man, and never turn a hair!" Whereunto the honest sergeant-major would retort, "Ah, Lucas, we know what a power of suction you have without showing the drink, but remember it's not a fortnight since when you were walking pack-drill for being as drunk as a boiled owl." Lucas thus suppressed, the sergeant-major would proceed: "Now, men, take a day or two to make your minds up what you prefer for dinner—geese, turkeys, roast pork, veal—whatever delicacies of the season you may fancy, and then let the orderly corporal know your choice, so that he may give the order in good time. The materials for the plum-pudding—they are—of course you know."

Then the artistic genius of the room would betake himself to mural decorations, representations in colours of the banners of the regiment, the captain's coat-of-arms, such legends as "A Merry Christmas to all!" "Long life to our worthy Captain!" "The 'Skilamalinks' take the right of the line!" and so forth. Adjacent plantations are harried of Christmas trees, holly, and mistletoe, and each room becomes an evergreen bower. Christmas Eve is the period of busy labour, skill and triumph on the part of the pudding-compounder, whose satellites pick raisins of their stones, chop the lemon-peel, and heroically refrain from taking surreptitious sips of the brandy destined to invigorate the pudding. Volunteers are ready with their clean towels to serve as pudding-cloths, and then a procession marches to the cookhouse, where the puddings are consigned to the copper over which the conscientious compounder holds his long vigil. It is a pleasant time when on Christmas Day the bountiful fare is spread on the barrack-room table, and when the captain goes round the rooms, and says a few genial words to the men standing at attention while they listen. Then the oldest soldier, nudged by his mates, takes one pace to his front, halts, comes to preternaturally rigid attention, and shoots out the words, "Captain Jolliffe, sir"—then stammers painfully for the space of about a minute, and finally blurts out—"wish to thank you, sir—most liberal dinner, stout, sir—drink your health, sir—proud of our captain, sir—wish you and yours Merry Christmas and many of 'em!" "Same to you, men," replies the captain—genially tastes the stout which the cheekiest man tenders him in a stoneware soup basin, and with, mayhap, the words "Be merry but be wise" clanks out of the room, followed by a cheer.

The inmates of the "Gentlemen's Room," it was always understood, preferred not to be beholden to their captain for their Christmas dinner. They were not indeed bloated plutocrats, but most of them had their pittance of army pay supplemented by remittances from home, some stated, some occasional; and some little expenditure was made in modest amenities. They luxuriated, for instance, in tablecloths, and in cups and saucers in lieu of the rough stoneware basins supplied to the other barrack-rooms by the contractor for the mess-table refuse. But although the gentlemen chose to be independent in regard to the Christmas dinner, they were glad to accept in the spirit in which it was tendered the dozen of wine which Captain Jolliffe sent over from the officers' mess with his compliments and the good wishes of the season. We had dined, and had formed a wide circle round the cheerful fire as we sat over the captain's wine, whose array of bottles was marshalled on the table which we encircled—we were drinking the Château Margaux out of teacups, I remember—when all at once there was a timid little knock at the door. "Come in!" cried Corporal Hayward; the door opened, and there entered into the barrack-room a handsome white-haired lady, with scared, wistful eyes, and a worn face the expression of which had for me something vaguely familiar. She was in a state of manifest agitation, and for the moment, as she stood catching her breath as if to keep down the sobs that were rising in her throat, she was unable to utter articulate sounds.

We all rose to our feet, opening our circle. With high-bred courtesy and genuine concern, Corporal Hayward hastened to her side, and led her to the chair which he had vacated—the only one in the room. Then in a measure she regained her composure, and asked, still rather flutteringly—

"Is this what is called 'The Gentlemen's Room?'"

"The fellows call it so," replied Hayward, "but we make no pretensions."

"The corporal of the guard sent me here," said the lady, "as the likeliest place— —" and then she burst into tears and broke down.

"Likeliest place for what, madam?" inquired Hayward, with sympathy and concern in his accents.

"I—I am searching for my lost son," she answered through her tears, "for the only son of his mother, and she a widow."

"Pray tell me his name," said Hayward.

"Josceline L'Estrange," replied the lady more firmly, "twenty-three years of age, tall, slight, with light wavy hair, and blue eyes. My boy! my boy!" and the sobs came again thick and fast.

"There is no man of that name among us, or indeed in the regiment. But men do not always enlist in their own names. Look around you—but, no, I am sure your son cannot be one of us, else long before now he would have been on his knees before you!"

The lady scanned face after face in vain. Hayward undertook that she might be present at muster parade on the following morning, so that she might have the opportunity of seeing every man in the regiment. This gentleness, and the concern of all of us, seemed to soothe her; she sat quiet and silent with folded hands. Jack Dalrymple—I saw him the other day on the box of his drag at the parade of the Coaching Club—boiled some water in a pannikin and made the lady a cup of tea. As she sipped it, she began to talk—to tell us the story of her lost son.

He had been for two years in India, a subaltern in one of the Company's native cavalry regiments. She had not heard from him for several months when, in the late autumn of '53, she read in an Anglo-Indian newspaper that he had resigned his commission. Greatly distressed, she wrote out to one of his brother-officers begging for tidings of him. The reply came that he had got into a scrape in which there was nothing dishonourable, but which had ruined him financially, that he had persisted in throwing up his commission and returning to England, intending, so his comrade stated, to enlist in one of the Queen's light cavalry regiments in time to take part in the war with Russia which he had assured himself was impending. Before those tidings reached England, the light cavalry brigade had already sailed for the East; but the poor mother had gone to London and devoted herself to inquiries among the recruiting sergeants in Charles Street, Westminster. One of the fraternity had professed to recognise the son by the description given by the mother, and from the circumstance that the former had told him he had been an officer in the Company's native cavalry; but since the old sergeant had forgotten the name of the intending recruit and did not recollect in what regiment he had enlisted, the quest had run to ground. After the return of the brigade to England on the termination of the Crimean War, the mother had been searching without result among the regiments of it quartered in the South-country stations, and it was finally, on the advice of a Lancer major, who had recently exchanged from the "Skilamalinks," that she should visit Captain Jolliffe's troop in that regiment, since in it there was an exceptional number of gentlemen rankers, that she had come to Sheffield. And now, she piteously said, her last hope seemed dead; she would search no further, but go home and die, the light of her life gone out.

Hayward, tender and anxious as he was, did not dare to speak words to her that might inspire her with false hope. But it had been growing upon me, as she told her simple mournful story, that I had the power to do more than inspire her with hope—to give her, in very truth, the sweet joy of its realisation. Stronger and more strong had grown my conviction, as I listened to her, that my chum was none other than her lost son. Everything of his life that he had confided to me—and to me alone—tallied closely with the story related by the white-haired lady sitting in Hayward's windsor-chair. Soon after dinner he had become silent and abstracted, and presently he had risen and left us. But I knew perfectly well where to find my poor brooding comrade—up in the stall alongside that vicious old chestnut jade which had carried him through Russian cannon-fire and Cossack spears on the sad, glorious day of Balaclava.

I had only to descend the staircase and go a little way to the left, to reach the door of the stable in which was old "Termagant's" stall. Before I threw open the door, indeed before I reached it, I heard an unwonted din of hoofs clattering on the cobblestones, of vicious kicks against bales and pillar-posts, of scared snortings and squealing. The usually quiet troop horses I found infected with a wild delirium of mingled fury and panic, as the sweat poured down their flanks, and as they snuffed a strange fresh odour which pervaded the stable. I called my chum; there was no answer. No; but in the farthest stall I found him—found him down among the infernal hoofs of that vicious old hell-jade, the chestnut of the Balaclava Charge. She had trodden him almost into pulp. The odour which was maddening the other horses was the smell of his blood. She was kneeling on his chest with her forelegs. She was off the short jib, and was tearing pieces off his face and skull with her cursed long yellow fangs.

The sight whirled me into a reckless fury. I dashed at her head, caught her hard by the nose, half stunned her with swinging blows from the horse-log that sent her bloody tusks down her throat as she came at me, forced her back into the gangway, and fastened her up in a spare stall. Then, dodging her final vicious lash out, I ran to where my comrade lay. No one could have recognised him; hardly in the crushed, torn, and bleeding mass could there be discerned aught of human being. Yet he was not quite dead. I felt the last beats of his heart, and it seemed to me that he tried in vain to speak ere his shattered head fell back over my knee. I laid him quietly down, ran under the window of our room, and called for Hayward.

He came down. We went into the stable together where my comrade's remains lay, and I told him I was sure that the dead man was the old lady's son. He went across the barrack-yard to Captain Jolliffe's quarters, and told him of the double tragedy of this Christmas afternoon. His wife put her bonnet on, went with her husband to the "Gentlemen's Room," and carried the white-haired lady with her to her own quarters, her guest for the night. Four of us took a table-slab off its trestles, and on it carried the mangled corpse to the little hospital in the corner of the barrack-yard, Captain Jolliffe accompanying us. There was no need to send in a hurry for the civilian doctor who had medical charge of the detachment. We gently cut the clothing off the wrecked form, and straightened the mangled limbs. Then my assurance became doubly sure. On the crushed chest, yet itself intact, hung by a ribbon round the neck a locket containing a miniature of the white-haired lady who had come to the "Gentlemen's Room" in search of her son. It was her likeness to him that from the first had made her face seem familiar to me, although I did not grasp the resemblance until she was telling her story.

The woful task fell to Mrs. Jolliffe of breaking to the poor mother the grievous tidings that she had found her son only to lose him for ever in the grave. But God in His mercy averted the blow. The Captain's wife began the duty devolved on her by showing to the mother, without a word, the locket and the miniature. The poor woman devoured it with eager eyes, made a futile clutch at the trinket she recognised: her arms fell, she heaved one quick, sudden sigh, and fell back dead in her arm-chair. We knew afterwards she had been suffering from advanced heart disease.

Friends came to carry home to the Wiltshire village the dead mother and son. Captain Jolliffe went to be present at the funeral of the gentleman private of his troop, who had been a good soldier in war-time and peace-time; and he took Hayward and myself with him that we might lay our comrade's head in the grave. There was no Dead March in *Saul* to which to keep the measured time as the little procession wended its way under the gaunt elm-trees to the rural churchyard, nor did any firing-party ring out the triple volley over the soldier's corpse; but there lay on his coffin the sabre whose edge his country's enemies had felt, and from under the busbies of hussar-comrades tears dropped on his coffin as it lay in the open grave.

JELLYPOD; ALIAS THE MULETEER

I need not say that neither of these was the name by which he appeared in the Army List. The Muleteer was not his original by-name, although there may be a good many people who never knew him by another. When I remember him first—that was about thirty years ago—he was familiarly known in the cavalry regiment he had then recently joined, as Jellypod. I knew more of him as Jellypod than I did of him after he came to be known by the other name; but have you never noticed how completely a later by-name supersedes an earlier? I think of him habitually as the Muleteer, and had even to tax my memory to recollect the earlier Jellypod appellation.

He came to the Potterers from a militia regiment. Nowadays the militia is a chartered and approved vestibule to the regular army: and it is quite the thing for a youngster to go straight from the Outlandshire Rurals into the Grenadier Guards or the Blues. But it was a different matter thirty years ago, when the aspiring militiaman had to purchase, and when it was regarded as a mild form of impertinence on his part if he did not creep humbly into some unpretentious high-low regiment. But this man had actually bought into cavalry, and what made his *outrecuidance* the more marked was that he had come from a London militia regiment. No doubt times are changed, and the salt of the earth do their mimic soldiery in the corps which now swaggers as the 10th battalion of the Royal Fusiliers or the 21st battalion of the Rifle Brigade. But thirty years ago the metropolitan and suburban militias were not held in lofty esteem. In a county militia regiment you might lay your account with finding a considerable sprinkling of younger sons of the territorial families, and probably the major would be a man who had served in the regulars, and had gone in for the local corps when he married and retired to settle down on his patrimonial estate. But the London regiments had not this stamp of officer-hood. As like as not the Colonel Commandant would be a soap-boiler engaged in the active duties of his odoriferous profession. You would find no doubt ex-regulars holding commissions, but they were rather of the copper captain variety, who bound their militia commissions as phylacteries on their foreheads in evidence that their claim to the title of officer and gentleman was unimpaired by the little cloud under which they had retired from more active service. A militia commission has always been more or less of a useful item of stock-in-trade to a man living by his wits; and gentlemen of this type were sandwiched freely in the old days in the London regiments between the dashing scions of aldermen and the *jeunesse dorée* of the Stock Exchange.

Jellypod was a good sort of fellow in his way, but he did not hit it off with the Potterers. For one thing he was a married man with two children. Now in the matter of matrimony among the officers, the Potterers might have belonged to the army of the late lamented Cetewayo. Old Growler the colonel—he had been chief ever since the Crimea, and it was currently believed that he had sworn to live to a hundred and to die in the command of the Potterers, resolutely refusing promotion—old Colonel Growler had laid down the rule that no officer should marry and remain in the regiment who was not at least half-way up among the captains. A junior captain might wed, although frowned upon, on giving his pledge to send in his papers within the year; but lo! here was a cornet joining, not only with a wife, but with a wife who was a foreigner, and there was the additional aggravation of brats.

Then Jellypod, subsequently the Muleteer, had a modest confidence in himself. Among his burglars and pickpockets he had learnt foot drill thoroughly, and the first time he turned out to recruits' drill in the barrack square, had affably set the "regimental" right in regard to a word of command. He had studied Jomini, had detected the superficiality of Hamley's *Operations of War*, and had visited scientifically the battlefields of 1859 in Northern Italy. He had not been in the Potterers a week before he had tendered every officer a printed copy of an (undelivered) lecture before the United Service Institution on the utility of cavalry as a support to infantry. Before a fortnight was over he had confided to the adjutant, who—of course I mean the fine old ranker adjutant—was always very friendly and confidential with newly joined officers, that he regarded the regimental system of the Potterers as reprehensibly slack; and that he thought every one under the rank of field-officer should invariably attend morning and evening stables. One fine day after luncheon he followed the chief into the anteroom and asked him whether he would have any objections to a project he (Jellypod) had conceived, that he should give a course of evening lectures in the garrison library to the non-commissioned officers of the regiment on the German cavalry method of working by "fours." Old Growler stared at him grimly from under his shaggy eyebrows for the space of about a minute, deliberately expectorated into the grate, then rose, and, without a word, stalked out of the room. Jellypod did not win much favour from the fat old quarter-master when he suggested to that worthy that the regimental meat should be cast every morning, until the contractor realised that the second class beef he was in the practice of sending in would no longer be accepted.

With all the goodwill in the world, Jellypod did not stand well in the eyes of the men of the troop to which he was posted as cornet. He began badly. As is usual when a new officer's furniture arrives, a squad of men under a corporal were detailed to unload the Jellypod furniture from the vans in which it had come down from town. The work done—you may be sure the fellows had some chaff among themselves about the cradle, which presented to them a strange anomaly in being part of a cornet's goods and chattels—the oldest soldier, as the custom is, formed up to Jellypod, and, saluting, intimated the anxiety of himself and his comrades to drink that officer's health. Jellypod wasn't a bit mean, but he regarded this attempt to "pike" him as an impertinence, and ordered the man about his business, threatening to report him. He did report him to the corporal, who told him bluntly he thought the "kick" quite natural—the work being outside the men's regular duty, and it being an invariable custom to reward a fatigue-party on this kind of service with the price of a drink round. In fact the honest corporal as good as hinted that he himself felt rather dry. But Jellypod stood on the principle of the thing, and refused to contribute toward the consumption of intoxicating fluids; he himself was a teetotaler. It was a high sense of principle, again, which impelled him to refuse to fall in with the immemorial practice of paying his footing the first time he entered the riding-school. He would have stood out even against the fee to the riding-master, taking the ground that among the duties for which he drew his pay was the instruction in equitation of the officer-recruit as well as of the soldier-recruit; but old Voyage had taken his grievance to the colonel, who curtly ordered Jellypod not to let him hear any more "of this d—d nonsense." But he stood out against the *dustoor* to the underlings of the riding-school. Then the grim old rough-riding sergeant swore a grizzly oath, and took the corporal and the rough-riders to witness that if Mr. Jellypod did not rue his meanness before he was dismissed riding-drill, then his name was not old Tom Bridoon. And in truth it was a bad morning's work for Jellypod when he declined to fork out that sovereign as he trod the tan for the first time; for it came to pass that he and that same tan became and remained exceptionally intimate.

The universal wonder was why Jellypod should have come into cavalry. He was a fine-looking florid man of some seven-and-twenty, with a full round face, encircled by long chestnut whiskers. He was straight and square-shouldered, but had already begun to run into flesh, displaying a not inconsiderable protuberance in front, whence his by-name; and in point of fact exhibiting the reverse of attenuation when taken in reverse. With his round fleshy thighs, he looked just the sort of man to have a washball style of seat in any position, and bound to endure much in the effort to obtain the correct cavalry seat of the period, then much longer and less easy to acquire than now.

The Potterers hunted to a man; they would have hunted every day of the week, including Sunday, if their studs had run to it, and if there had been a sufficiency of attainable meets. The chief was the keenest of any; the prime article of his simple faith was that so long as unfortunately there was no fighting to be done, the chief end of the cavalryman was to gallop after hounds. So, the day Jellypod came to the regiment, the chief, never dreaming that there was any need to ask him whether he hunted, simply put the question, "How many hunters are you bringing; how many days a week do you care to hunt?" You might have knocked him down with a feather—he was stricken absolutely dumb, when Jellypod in the most matter-of-fact way replied:

"I am bringing no hunters, sir. I don't think hunting is an amusement I should care about. The fact is, I really don't know how to ride. I don't believe I was ever on the outside of a horse in my life. Of course I must learn now that I am in a cavalry regiment; and I daresay I shall find no difficulty in purchasing a steady, docile charger."

When he joined he had bought the first charger of the officer whose retirement created the vacancy which made room for him, a perfectly broken thoroughbred old chestnut, cunning in riding-school drill, knowing every command as if it had studied the book of the *manège*. This was a great pull for Jellypod; if only he could have kept in the saddle, the gallant old horse would have kept him right. But with "stirrups up" he couldn't keep in the saddle had his life depended on doing so. At a walk he was all right; but as soon as the word "Trot!" was given, he was all over the place. If he hung on by his eyelids for a round or two, old Bridoon, the non-payment of footing rankling in his mind, would touch up the old chestnut with the long whip; and then Jellypod would shut his eyes and gently roll off the saddle on to the tan. The man, however, had both pluck and perseverance. He never did get his seat without stirrups, but when these were allowed to the ride, he did better; trusting to them and to the reins to an unjustifiable extent, and rolling about, as old Bridoon used to say, "like an apple in a bucket"—only the expression was mostly a good deal coarser; but coming to grief altogether with much greater rarity. To the last he was the most abject duffer at "heads and posts," and it was well that the old chestnut carried a good head, else every time he and his rider went over the bar, the latter would have shot bodily over the former's ears. Altogether, Jellypod had a good six months in the school before he was dismissed riding-drill, and then it was only because, as the riding-master said, he could not be bothered with him any longer.

Jellypod had developed into considerable of a martinet even before he ceased to be a recruit and blossomed forth as a "duty-soldier." There was not an officer in the regiment who had so keen an eye for specks of rust in that awkward cranny at the back of a big bit, as it hung with specious resplendency between the burnished stirrup-irons. Trouble was no object to Jellypod in his quest after evidences of the dragoon's perfunctoriness. He was the first officer in the British cavalry—ex-rankers in a bad temper excepted—to unfasten a buckle in order to ascertain whether that recondite crevice at the root of the tongue was free from rust. The men of his troop rejoiced to see him cured of the practice of searching for scurf in the tails of horses shown out to be passed as clean, by a kick on the knee which he received from Tom Maguire's vicious chestnut mare. With all this bustle of thoroughness, Jellypod had no intention of posing as a tartar; he was simply full of exuberant zeal to do his duty to the extremest tittle. But he got himself, all the same, heartily disliked and a good deal despised. You see he was in such a hurry to be critical that he had not always acquainted himself with the right names of things. The whole stable burst into a roar of involuntary laughter once, when he spoke of a crupper as a "breeching"; and he "mulled it" severely on another occasion when he spoke of a horse's "left foot."

He was such a glutton for work that he was always ready to take "the belt" for another officer; I have known him orderly officer for a week on end, and he performed the duties of the "orderly" function in the most thorough manner. He would "take the guard" twice in the course of a night, and never omitted to make the round of the sentries with the corporal. So full of zeal was he that when living for a while in barracks during the absence of his wife at the seaside, he began the reprehensible practice of sneaking stealthily round the posts in order to detect any sentry who might be indulging in a few winks. He found it advisable, however, speedily to desist from this species of enterprise, because of an unpleasant experience he met with. Approaching a sentry, he had bidden him "give up his orders." Now the orders to sentries are that they are to give up their orders to nobody unless accompanied by the non-commissioned officer of the guard; and the sentry refused. Jellypod, bent on testing the soldier's knowledge of and fidelity to his orders, announced himself an officer and repeated his demand. The soldier recognised him, and saw his way to make reprisals on this man who pried by day into the tongues of buckles, and by night went on the prowl to trip up sentries.

"Here," exclaimed the sentry, "I don't care who you are; officer or no officer, you have no business comin' molestin' me on my post, an' tryin' to make me commit myself by givin' up my orders. Into the sentry-box with you, or I'll fell you with my carbine. Jump lively, or I'll brain you!"

Jellypod was not a hero, and it was clear to him that the man was in earnest and his monkey up. Severely crestfallen, he got into the sentry-box, and then begged of the sentry to summon the sergeant of the guard.

"See you d—d first," said the soldier; "you ain't 'fire,' so I've no call to give 'immediate alarm.' You'll stop there and cool till the relief comes round, and that will be in about an hour and a half."

There was no help for it, Jellypod had to dree his weird. When the sergeant came with the relief, he wanted the sentry made a prisoner of for insubordination and threatening violence to his superior officer; but the sergeant refused, saying he considered the man had acted within his duty. He put the occurrence into his report; and next forenoon Jellypod was sent for to the orderly room, and had the opportunity of realising with what emphasis and fertility of invective old Growler could administer a wigging. He never skirmished around any more among the night sentries, and for at least a week desisted from screwing his eyeglass into the crevices of big bits and turning buckles inside out. The chief was always down on him, but worse than ever after this episode. Two days after it, out at squadron drill, he told him he rode like a cross between a tailor and a sack, and sent him back to riding-school till further orders.

The truth was that the chief was most anxious to see the back of Jellypod, and the aspiration was shared in by every officer in the regiment. He was not detested; it was recognised that there was nothing of the actual cad about him; but the feeling was intense that he was the wrong man in the wrong place as an officer in the easy old confraternal Potterers, who did not believe in new-fangled notions, and who, as regarded most of their professional ways, had moved very little since they charged in the Union Brigade at Waterloo. Colonel Growler was a just man, and under no temptation would he resort to tyranny, or allow his officers to indulge in hazing; but he was not backward in administering strong hints to Jellypod that he was not in his proper sphere as a cornet in the Potterers. As soon as that subaltern was dismissed from riding-school, it became imperative that he should provide himself with a second charger—indeed he ought to have done so earlier. Beast after beast was sent him on approval, any of which he thought quite good enough, and it is true that any of them was good enough for the price which was Jellypod's figure. But the right vests in the colonel of a cavalry regiment to pass or reject horses intended for officers' chargers; and Growler ruthlessly cast candidate after candidate for the position of Jellypod's second charger. At last he was told he must get a proper second charger, and no more nonsense; Jellypod piteously urged that it was the colonel who was standing in the way of his possessing that requisite animal.

While matters stood thus, the Potterers got the route. I should have said they had been in Newbridge for a couple of years, and now they were ordered to Birmingham, Coventry, and Weedon. Jellypod's troop was in the detachment assigned to Weedon under the command of the major. Jellypod, whose first charger was lame, went by train into Dublin, where the detachment spent the night before embarkation. Next morning he appeared in complete marching order, on the back of a big underbred young horse, as soft as butter, for it was just off the grass, and with quarters as round — well, as Jellypod's own. The beast fretted itself into a lather on the march down to the North Wall, where, to the dismay of Jellypod, Colonel Growler was very much in evidence to see the detachment duly off. The chief no sooner caught sight of Jellypod's mount than he denounced it as a cross between a cow and a camel, and cast it on the spot, so Jellypod crossed St. George's Channel a cavalry officer on the line of march without a horse to his name.

He was the only subaltern with his troop, and it was thought imperative by the major and his captain that he should go on the road. The only resource was to dismount one of the men, and put Jellypod on the troop-horse. There was a good deal of malice in the selection of the quadruped. Throughout the regiment "F. 23" had a malign reputation for unapproachable roughness. She was satirically known as "the Bonesetter," and was understood to have dislocated every articulation in the framework of one recruit, and jerked the teeth out of the head of another. This was the mount which on the Liverpool jetty was given to Jellypod, to carry him for nine long marches till Weedon should be reached.

"F. 23" was a pleasant horse at a walk, and not at all a bad-looking beast in the summer time, when her coat was glossy. Jellypod clearly rather fancied himself as he paced up Compton Street under the eyes of the shop-girls. As soon as the town was cleared the trumpet sounded "Trot!" and his self-complacency rapidly disappeared. Apart from her roughness, "F. 23" was a hot old jade, and stiffly plunged and bucked as she fought against the officer's heavy hands tugging and jerking at the curb as he rolled and floundered all over the saddle, while the perspiration streamed from under his helmet. One need not dwell on the agonies of that march: suffice it to say that when Cornet Jellypod woodenly dismounted in front of the Grosvenor Hotel in the ancient city of Chester, the world has seldom contained a more saddle-sick man. As soon as saddles were removed, information came from the stable that the day's work had given "F. 23" a sore back, and that it was impossible that she could be ridden during the rest of the march.

Jellypod felt very like intimating that it was impossible that he could ride during the rest of the march. But he was of a resolute spirit, and first arnica and afterwards cunningly moistened pipeclay judiciously applied had improved matters by next morning. A second trooper was dismounted, upon whose horse Jellypod performed the second day's march to Market Drayton. The paces of this beast were suave and easy compared with those of the "Bonesetter," but Jellypod rolled about so in the saddle in the effort to favour his chafes, that when the day's march was over mount No. 2 was also reported to have a sore back. It was then that his captain, previously only grumpy, permitted himself the use of the strongest language in addressing the unfortunate Jellypod. This captain was known in the regiment by the pleasing appellation of "Hell-fire Jack," on account of the fervour of his objurgations when the spirit moved him. On this occasion the spirit moved him very much indeed, and rendered his remarks wholly unquotable. Suffice it to say that he swore Jellypod should have no further opportunity of bedevilling troop horses; but should be compelled to tramp on foot the rest of the way to Weedon, leading the two beasts which he had used up in as many days. This was a *brutum fulmen*; no doubt the captain would have been glad to carry out his threat; but the major pointed out that it would not do. So Jellypod was permitted to finish the journey by train, and his abrasions were all but whole by the time the detachment rode up the slope by the military prison, and defiled through the fine old gateway of wrought-iron that leads into the Weedon barrack-yard.

A few months later the Potterers quitted the midland stations, and were concentrated in the lines at the Queen's Hotel end of Aldershot North Camp. A very brief experience of the Long Valley sufficed for Jellypod. He had not nerve enough for a troop leader in a charge over its broken and dust-smothered surface. One day he pulled his horse back on to him in a half-hearted attempt to jump one of the little cuts which the rain-storms wash out in the friable black dust, and as he lay prone in the V-shaped trough of it, a couple of squadrons rode over him. Next day he opened negotiations for an exchange to India, and presently he was gazetted to one of the ex-Company's hussar regiments.

Jellypod appeared to thrive in India. He had got his lieutenancy before his exchange, and some two or three years later an opportune snap of cholera made a captain of him. But his great chance came when Sir Robert Napier set himself to organise that Abyssinian expedition which brought him his fairly earned peerage. Jellypod—I ought to say here that I believe the familiar old Potterer nickname did not follow him to India—had the luck to get a special service billet. It did not promise much glory, since its function was the command of the mule transport train of one of the divisions, but he was thankful for minor mercies and accepted it with avidity. Now as a beast of burden the mule has its idiosyncrasies and peculiarities which, it is averred with considerable show of authority, no white man has ever fully comprehended. If this be indeed so, our friend was the exception that proves the rule. He seemed to have a natural affinity with mules, and could do anything with them he pleased. No Alabama nigger ever had a closer *rapprochement* with the mule than had this gallant officer; and it was the universal recognition of this accomplishment that earned for him the *sobriquet* of "the Muleteer," by which hereafter I shall denominate him.

He was zeal itself. Staveley somewhat roughly sat on his project of giving evening lectures on the sandy beach of Annesley Bay to the Smytches, Rock Scorpions, Cypriotes, Syrians, Fellaheen, and other miscellaneous scum of the Levant who were serving as mule-drivers, on the expediency of the construction of a common language to be used in addressing the mules in their charge. I have reason to believe that the story was a "shave," that he sent in a memorial to Sir Robert Napier, suggesting that a number of mules of both sexes should be left behind in the Abyssinian villages, with intent that a stock of transport animals should be thus propagated. But he certainly was a most zealous and active transport officer. It is reported of him that on one day he personally flogged upwards of three hundred mules up the steep slope on the landward side of Zula. Had there been any fighting in the Abyssinian expedition—it is really the case, I believe, that one man was killed—he of course would have been out of it in the rear among the baggage. But he was no greater distance off the final amusement than the south side of the Bashilo; he was mentioned in despatches, as is the modern fashion in regard to every one above the rank of lance-corporal; the Director of Transport strongly recommended him for "extent and value of assistance," and the Muleteer looked forward with a modest confidence to a brevet majority, and thought it not unlikely that he would get the C.B. as well. The Muleteer had the happy fortune to live, not in the bad old days, but in the good new days. In the bad old days, the only service that assured to a man a brevet—if he came out alive—was to lead a forlorn hope. Then, an officer might own a carcase as full of holes as a cullender, and never have the impertinence to dream of a brevet. The Napier brothers, for instance, got pretty well shot to pieces in the Peninsular war. Charles was a major at Vimiera in 1808; he was still a major after Fuentes de Oñoro in 1811, never having missed a battle, and having been wounded six times. George got his captaincy in 1804; he was all through the Peninsular fighting, from Corunna to Toulouse, in which latter battle, fought in 1814, he was but a substantive major, having in the interval lost an arm and been wounded otherwise repeatedly. Henry Havelock soldiered twenty-nine years before he obtained the rank of a field-officer. The officer of these brighter days lives under a régime the virtual head of which was a full major-general in twenty years after he got his first commission. Nowadays, every staff officer who has been within sound of a skirmish, the wind blowing his way, gets his brevet as a matter of course. There is a fortunate young gentleman in the service to-day (he is in "the ring," of course) who has three medals for as many campaigns, the C.B., the Khedive's Octopus, and the Osmanlie, who has been the recipient of two steps in rank by brevet, and who has never seen a shot fired in anger.

Well, the Muleteer was earning his Abyssinian laurels a few years before "the ring" became the pride and ornament of the British army, else, supposing him to have been of the elect, he no doubt would have got the C.B. As it was, he got a brevet majority, and when the expedition returned to India, he said farewell to regimental duty and got a billet on the staff; and such was his good fortune, that for some ten years he continued to hold staff appointments with perfect satisfaction to himself, and with no perceptible detriment to the interests of the service. Being on the Madras side, he gradually fell into the easy-going fashion of the "benighted Presidency"; no doubt his zeal had not departed from him, but it had fallen latent. His portliness had increased with years and ease, and it was only once in a blue moon that he was seen in the saddle. A second brevet had come his way in some inexplicable fashion, and he was now for some time past a lieutenant-colonel. But his substantive rank still remained that of captain, and as his original Indian regiment had gone home and he had exchanged into its successor, so as to keep on in his staff billet, he was regimentally a very junior captain. But this gave him no disquietude, since nothing was further from his intention than to revert to regimental duty.

I don't quite know how it happened, but in negotiating a second exchange so as to keep his staff berth, he somehow missed stays; found himself all at once on half-pay, and no longer in staff employ. The story was that he was manœuvred out of the brigade-majorship, or whatever it was he held, by an intrigue at Presidency headquarters, where the post he had been occupying was wanted for somebody else. Anyhow, the poor Muleteer had no alternative but to return to England. He came back very disconsolately, and tried in vain for some staff employment. He would have left the service altogether, if he could have found anything to do worth his while in civilian life, but nothing offered. He thought himself too poor to scratch along on half-pay, and made interest for reinstatement to full pay and duty. His substantive rank being still that of captain merely, he could of course aspire to no higher regimental position; and one fine day he was gazetted to a troop in the old familiar Potterers. Of course he came in as junior captain. Certainly as a junior captain he was a good deal of an anachronism, for he was a grandfather, he weighed sixteen stone, there was a deep tinge of gray now in the chestnut whiskers, and he was senior in the army to the commanding officer of the regiment. But now in the Potterers, he met with a good deal of consideration. Most of the old hands who remembered him in his cockolorum days were now out of the regiment. Old Growler was by this time a lieutenant-general; the major of his early days had gone into brewing; the adjutant was drilling a yeomanry corps; and the quarter-master had retired on his plunder.

The regular drill season was over, and the Potterers had come from Brighton to Aldershot, exchanging with a regiment that had borne the heat and burden of the summer in flying columns and Long Valley field-days. So it seemed that the Muleteer had at all events a quiet winter in front of him, before the season should come round when he should have to encounter the chances of the Long Valley, the pitfalls of the Fox Hills, and the grips and fissures of the Devil's Jumps. But it happened that early in October a continental cavalry officer of distinction visited England, and orders came down from Pall Mall for a field-day of the Aldershot cavalry brigade in honour of the stranger. The general commanding the brigade was away on leave, shooting grouse in Scotland. The three regiments paraded, and lo! the junior captain of the Potterers, senior as he was in army rank to any other officer on the ground, quitted his subsidiary position of squadron leader in the Potterers, rode out to the front, and assumed command of the brigade.

It must quite frankly be allowed that he made a deuce of a mess of it. The Duke addressed him in those bland phrases and mild tones which are so characteristic of the head of the British army when things do not go smoothly. The Muleteer, for his part, lost his temper as well as his head, and pitched vehemently into his own regiment, denouncing it for all sorts of faults and shortcomings. The lieutenant-colonel commanding it bore his expletives with a grim submissive silence, biding his time. At length, the Duke and the Muleteer both equally hoarse, the distinguished stranger fluent in encomia while an amused smile played over his features, the field-day came to an end. The Muleteer ceased from his temporary pride of place as acting brigadier-general, and reverted to his position as junior captain of the Potterers; and that honest old corps stolidly returned to barracks. No sooner had the men dismounted than "officers' call" was sounded. The officers, still with the grime of the Long Valley on their faces, crowded into the orderly room, where they found the chief already seated in his chair, with that look in his face which it wore when he was not amiable. He directed the Muleteer to come to the front, and thus addressed him:—

"When in command of the brigade to-day, you used, sir, a considerable variety of forcible expressions in the denunciation of the regiment which I have the honour to command. To some extent, I am prepared to admit the force of your strictures, although it might be the opinion of an impartial critic that the fault did not wholly lie with the regiment. The squadron of which your own troop, sir, was a part, was the chief sinner in slackness and blundering. You will, sir, till further orders, take that squadron out into the Long Valley for drill every morning, from nine to eleven. And, sir, I observed to-day that your seat on horseback was excessively bad, and that when your charger knocked about a bit, you were all over the place. You will, therefore, until further orders, go to riding-school every morning, from seven to eight, along with the junior class of recruits. That is all I wished to say. Good-morning, gentlemen."

The same afternoon the Muleteer sent in his papers, and next morning he went away on leave, pending his retirement from the service. I believe he is now living in the Poictiers district, engaged in the occupation of breeding mules.

THE DOUBLE COUP DE GRÂCE

In an earlier article I have tried to describe the "Old Sergeant" of my native parish. In a neighbouring glen which formed another parish of our local presbytery, there dwelt during my boyhood another veteran of the grand old type, that stout ex-warrior, Sergeant Davie Russell. I lived a good deal from time to time with the minister's family of the parish in which the sergeant dwelt, and to the elderhood of which it was his pride to belong; and the manse boys of Glenvorlich used often to take me with them to visit the still stalwart veteran in his comfortable cottage under the shadow of the great mountain with the twin wens on its summit. The Sabbath evening was the time when he was best pleased to see us; and for the sake of the interesting stories which were sure to follow, we were content to endure a cross-examination in the toughest problems of the Shorter Catechism, and listen to a dissertation on the faulty tactics of Amasa, the captain of the host of Absalom, who, the sergeant contended, would not have suffered so severe a defeat if he had posted his troops out in the open to encounter the onslaught of Joab instead of taking up a position in the heart of the wood of Ephraim. On Sundays Sergeant Davie Russell always wore his pensioner's blue coat with the red facings, the Waterloo Medal hanging by the faded crimson ribbon on its left breast, and the empty sleeve tacked to the right lapel of it. It was in the memorable battle which ended Napoleon's career that he had lost his right arm, and ever since he had enjoyed his sergeant's pension, with a trifle extra for his wound. Forty years of peace-time had no whit dulled his recollection of the old fighting days, and we boys hung on the old soldier's lips as he told us stories of his battles. Wellington was his hero. "His soul was as a sword, to leap at his accustomed leader's word"; to finish the quotation, "he knew no other lord."

He used to talk to us of the young general's calm face at Assaye, when he ordered forward the seventy-fourth regiment—the sergeant's old corps—through the hurricane of Mahratta cannon fire to retrieve the mischief of the pickets' reckless advance; and how, when the Mahratta batteries had been captured with a rush, the keen tulwars of the swarthy horsemen were slashing into the disordered ranks, until in the nick of time the eagle-eyed chief sped Maxwell's light dragoons to the relief. Then he would speak of Wellington on the Busaco ridge; how, just as Loison's supple Frenchmen had climbed the steep and rugged slope, and were re-forming on the edge of the upland, he gave the word to the Scottish regiment, which advanced at the double, halted, and poured in a volley, and then, bringing the bayonets down to the charge, literally pitchforked the Frenchmen headlong down the abrupt declivity. I think we used to like best to hear the sergeant tell of the desperate fighting in the storming of Peninsular fortresses besieged and taken by Wellington; of "the deadly breach in Badajos's walls," when the stormers leaped down into the ditch and struggled up the steep face of the battered masonry, only to find themselves confronted by the grim tiers of sword-blades projecting from massive beams, behind which stood drawn up the staunch defenders, sweeping the ascent with their musketry fire; of the fierce storm of Ciudad Rodrigo, where George Napier lay on the slope of the breach, struck down by the wound that shattered his arm, and still as he lay, waving his sword with his sound arm, and cheering on those whom his fall had for the moment caused to falter; of that strange quarter of an hour on the breach of Saint Sebastian, when the stormers, beaten back by the fire and steel of the serried defenders, lay down by order on the face of the breach, while Graham's artillery played over them on the French masses defending the crown of it, the aim so fine that one of the leading men of the prostrate stormers, rashly raising his arm, had his hand carried away by a cannon-ball.

Waterloo, too, was a theme on which we used to incite the old sergeant to enlarge; and I delight to remember as it were yesterday how the veteran's cheek would flush as he told of Wellington slowly riding along the line before the battle began, amid the cheering of the troops as he passed, cool and calm, as had been ever his wont in the old Peninsular days, with the high-souled confidence of success on the face of the man who had never known what it was to lose a battle. Then he would go on to tell of the advance of the massive French column up the slope on the left of La Haye Sainte, its broad front fair against Picton's weak division; how that warlike chief sat on his charger in front of the Cameron Highlanders, to which regiment the sergeant then belonged, and vehemently damned as wretched cowards the Dutch-Belgian runaways, who fled through the firm British line; how, when he saw that the right moment had come, he shouted, "A volley, and then charge!" and how, at the word, the volley sped, and the Highlanders, springing through and over the ragged hedge, struck the head of the French mass with the cold steel. It was in the hand-to-hand fight that followed, the sergeant would recount with a jerk and twitch of his stump, that he lost his arm and gained his wound-pension; and as two comrades helped him to the rear when the French were routed, he saw Picton lying dead with a bullet-hole in his forehead.

Sergeant Russell's family consisted of twin sons, who, when I knew them, were already grown men. From childhood both had ardently looked forward to follow in their father's footsteps, and when in 1846 the country was ringing with the news of the victories of the first Sikh war—when "Moodkee," "Ferozeshah," and "Sobraon" were in every one's mouth—the brothers, then of fit age to take service, had been frantic to accept the Queen's shilling and take a share in the stirring doings. But they were entreated of their father to stay at home with him while he lived, for he was an old man and could not long survive. Filial affection constraining the lads, they reluctantly consented, and betook themselves to civilian avocations. John Russell, the elder twin, a taciturn, resolute man of strong character, became a stone mason; Aleck, the younger brother, of a lighter and less stable nature, took to the trade of a carpenter. Both were men of blameless life, and the mothers of the parish held up their mutual love to the admiration and imitation of their offspring.

But a shadow was to come between the brothers. They both fell in love, and, as ill fortune would have it, they both fell in love with the same girl. I remember her well, a pretty, airy creature, the daughter of the petty local shopkeeper up in the throat of the glen. In her reckless waywardness she played the brothers off against each other, and a bitter jealousy supplanted the old loyal affection. They did not quarrel outright, and both still lived under their father's roof; but the elder brother glowered sullenly at the younger, and the younger would shoot galling jibes at his silent senior. The old sergeant noticed the alienation, and took it so to heart that he fell ill, and in a few days a long straggling procession came winding down the brae to the little graveyard by the burnside, and the old soldier of the Peninsula and Waterloo was lowered into his quiet grave under the willow trees.

The brothers walked home together, drawn together again by their loss. That same evening a long silence was broken abruptly by the elder brother.

"See here, Aleck, it can never mair be wi' you an' me as it used to be. If ye win that lassie, I s'all hae murder in my heart against you; if I win her, ye'll nourish against me the hate o' hell. Suppose we agree tae lay aside thoughts o' her, heave awa' thae trowels an' plummets an' planes an' augers, an' gae to the wars as the auld man did afore us. That's the trade for us, lad; Brown Bess an' the bayonet afore gimlets an' gavels!"

The brothers shook hands on the compact, and resolved to 'list without delay. They were stirring times, those early months of 1849, when news was coming home of the outbreak of the second Sikh war, and we were reading of the glorious death of Cureton, "the fair-haired boy of the Peninsula"; of young Herbert Edwardes' ready prowess—a junior lieutenant, yet in command of an army with which he had won victories and was beleaguering Mooltan; of William Havelock's wild gallop to his death across the Ramnuggur sands, and of stout old Thackwell's stiff combat at Sadoolapore. The old sergeant had not been buried a week when his sons were tramping over the hills to Aberdeen, where was the nearest recruiting station, and presently we heard that both had enlisted in the same regiment, a corps which was in sore need of recruits, for it had suffered terrible losses in the desperate struggle of Chillianwallah. That news would have been the last tidings of the brothers that ever reached the highland glen, but for one letter from John to the minister of the parish, written about the end of 1850. He was doing well in the regiment, being already a full corporal; but now that there was peace and idleness, Aleck had grown restless and had volunteered into another regiment, since when he had not heard of him. No word more came of, or from, either of the brothers, and as the years passed they fell out of memory.

Many years later I paid my first visit to India. The seven years of peace, after Chillianwallah and Goojerat and the annexation of the Punjaub, had been followed by the ghastly period of the great Mutiny, and now the blood of the Mutiny had been long dry. On the maidan of Cawnpore one could scarce discern the traces of the poor earthworks that had constituted Wheeler's intrenchment, and Marochetti's marble angel spread pitying wings over the well which had been filled to its top with our slaughtered ladies and their children. The shot-wrecked Residency of Lucknow stood, and still stands, in the condition the relieved garrison left it, a monument of that garrison's heroic constancy; but otherwise the stains of battle had been wiped from the beautiful capital of Oude, and gardens bloomed where the dead had lain thick. The subalterns of Chillianwallah and Goojerat were general officers now—those whom the climate and the Mutiny had spared—and the talk in the clubs and at the mess-tables was no longer of old Gough and his "could steel," and of the "Flying General" chasing the fugitives of Goojerat into the Khyber Pass, but of Clyde and Hugh Rose and William Peel and John Nicholson.

In the course of my travels I was the guest for a week of a general officer who was kind enough to recount to me many reminiscences of his long period of soldiering in India. One of those narratives had for me a special pathetic interest, and perhaps the emotion may be in a measure shared in by the reader who shall have already accompanied me thus far. I wrote down the story the same night it was told me, when the old soldier's words were fresh in my memory.

"In the early 'fifties," said the general, "our European troops serving in India were not in good case. In those days they were constantly quartered in the plains, the barracks were dismal, pestilential, thatched sheds, there were none of the comforts the soldier now enjoys, and in the dismal ennui his only resources were his canteen and the bazaar. The revulsion from the stir and variety of marching and fighting, superinduced widespread discontent, and in many instances depression intensified into actual despair. Quite an epidemic of suicide set in, and was but partially cured by Sir Charles Napier's very Irish expedient of sentencing a man to be shot who had unsuccessfully attempted to take his own life. At this time transportation to West Australia was the usual punishment in the army for the military crime of grave insubordination. So low had sunk the morale of too many of the rank and file, and so ardent was the desire for change of any kind, no matter what or where, that men deliberately laid themselves out to earn the punishment of transportation. This was not a difficult task. The soldier had only to make a blow at his superior officer—and all above him from a lance-corporal to the colonel were his superior officers—or even to throw a cap or a glove at him, to have himself charged with the offence of mutinous conduct. The *pro forma* court-martial sat; the soldier pleaded guilty; the sentence of transportation was duly 'approved and confirmed,' and presently the man was blithely on his voyage to join a chain gang at Perth or Freemantle.

"This state of things was too injurious to the service to be allowed a long continuance. The Commander-in-Chief promulgated a trenchant order, denouncing in strong terms the utter subversion of discipline that seemed impending, and sternly intimating that death, and not transportation any more, should in future be the unfailing penalty for the crime of using or offering violence to a superior officer. The order was read aloud at the head of every regiment in India, but its purport did not seriously impress the troops. The men were fain to regard it in the light of what the Germans call a stroke on the water, and they did not believe that it would be actually put in force. They did not know the nature of Sir Charles Napier.

"It was in my own regiment, then quartered in Meerut, that the first offence was committed after the promulgation of the order. A young private named Creed, who had joined us in India from another regiment, one morning casually met on the parade-ground a young officer on the staff of the General, and without a word threw his cap in the face of the aide-de-camp. He was made a prisoner, and when brought before the colonel, frankly owned that he had no ill-feeling against the officer, whom, indeed, he did not know that he had ever seen before, and his simple explanation of his conduct was that he had acted on 'a sudden impulse.' It was proved, however, that the night before the assault he had been heard to say in the canteen that he meant to 'qualify for West Australia' within the next twenty-four hours. The case was reported to the Commander-in-Chief, who directed that the prisoner should be tried by a general court-martial, the attention of which he called to his recent orders. The sentence of the court was 'death,' which his Excellency approved and confirmed. It was read to the prisoner by the colonel, in front of the regiment, and he was informed that the sentence would be carried into execution on the morning of the next day but one.

"The night before the morning fixed for the execution there reported himself to me as having joined, a non-commissioned officer whose arrival I had been expecting for some days. Wishing to remain in India he had volunteered to us from a regiment which had been quartered at Agra, and which had been ordered to return to England. He was scarcely a prepossessing-looking man, but looked every inch a good soldier, and his face indicated self-command and dauntless resolution. Standing composedly at attention, he handed me the documents connected with his transfer and a private note from the adjutant of the regiment he had quitted. It ran thus—

"'Sergeant Russell will hand you this note. We lose him with great regret; he will do you credit. I never have known a better non-commissioned officer. Duty to its last tittle is the man's watchword and what he lives for. I verily believe were he detailed to the duty of shooting his own brother, he would perform the service without a word of remonstrance. I own that I grudge him to you.'

"I told the newcomer that his late adjutant had given him a high character, and that I was glad to have in the regiment a man so well recommended. He saluted silently; I detailed him to a company and told him he might go. But as he was leaving the orderly room a thought struck me and I recalled him. I knew how strong throughout the regiment was the sentiment in favour of the poor fellow who was waiting his doom; and it occurred to me that this new sergeant, who in the nature of things could not be a warm sharer in this sentiment, was a fitting man to detail to the command of the firing party. I briefly explained to him the circumstances, and then told him to what duty I purposed assigning him. 'Very well, sir,' was his calm remark; 'it is an unpleasant duty, certainly, but I can understand the reason why you put it on me.' Then, telling him to apply to the regimental sergeant-major for details, I let him go.

"I need not ask you whether you have ever seen a military execution; it is the most solemn and fortunately the rarest of all our military spectacles. It was not yet daylight when all the troops of the garrison, both European and native, were on march to the great parade-ground. The regiments, as they arrived, wheeled into position, the whole forming three sides of a vast square, the dressed ranks facing inwards. The dead silence was presently broken by the roll of the drum, announcing the approach of the procession escorting the doomed man, and a moment later the head of it rounded the flank of one of the faces of the great hollow square. In effect the yet living soldier was marching in his own funeral procession, his step keeping time to the swell and cadence of his own dirge. At the head of the sombre cortège was borne the empty coffin of the man whose sands of life were running out; there followed in slow march, with arms reversed, the execution party of twelve privates and a corporal, under the command of Sergeant Russell; and then a full military band, from whose instruments there pealed and wailed alternately the Dead March in *Saul*. There was a little interval of space, and then, alone save for the Presbyterian chaplain walking beside him in his Geneva gown, and praying in low, earnest accents, marched with firm step the condemned man, his face calm, but whiter than the white cap on his head. Close behind marched, with fixed bayonets, a corporal and a file of men of the quarter-guard. Thus was constituted what, save for the central figure of it, who still lived and moved and had his being, and for the empty coffin, was in every attribute a funeral procession.

"The parade came to the 'shoulder' as the little column, wheeling to its right after clearing the flank by which it had entered the square, began its slow, solemn progress along the front of the left face. I felt the throbbing strains of the Dead March becoming actual torture to me long before the procession, moving in its measured march along the successive faces, had reached the front of the centre, where stood the regiment to which the prisoner and myself belonged. 'Steady, men!' shouted the colonel hoarsely, as he felt rather than heard or saw the involuntary shiver that ran along the ranks as the firm, pale face slowly passed. With an upward glance at the chief, the poor fellow straightened himself and set his shoulders more square, as if he took his officer's word of command to include him also. His chum broke into noisy weeping, and a young officer swooned, but the doomed man strode steadily on, without the quiver of a muscle of his set face.

"At length the long, cruel progress was completed, and the head of the procession drew off to the centre of the unoccupied fourth face of the square; the coffin-bearers laid down their burden there and retired, and Sergeant Russell drew up his firing party into two ranks fronting toward the coffin, at a distance of about thirty paces. The band ceased its sombre music and wheeled aside. The prisoner, accompanied still by the clergyman, marched steadily up to his coffin, on which the two knelt down.

"The clergyman's ministrations were almost immediately interrupted. At a signal from the general the judge-advocate rode out from the staff, and, moving forward to the flank of the firing party, read in sonorous tones the warrant for the condemned soldier's execution. Universal admiration and compassion were stirred by the soldierly bearing of the man as he listened to the official authorisation of his doom. As the judge-advocate approached he had risen from the kneeling position, doffed his cap, and sprung smartly to 'attention,' retaining that attitude until the end, when he saluted respectfully and knelt down again as the minister rejoined him. There was a short interval of prayer; then the judge-advocate beckoned to the chaplain to retire, and the soldier remained alone, kneeling on his coffin-lid there, face to face with imminent death in the midst of the strained and painful silence.

"Marching at the head of the procession, the members of the firing party had no opportunity of seeing their unfortunate comrade until he had reached his coffin and was kneeling in front of where Sergeant Russell had drawn up the party of which he had the command. I should tell you that the sergeant of an execution party carries a loaded pistol, with which it is his stern duty to fulfil the accomplishment of the sentence if the volley of his command shall not have been promptly fatal. The corporal of the party told me afterward that after it had taken position Sergeant Russell spent some time in examining their muskets, and that the prisoner had for some little time been kneeling on his coffin before the sergeant looked at him. As he gazed he suddenly started, became deadly pale, muttered more than once, 'My God, my God,' and was for several minutes visibly perturbed; but later, although still ghastly pale and having a strange 'raised' expression, he pulled himself together and was alert in his duty. What I myself saw and heard was, that after the parson had withdrawn, and Sergeant Russell approached the prisoner to fulfil the duty of blindfolding and pinioning him, the latter gave a great start and, throwing up his arms, uttered a loud exclamation.

"The feeling in the regiment, as I have told you, was exceedingly bitter against the sentence, and there happened just what I had apprehended. In the dead silence Sergeant Russell's deliberate order, 'Make ready!' 'Present!' 'Fire!' rang out like the knell of fate. The volley sped; the light smoke drifted aside; and lo! the prisoner still knelt scatheless on his coffin.

"There was a brief pause, and then Sergeant Russell, with his face bleached to a ghastly pallor, but set and resolute, his step firm, strode up to the kneeling blindfolded man, pistol in hand, and—did his duty. But he did not return to the party he commanded. No, he remained standing over the prostrate figure, and was deliberately reloading the pistol.

"'What the devil is the man doing?' cried the general testily.

"'Probably, sir,' answered the assistant adjutant-general, 'he has not fully accomplished his duty. He seems a man of exceptional nerve!'

"'Well,' said the general, 'I wish he'd be sharp about it!'

"Sergeant Russell did not detain the chief unreasonably long. Having reloaded it, he put the pistol to his temple, drew trigger, and fell dead across his brother's body.

* * * * *

"For that they were brothers," continued the general after a pause, "the papers found in their effects proved conclusively. The younger one, Alexander, had joined us in a false name. By the way, they were countrymen of your own—natives of Glenvorlich in Banffshire."

BILL BERESFORD
AND HIS VICTORIA CROSS

Some fifteen years ago the prevailing opinion regarding the brothers Beresford—Lord Charles and Lord William—probably was that they were both more or less crazy. Their father, the fourth Marquis of Waterford, was a clergyman. It is not alleged that this circumstance contributed to intensify the impression; and in point of fact the clerical marquis was a sedate well-ordered divine, who was a dean, and no doubt might have been a bishop had he aspired to that dignity. But their uncle, the third Lord Waterford, had earned by sedulous exertion the popular appellation of "the mad marquis." He rode his horse over toll-gates by lantern light, distinguished himself in miscellaneous pugilistic encounters, made and won the wildest wagers, and finally broke his neck in the hunting-field. It was supposed that the spirit of this ancestor had revived in his madcap nephews. Lord Charles—far better known as "Charlie"—was a midshipman who appeared to live for larks. Lord William—whom all his world knew as "Bill"—was a lieutenant in a lancer regiment who in the hunting-field and in steeplechase riding had broken pretty well every bone in his body, and some of them several times over. Men who knew the brothers well realised that behind their madcap daring and their wild recklessness lay a capacity for earnest work when the opportunity should offer. It should be said that their eccentricities were never sullied by taint of anything gross or dishonourable; it lay in no man's mouth to say that a Beresford ever did a coarse, a shabby, or an ungenerous thing.

People had grown to comprehend that Charles Beresford was something other than a merry-andrew, before that critical moment of the bombardment of Alexandria, when he laid his little *Condor* right under the guns of a hostile battery, and not less by skill than by daring contributed materially to the successful issue. Since then he has served as a minister of the Crown, and when until lately he spoke from his place in Parliament, he was listened to as a leading practical authority on naval reforms. William has three medals for as many campaigns; has won the Victoria Cross by the deed of splendid valour I am about to narrate; was the sole and most efficient staff officer to a brigade composed of uniquely heterogeneous elements out of which good work could be got only by a rare combination of tact, firmness, and veritable leadership; and is now fulfilling adequately the important duties of Military Secretary to the Viceroy of India. Under these circumstances people have now for some time left off regarding the brothers Beresford as crazy.

Lord Charles I only know; Bill—I won't call him Lord William any more—has been my comrade *per mare et terras* for more years than either he or I care to reckon. I met him first on a night march in the autumn manœuvres on Salisbury Plain in August 1872. He was then a "galloper" to the general commanding the cavalry brigade. General and brigade had lost their way in the darkness, and Bill got the order to go and find it. He was riding a violent cross-grained mare, which resented being forced to leave the other horses. I gave him a lead for a little way. As I turned, his mare reared straight on end; I knew it, dark as it was, because her fore-foot touched my shoulder. Then there was a thud on the short thick grass carpeting the chalk of the great plain. The brute had "come over" on Bill. There was a groan, but it was from the mare as she fell heavily, not from her rider. He was out from under her somehow before she began to struggle, was in the saddle as she scrambled to her feet, gave her the spur, and forced the cowed brute at a gallop out into the darkness.

Bill and I went up the gruesome Khyber Pass together, in November 1878, with the little army which gallant one-armed old Sir Sam Browne led to the invasion of Afghanistan. Across the narrowest gut of that gloomy defile, perched high on its isolated rock, stands the fortress of Ali Musjid, held against us by a strong Afghan garrison. Ali Musjid was the impediment which had to be subdued before we could penetrate farther into the bowels of the Afghan land. Two long broken ridges reach up to the base of the Ali Musjid rock, separated from each other by the valley down the centre of which flows, or rather rushes, the Khyber stream. At the head of one brigade Sir Sam himself moved on the fortress along the rugged right-hand ridge; the other brigade, commanded by General Appleyard, had its route along the left-hand upland. Rather late in the day, when the force was fully committed to this movement, it became apparent that because of the intervening ravine, quick inter-communication with Appleyard was rendered difficult. The Afghans in the fort were no fools; they had recognised the existence of the interval between the two brigades; and they did their level best to keep the force bisected by pouring a steady stream of artillery and musketry down the valley.

Sir Sam wanted to send a message to Appleyard. Beresford, who was then an aide-de-camp to the Viceroy of India, and had got a month's leave from his duties in that capacity to take a hand in what fighting might occur, was a sort of "odd man" on Sir Sam's staff. He never was oppressed with shyness, and when Sir Sam spoke of his wish to communicate with the left brigade, he put in his word. "I'm an idle man, sir; won't you send me across to General Appleyard to tell him what you want him to do?"

"Very well, Beresford," replied Sir Sam; "I want you to get over as quickly as may be; but you'd better make a bit of a detour to the rear before you cross the valley. By crossing below the bend you'll avoid most of the fire that is sweeping the direct way across."

"All right, sir," said Bill, with a wink of the eye on the chief's off side that seemed to say, "I think I see myself detouring."

He took his sword-belt in a couple of holes and started. To begin with, he had to clamber into the valley down the face of an all but perpendicular precipice, on the projections of which the Afghan shells were striking with malign freedom.

Looking down from the upper edge I watched him complete the descent, and then start on the dangerous journey across the valley. No doubt he was making good speed; but it looked to me, anxious as I was, as if he were sauntering. Now and then he was hidden altogether by the smoke and dust of an exploding shell.

Cool hand he was, to be sure! When he reached the hither bank of the Khyber stream, he deliberately sat himself down on a stone, and unlaced his boots, took them and his stockings off, and waded the stream barefoot. Having crossed, he sat down and replaced these articles of attire—how abominably particular he seemed, sitting right in the fair-way of that belch of fire, about the correct lacing of his ankle boots! Finally he lit a cigarette, resumed his tramp across the rest of the valley, and clambering up the rocks bounding its farther side, disappeared among Appleyard's red-coats. That officer was already committed to an attack, so Bill remained with his force and took part in the effort in which Birch and Swettenham went down.

When Sir Sam Browne was halted in Jellalabad, and there was no chance of any further fighting that winter, Bill went back to Simla to his duties about the Viceroy. Presently I, too, tired of the inaction in the Khyber, and travelling down country to Calcutta, and voyaging across the Bay of Bengal to Rangoon, went up the Irrawaddy River into native Burmah, bound for Mandalay, the capital of King Theebaw. While "worshipping the Golden Feet" there, and investigating the eccentricities of the monarch who not long after lost his throne, a telegram came to me from London, ordering me with all speed to South Africa, where the Zulu war had broken out and where the massacre of Isandlwana had just occurred. Hard on it came a message from Bill, telling he too was off to Zululand, and proposing we should travel down there together. I wired him back a *rendezvous* at Aden, the port at the mouth of the Red Sea whence once a month a steamer starts on the voyage along the east coast of Africa as far as Zanzibar; from which place there is connection with Port Durban in Natal by another steamer.

Down the Irrawaddy, across the Bay of Bengal, athwart Hindustan to Kurrachee at the mouth of the Indus I hurried; at Kurrachee caught the steamer for Aden, and at Aden there was Bill, impatiently grilling in that extinct volcano-crater till the Zanzibar packet should start. We dodged into every little obscure Portuguese-negro port along that coast—Quillimane, Mozambique, Magadoxa, Melinda, Lourenço Marquez—stagnant, fever-stricken, half barbarous places where, as it seemed, nobody was either quite black or quite white. We reached Port Durban about the middle of April 1879, to find its roadstead crowded with the transports that had brought the reinforcements out from England, and its hotels crammed with officers of all ranks and all branches of the services. General "Fred" Marshall, an old friend of Beresford and myself, commanded the regular cavalry brigade, and Bill hoped for a berth on his staff. But a better billet fell to him. Far up in the Transvaal Sir Evelyn Wood's little brigade had just gained a brilliant victory over some 20,000 Zulus, who had made a desperate attack on its position. Colonel Redvers Buller commanded Wood's irregular volunteer cavalry, and in the recent fight his staff officer, Major Ronald Campbell, had been killed. It was a peculiar and difficult post, and Campbell was a man whom it was not easy to succeed. The assignment rested mainly with Marshall, and on the night of our arrival, he, knowing Beresford better than most men then did, named him for the post.

Full of elation;—Bill because of being chosen for a duty that assured him responsibility and plenty of fighting; I because my chum had so fallen on his feet,—we returned to our hotel. As we sat a while in the public room before retiring, there entered a couple of men far from sober. At first they were civil, and told us that one was the second officer, the other the ship's surgeon, of a transport in the roadstead. Presently the sailor-man's mood changed, and he became grossly insulting to Beresford; who for a while treated him good-humouredly. At last the fellow said he believed Bill was a coward. Then Bill quietly rose, and simply requested the nautical person to "come outside." I did not half like the business, for the sailor was a big slab-sided fellow; whereas Bill is one of the light weights, and it was not pleasant to think of his carrying a black eye to his new appointment. But intervention did not seem possible; and it remained for the doctor and myself to "see fair." In front of the hotel was a garden studded with rose-bushes. At it they went hammer and tongs; Bill fending off the big sailor's "ugly rush" with skill and coolness—he had not been at Eton for nothing. In the third round the sailor was down, his head in a rose-bush, and Bill sitting thereon—the head, not the bush. The sailor did not want any more; every one shook hands round, and perhaps there was a drink of conciliation.

Bill next day went off up country to his billet; and not long after I joined Wood's force up at Kambula. I found Bill too busy to do more than give me a hurried hand-shake. He was Buller's only staff-officer, and the force Buller commanded, about a thousand strong, was the strangest congeries imaginable. It consisted of broken gentlemen, of runagate sailors, of fugitives from justice, of the scum of the South African towns, of stolid Africanders, of Boers whom the Zulus had driven from their farms. Almost every European nationality was represented; there were a few Americans, some good, some bad; a Greaser; a Chilian; several Australians; and a couple of Canadian voyageurs from somewhere in the Arctic regions. There were Frenchmen who could not speak a word of English, and Channel Islanders whose *patois* neither Englishmen nor Frenchmen could fully understand. One and all were volunteers, recruited for the campaign at the pay of five shillings a day. What added to the complication was that the force comprised a dozen or more sub-commands, each originally, and still to some extent a separate and distinct unit. There were "Baker's Horse," and "D'Arcy's Horse," and "Beddington's Horse," and "Ferreira's Horse," and so on; each body asserting a certain distinctive independence. Beresford had to arrange all details, keep the duty rosters, inspect the daily parades and the reconnaissance detachments, accompany the latter, lead them if there was any fighting, restrain the rash, hearten the funkers, and be in everything Buller's right-hand man. The volunteer officers, some zealous, some sluggish, some cantankerous, were, as regarded any knowledge of duty, for the most part quite useless. In effect the force, which in numerical strength reckoned as a brigade, was "run" by those two men—Redvers Buller and Bill Beresford. Buller was a silent, saturnine, bloodthirsty man, as resolute a fighter as ever drew breath—a born leader of men—who ruled his heterogeneous command with a rod of iron. Beresford, to the full as keen a fighter and as firm in compelling obedience, was of a different temperament. He was cheery; with his ready Irish wit he had a vein of genial yet jibing badinage that kept queer-tempered fellows in good humour while it pricked them into obedience. In fine he disclosed the rare gift of managing men—of evoking without either friction or fuss the best that was in them. And, strangest wonder of all wonders, the fellow whom all men had regarded as the most harum-scarum of mortals—the most "through-other," to use a curious Scotch expression—was found possessed of a real genius for order and system. I admired him excessively in his novel development, but must confess that, being selfish, I did not enjoy it. For he was very busy and I was rather idle, and I grumbled at the deprivation of the brightening of my life that had been contributed by the humour and gaiety of his leisure time.

The campaign, on which almost at its outset had fallen the shadow of the poor Prince Imperial's hapless fate, drawled sluggishly along, till at length as, on the 1st of June, the column wound down into the valley from the bluff of Etonganeni, there lay stretched out beyond the silver sparkle of the river among the trees, the broad plain on whose bosom lay the royal Kraal of Ulundi, encircled by its satellites. Over the green face of the great flat there flitted what, seen through the heat-haze, seemed dark shadows, but which the field-glass revealed as the ïmpis of Cetewayo practising their manœuvres. There are times when the keenest fighting man is not sorry that between his enemy and himself there lies a distance of ten miles. Whether in the spirit or only in the stupid deed, those Zulus were quixotic in the chivalry of their manner of fighting. At Isandlwana only had they been *rusés*. At Kambula, at Ginghilovo, they had marched straight up into the eye of our fire; at Ulundi they held their hands while we scrambled in dislocation through the broken ground that was the vestibule to the plain; waited with calm patience till our square was methodically formed and locked up; then, after the short hesitation that seemed to ask that question, "Are you quite ready now, gentlemen?" they came at us with surpassing valiantness and a noble ardour, as over the fire-swept plain sped the whirlwind of their converging attack. There were cynics in our force who smiled grimly and quoted Bosquet's historical sneer, as they watched the evolutions of the ïmpis in the hazy distance. Magnificent in their swift precision those evolutions certainly were; but it was not war that the Zulu braves should be wheeling and massing and deploying away there on the plain, instead of taking us at a disadvantage as the long baggage-cumbered column painfully toiled through the dense bush that filled the valley for which we had forsaken the bare upland of the veldt.

Cetewayo was hesitating, to meet the proverbial fate of the hesitator. He sent in the sword of the poor Prince Imperial; and later came from him a drove of cattle, the live spoil of Isandlwana. But he would not definitely consent to the terms offered him; yet he refrained from absolutely refusing them. When the laager was formed on the pleasant slope stretching up from the rippling Umvaloosi, two days were accorded him in which to make up his mind. Meantime our attitude was that of vigilant quiescence. The laager was roughly entrenched; the guns were got into position; the outposts were strengthened; and arms and ammunition were carefully inspected. During the advance the commands of Newdigate and Wood had marched apart; now for the first time they were united, or at least disjoined only by a subdivision of the laager, and there was much visiting to and fro; for it was comparative leisure time for all save Buller's irregulars, who from beginning to end of the campaign may be said to have been on the chronic scout. Some of us went bathing in the Umvaloosi, but had to "lave that"—a pun is not intended—because of a dropping fire from Zulus concealed in the crannies of a rocky hillock or kopjie, just across the river from the camp. Not alone for the bathers was this fire a nuisance; a part of the laager was within range of the Martini-Henrys got at Isandlwana, which the Zulus on the kopjie were using; and one or two casualties occurred.

We had good information as to Cetewayo's strength, thanks to the brave Dutch trader who was his prisoner, and whom he had utilised to write the communications he sent to Lord Chelmsford; at the foot of the last letter the honest fellow, disregarding the risk, had written—"Use caution, he has 20,000 men here." But it was desirable, in view of the contingency of Cetewayo proving stubborn, to gain some detailed knowledge of the ground in our front, over which the final advance would have to be made. So on the morning of 3d July, orders were issued that Buller at mid-day should take out his irregulars across the river, and make a reconnaissance of as much of the plain beyond as the Zulus might see fit to permit. He was not to bring on an engagement, since Cetewayo's "close-time" was not yet up; he was to disregard straggling opposition, but was at once to retire in the face of serious resistance.

These droll irregulars never took much pains about parading. Neither smartness nor uniformity was a desideratum. The fellows dressed how they liked, or rather, perhaps, how they could: their only weapon, besides the revolver, a Martini-Henry rifle, each man carried as seemed unto him best, providing that he carried it somehow, somewhere about himself or his pony. The only uniform accoutrement was the bandoleer in which the cartridges were carried. When they got ready, they mounted; when he found around him a reasonable number of mounted men, the leader of the corps started; his fellows followed in files, and the men who were late overtook the detachment at a canter. No man skulked; the majority were keen enough for fighting, and the funkers, if there were any, had to pretend to be as zealous as their comrades. Buller and Beresford were always in the saddle early, waiting for the firstlings of the muster. Buller's favourite mount was a fiddle-headed, brindled, flat-sided, ewe-necked cob named Punch. He was perhaps the very ugliest horse of his day and generation in all South Africa, but he was also among the most valuable. Although not very fast, his endurance was wonderful; he made nothing of a hundred miles at a stretch, with an occasional "off-saddle" and a roll as the only relief; but it was neither his endurance nor his ugliness that constituted his special value. He was "salted" to the third degree of saltness; he was a veritable "mark mason" among "salted" horses. Now salt-horse in the South African sense has no affinity with the salt-horse at which sailors grumble. The "salted horse" of the veldt is an animal which is proof against the pestilence known as "horse-sickness." He rarely survives the attack; after one attack he is still liable to another, but less liable; he may have three attacks, and if he yet lives, he is of the loftiest aristocracy of "saltness," and proof for all time against horse-sickness. If that were the only ill that horse-flesh is heir to, he would be immortal. Beresford had lost one horse by a Zulu bullet, another by horse-sickness; but cavalry-man and steeplechase rider as he was, he was not the man to be badly mounted. He rode a smart chestnut, with the Irish Birdcatcher white ticks on his withers and flanks. The leader of the irregulars and his staff-officer sat on their horses in front of Evelyn Wood's tent, waiting for their fellows to come on the ground. Wood, standing in his tent-door, chatted to the laconic Buller, while Beresford and "the boy"—young Lysons, Wood's A.D.C., was "the boy"—gossiped a little apart. Presently Baker came along at the head of his assortment of miscreants; Ferreira leading his particular bandits, was visible in the offing, and Buller, alongside of Baker, headed the procession of horsemen down toward the river, Beresford temporarily remaining to see the turnout complete and close up the command. Before Buller was at the waterside, he had galloped up to the head of the column, for it was his place, as ever, to lead the advance; Buller bringing on the main body behind the scouts.

The arrangements were simple; and there was no delay down by the Umvaloosi bank, where the accelerated fire from the Zulus in the kopjie over against them whistled over the heads of the horsemen; over whom too screamed the shells from the guns in front of the laager that were being thrown in among the crags where the Zulus lurked. The spray of the Umvaloosi dashed from the horse-hoofs of the irregulars, as they forded the river on the right of the kopjie, and then bending to the left round it, took it in reverse. The Zulus who had been holding it had not cared much for the shell fire, ensconced among the rocks as they were, but were quick to notice the risk they ran of being cut off by the movement of the horsemen, and made a bolt of it. Beresford's fellows galloped hard to intercept them, Bill well in front, sending his chestnut along as if he were "finishing" in front of the stand at Sandown. The Zulu ïnduna, bringing up the rear of his fleeing detachment, turned on the lone man who had so outridden his followers. A big man, even for a Zulu, the ring round his head proved him a veteran. The muscles rippled on his glistening black shoulders as he compacted himself behind his huge flecked shield of cowhide, marking his distance for the thrust of the gleaming assegai held at arm's length over the great swart head of him. Bill steadied his horse a trifle, just as he was wont to do before the take off for a big fence; within striking distance he made him swerve a bit to the left—he had been heading straight for the Zulu, as if he meant to ride him down. The spear flashed out like the head of a cobra as it strikes; the sabre carried at "point one" clashed with it, and seemed to curl round it; the spear-head was struck aside; the horseman delivered "point two" with all the vigour of his arm, his strong seat, and the impetus of his galloping horse; and lo! in the twinkling of an eye, the sabre's point was through the shield, and half its length buried in the Zulu's broad chest. The brave ïnduna was a dead man before he dropped; the sword drawing out of his heart as he fell backward. His assegai stands now in the corner of Bill's mother's drawing-room.

Beresford's Zulu was the only man slain with the "white arm" in hand-to-hand combat during the day, but of the fugitives whom the dead ïnduna had commanded, several fell under the fire of the fellows who followed that chief's slayer. The surviving Zulus ran into the nearest military kraal, Delyango. Out of it the irregulars rattled them, as well as the few Zulus who had been garrisoning it. A detachment had been left behind—a fortunate precaution taken by Buller—to cover the retreat by holding the kopjie in the rear; and then the force—Beresford and his scouts still leading, the main body spread out on rather a broad front—galloped on through the long grass across the open, bending rather leftward in the direction of the Nodwengo, the next military kraal in the direction of Ulundi. In front of the horsemen there kept retiring at a pace regulated by theirs, about two hundred Zulus, all who were then visible anywhere on the face of the plain. These shunned Nodwengo, leaving it on their right, and heading straight for Ulundi. The irregulars drew rein long enough for a patrol to ride into Nodwengo and report it empty. Then the horses having got their wind, the rapid advance recommenced. It really seemed a straight run in for Buller and Beresford as they set their horses' heads for Ulundi and galloped on. The idea had occurred to many in the force that Cetewayo must have abandoned his capital and withdrawn his army into the hill country close behind Ulundi.

Those irregular horsemen had no very keen sense of discipline, and in a gallop, a forward gallop especially, were rather prone to get out of hand. Buller's hardest task was to restrain this impulse, and it was well that day that he was exerting himself all he knew to curb the ardour of his fellows. Beresford's advance-detachment, scouts as they were, were of course straggled out rather casually over the whole front. Everything seemed prosperous. No enemy showed anywhere save the two hundred fugitive Zulus, falling back ahead of our fellows at the long easy run which takes the Zulu over the ground with surprising speed and which he can keep up hour after hour without a symptom of distress.

· Their flight was a calculated snare; those fugitives were simply a wily decoy. Suddenly from out a deep, sharply-cut water-course crossing the plain, and invisible at two hundred yards' distance, sprang up a long line of Zulus, some two thousand strong, confronting at once and flanking the horsemen. Simultaneously the whole plain around them flashed up into vivid life. Hordes of Zulus had been lying hidden in the long grass. Buller's alert eye had caught the impending danger, and his voice had rung out the command "Retire" ere yet the bullets of the sudden Zulu volley whistled through and over his command. Three men went down smitten by the fire. Two were killed on the spot and never stirred; we found their bodies next day shockingly mangled. The third man's horse slipped up in the abrupt turn, and his rider for the moment lay stunned. But Beresford, riding away behind his retreating party, looked back at this latter man, and saw him move up into a sitting posture.

He who would succour in such a crisis must not only be a brave man, but also a prompt man, quick to decide and as quick to act. The issue of life or death hangs at such a time on the gain or waste of a moment. The Zulus, darting out from the water-course, were perilously close to the poor fellow; but Beresford, used on the racecourse to measuring distance with the eye, thought he might just do it, if he were smart and lucky. Galloping back to the wounded man, he dismounted, and ordered him to get on his pony. The wounded man, dazed as he was, even in his extremity was not less full of self-abnegation than was the man who was risking his own life in the effort to save his. He bade Beresford remount and go; why, he said in his simple manly logic—why should two die when death was inevitable but to one? Then it was that the quaint resourceful humour of his race supplied Beresford with the weapon that prevailed over the wounded man's unselfishness. The recording angel perhaps did not record the oath that buttressed his threatening mien when he swore with clenched fist that he would punch the wounded man's head if he did not allow his life to be saved. This droll argument prevailed. Bill partly lifted, partly hustled the man into his saddle, then scrambled up somehow in front of him, and set the good little beast agoing after the other horsemen. He only just did it; another moment's delay and both must have been assegaied. As it was, the swift-footed Zulus chased them up the slope, and the least mistake made by the pony must have been fatal. Indeed, as Beresford was the first gratefully to admit, there was a critical moment when their escape would have been impossible, but for the cool courage of Sergeant O'Toole, who rode back to the rescue, shot down Zulu after Zulu with his revolver as they tried to close in on the rather helpless pair, and then aided Beresford in keeping the wounded man in the saddle until the safety of the laager was attained. There was danger right up till then; for the hordes of Zulus obstinately hung on the flanks and rear of Buller's command, and the irregulars had over and over again to shoot men down at close quarters with the revolver; more than once the fighting was hand-to-hand and they had to club their rifles. If the Zulus had kept to their own weapon, the assegai, the loss among Buller's men would have been very severe; but they had extensively armed themselves with rifles that had fallen into their hands at Isandlwana, with the proper handling of which they were unfamiliar. They pursued right up to their own bank of the Umvaloosi, and blazed away at our fellows long after the river was between them and us. Of course, cumbered with a wounded and fainting man occupying his saddle while he perched on the pommel, Beresford was unable to do anything toward self-protection, and over and over again on the return ride, he and the man behind him were in desperate strait, and but for O'Toole and other comrades must have gone down. When they alighted in the laager you could not have told whether it was rescuer or rescued who was the wounded man, so smeared was Beresford with borrowed blood. It was one of Ireland's good days; if at home she is the "distressful country," wherever bold deeds are to be done and military honour to be gained, no nation carries the head higher out of the dust. If originally Norman, the Waterford family have been Irish now for six centuries, and Bill Beresford is an Irishman in heart and blood. Sergeant Fitzmaurice, the wounded man who displayed a self-abnegation so fine, was an Irishman also; and Sergeant O'Toole—well, I think one runs no risk in the assumption that an individual who bears that name, in spite of all temptation, remains an Irishman. So, in this brilliant little episode the Green Isle had it all to herself.

It will ever be one of the pleasantest memories of my life, that the good fortune was mine to call the attention of Sir Evelyn Wood to Bill Beresford's conduct on this occasion. By next mail his recommendation for the Victoria Cross went home to England; and when he and I reached Plymouth Sound at the close of our voyage, the Prince of Wales, who was then in the Sound with Lord Charles Beresford, was the first to send aboard the *Dublin Castle* the news that Her Majesty had been pleased to honour the recommendation. Lord William was commanded to Windsor to receive the reward "for Valour" from the hands of his Sovereign. But there is something more to be told. Honest as valiant, he had already declared that he could not in honour receive any recognition of the service it had been his good fortune to perform, unless that recognition were shared in by Sergeant O'Toole, who he persisted in maintaining deserved infinitely greater credit than any that might attach to him. Queen Victoria can appreciate not less than soldierly valour, soldierly honesty, generosity, and modesty; and so it came about that the next *Gazette* after Lord William Beresford's visit to Windsor contained the announcement that the proudest reward a soldier of our Empire can aspire to had been conferred on Sergeant Edmund O'Toole, of Baker's Horse.

LA BELLE HÉLÈNE OF ALEXINATZ

A SKETCH OF THE SERVIAN WAR-TIME

I

It has been the fashion among soldiers to sneer at the fighting in the Turco-Servian campaign of 1876. I am ready to own that the strategy was a little mixed, and that the tactics were of the most rough-and-ready kind; but if ever a military writer cares to analyse its events crowded into the time between the beginning of July and the end of October, he will not fail to recognise that it was no bad work for the raw militia of a principality with a gross population of barely a million and a half, to make a stubborn stand against the forces of such an empire as Turkey, even in that empire's decadence. No State could have had a more vulnerable frontier line. From the confluence of the Drina with the Save on the west, round her border to the Danube at Widdin, Servia on three sides was, so to speak, embedded in Turkish territory. The fierce Bosnians threatened her on the west; Albania marched with her on the south; on her east loomed Abdul Kerim Pasha from his base at Nisch, and Osman Pasha, the hero of Plevna, was a standing menace on the Widdin side of the Timok river. Struck at on four different points, Servia was, nevertheless, able to hold her foes at bay till that October afternoon when, determining for once to lay aside Fabian tactics, Abdul Kerim's Turks pushed home their attack on the lines of Djunis, and turned the fire of the captured batteries on Tchernaieff's camp at Deligrad. It should be remembered that Servia began the contest with a single brigade of regular soldiers, which perished as a force in the earlier encounters; that she maintained the struggle with militia levies and untrained volunteers; that until the Russian volunteers came to her aid, she had not a dozen officers who had any save the most rudimentary knowledge of the profession of arms; and that the sum total of her public revenue from all sources scarcely exceeded half a million sterling.

II

From the point of view of the war correspondent, the campaign, at least on the Servian side, fairly bristled with adventure and with opportunities for enterprise. There were few days on which a man, keen for that species of pleasure, could not, somehow or other, find a fight in which to enjoy himself. If he stood well with the military authorities—and the easiest way to do this was to manifest a serene indifference to the possible consequences of hostile fire—he was impeded by no restrictions in regard to his outgoings and incomings. He would be told of an impending fight in time to be present at it; and, fighting or no fighting, he was always welcome to what fare might be the portion of a staff that certainly did not hanker after luxuries. If he were content to rough it cheerily, and was always ready to "show a good front" with the first line of an attack, and the rear of a retreat (which latter was occasionally extremely hurried), he was treated *en bon camarade* by every one, from the general to the subaltern. When Tchernaieff himself was eating that curious composition known as *paprikash,* and drinking the dreadful plum brandy which its makers call *zlibovitz,* the correspondent could live without beef-steaks, nor count it a grievance that there was no champagne to be had.

The easiest way into Servia for an invading force was down the valley of the Morava, a fine river, which, flowing close to the Turkish camp at Nisch, entered the principality a few miles south-east of the town of Alexinatz. Athwart its valley, some seventeen miles lower down than Alexinatz, stretched the lines of the entrenched camp at Deligrad, where, according to the original Servian plan, the great stand against the invading Turk was to be made. But as that person manifested little activity, and in fact, so far from invading, himself submitted to be invaded, time had served to devise and execute an advanced defensive line in front of Alexinatz. The position had the radical fault that it could be turned with ease, when there would ensue the danger that its defenders might be cut off from a retreat on Deligrad; but it had natural features of great strength against an enemy who might prefer a direct assault to a turning movement. South and east a great upland formed a continuous curtain to the quaint little town. Round the western bluff of this height flowed the gentle Morava, on the other side of which stretched a wide fertile valley, partly wooded, partly cultivated. It was this valley, prolonged as it was both to the north and south, that constituted the weakness of the Alexinatz position; nor was the hasty line of entrenchments drawn athwart it, or the earth-work covering the bridge of boats across the Morava, any adequate counterbalance to this weakness. As for the upland curtain, by the beginning of August that naturally strong position had been artificially strengthened by a continuous defensive line, studded by near a score of redoubts armed with twenty-four and twelve-pounders, emplacements intervening for the guns of the field artillery batteries. General Tchernaieff was himself in command, with some 13,000 Servian militia of the first levy, and a considerable number of Russian volunteers, both officers and men.

III

The days in Alexinatz were by no means dull. None of its population had as yet fled; and for the stranger who had acquired some Servian, there was even a little society. There were two hotels in the place—the "Crown," where most of us correspondents lived, because the people there did not insist on more than two persons occupying the same bedroom; and the "King of Greece," whither we used to betake ourselves to drink our coffee, since the *fille de comptoir* was a pretty Servian girl, whom the *Figaro* correspondent had christened "La Belle Hélène." Poor Hélène! before the armistice she had died of typhus fever in that rottenest of holes, Paratchin; but in her heyday at Alexinatz she was an extremely cheery young person, full of not wholly artless coquetry, and prone to stimulate rancorous jealousies among the idle suppliants for her smiles.

Villiers and myself took but few opportunities to bask in Hélène's smiles. One while we were away on the foreposts, actually inside the Turkish territory, and where from the hill-top on which, with a handful of reckless desperadoes like himself, Captain Protopopoff, a Russian soldier of fortune whom I had already known in the Carlist war, kept watch and ward, we could see the spires of Nisch itself, with the Turkish camps lying under the Sutar Planina and the fort-crowned Mount Goritza. Then we were off, through Fort Banja and Kjusevatz — where we found the gallant Horvatovitz in the very thick of a brisk fight with the Turks — to Saitschar on the eastern frontier, just in time to be driven out of that place along with Colonel Leschanin and its Servian defenders at the hands of Osman Pasha, abandoning momentarily that curious inactivity of his on the green heights on the other side of the Timok. It was a horrible nightmare, that night march from out the evacuated Saitschar. Cannon roaring, flames lighting up the valley, gusts of thick smoke driven athwart the hill faces, the heaven's lightning flashing in competition with the lightning of man; a narrow steep road crammed with fugitives fleeing from the wrath behind them; women clamouring wildly that the Turk was close behind them; children shrieking or sobbing; animals — oxen, sheep, goats, swine, and poultry — huddled in an inextricable entanglement in the road of retreat. Two months later, when the Servians made an unsuccessful attempt to retake Saitschar from Osman Pasha, Villiers and I were to listen again to the angry shriek of his shells, and the cruel bicker of his musketry fire.

IV

It was not till Saturday, August 19, that Alexinatz heard that species of music. On that day a Turkish column dashed into the Morava valley and fell upon the Servian advance-positions. There was some hard fighting, but the Servians for that day at least held their own, and prevented the Turks from getting farther forward than the village of Supovatz. But on the Sunday, the latter, reinforced from Nisch, renewed the offensive in force and with vigour. The Servians, who had also been reinforced, made a sturdy fight of it out in front of Tessica. From that village, where I had spent the night, I had early sent word back to the surgeons of the St. Thomas's Hospital ambulance, who had pushed up to the front at Alexinatz, that they would find plenty of employment about Tessica; and about noon had ridden back to meet them. Near the bridge-head I encountered them, Mackellar in command, with Sandwith, Hare, and poor Attwood in the waggon with him; and, turning, went forward with them to what seemed a suitable spot for a *Verband-platz*, at a cross-road where the wounded had already gathered pretty numerously. As they tumbled out, pulled off their tunics, rolled up their sleeves, and went to work, I took the precaution to turn their waggon round, with the horses' heads in the direction of Alexinatz, since the road was too narrow for quick and easy turning, if anything should occur to crowd it. But it was more from routine than from any serious apprehension that I did this; for the Servians seemed prospering fairly well in the long, hot struggle with their Turkish assailants.

After a rapid scurry to the front, I had returned to the *Verband-platz*, and was giving assistance there, when all at once I chanced to look up. I had become engrossed with the dressing business, and had been neglecting to watch the fighting. To my amazement, I could see no Servians out to the front. There were soldiers there, but they were blue-jacketed Turks, darting forward and firing at intervals. A straggling fire was discernible behind us, so that, in fact, we were between two fires. The Servians had melted away all of a sudden, and were in sudden, panic-stricken retreat. Our attention awakened, we could hear the scurry of the fugitives along the road flanking the field in which we were at work. Not a moment was to be lost, for already we could hear the shouts of the Turks; the wounded, unable to walk, were bundled into the waggon, from which the driver had fled without warning us; the surgeons scrambled up somehow; and I, hitching my saddle horse behind, took the reins, because I knew the roads and also how to drive. Our waggon was the rear-guard of all the force that had been holding the Tessica front. The Turks made a dash to intercept us; but the little horses could gallop, and it was a time to let them out. Presently we overtook the wreck of the stampede, and bored our way into the chaos. Provision waggons, cannon, tumbrils, and waggon-loads of wounded men were hurrying in pell-mell confusion among galloping cavalry-men and running foot-soldiers. The rout lasted till within two miles of the bridge-head, and there was a time when I thought the Turks would enter Alexinatz with the Servian fugitives. But a fresh front had quickly formed by troops rapidly drawn from out the Alexinatz defensive line; the officers exerted themselves vigorously to arrest the stampede, and the Turks did not seem to care to profit by their good fortune.

<h1 style="text-align:center">V</h1>

The isolated combat of this Sabbath was but the prelude to four days' as stubborn fighting as I have ever witnessed. The Turks seemed to have made up their minds to carry Alexinatz at any cost; but apparently failed to recognise at how little cost the position might be made untenable for the Servians by a wide turning movement down the valley on the left bank of the Morava. They had hardened their hearts for the desperate effort of winning by sheer direct fighting a position of extraordinary strength when so assailed. The Monday opened with a fierce cannonade from the Turkish batteries directed against the Servian troops holding the broken *terrain* in front of the entrenched position, and this artillery preparation was followed in the afternoon by a series of furious infantry attacks. With flaming volleys the Turks swept forwards over the hedges and through the copses, with a confident steadfastness that boded ill for the militiamen waiting waveringly to confront them. As the Turks came on, I watched the Servian line give a kind of shudder; then it broke, the men huddling together into groups, as if they had thought of forming rallying squares, firing the while wildly. They rallied again on the edge of a wood, but the Turkish cannon had followed fast in the track of the Turkish fighting line, and opened fire on the Servians just in the act of attempted re-formation. As they broke and ran, courting the cover of the woods, the Turks followed them up steadily, slowly, inexorably! By nightfall the Turkish skirmishers were holding the wooded bottom of the valley, out of which rose the long bare slope that constituted a natural glacis to the line of Servian entrenchments drawn across the crest of the upland-curtain which covered the town of Alexinatz. That entrenched line carried, the Bashi-Bazouks would be in the streets of Alexinatz half an hour later.

There was no lull in the fighting on the following day, although the Turks held their hand for the time from the effort to storm the entrenched position. They fought their way on the left bank of the Morava, closer in towards the bridge-head, and got so forward with their artillery as to be able to throw shells into the town itself. On the Alexinatz side of the river they concerned themselves with driving in the Servians from their advanced positions round towards the south-eastern flank of the entrenched face, fighting hard for every step of ground which they were able to gain.

Of the detached incidents of this day I have no record. I wrote as I rode, making short notes as events occurred, and tearing the leaves out of my note-book and sending them into the town for despatch by the post to my colleague at Belgrade, who telegraphed from the Austrian side at Semlin everything that reached him from the front. But no post went out that night, nor would it have carried my leaflets if it had, since the officer who undertook to deliver my letter at the post-office was killed by a shell when crossing an exposed point in his way into the town. My memory of the day is a blurred confusion of continual musketry fire, of short stands ever to lapse into sullen retirements, of wounded men who had to be abandoned to the cruel fate that awaited them from the ruthless Turks, of burning thirst, of blistering heat, of that sense of depression which reverses always give to the spectator, alien though he may be. Villiers, worn with fatigue and exposure, had gone back into the town with the English surgeons, who, with the gallant and energetic Baron Mundy for their coadjutor, had been toiling all day long in a hollow until the Turkish shells began to fall thick and fast among the wounded whose condition they were striving to ameliorate.

<h2 style="text-align:center">VI</h2>

After nightfall I followed them; but not to eat or to rest. For nobody in Alexanitz that night was there either food or rest. Poor little Hélène was sobbing in a corner over a young Servian sergeant who had been brought in sore wounded, and who, she told us with streaming eyes, was her sweetheart. The townsfolk, spite that shells were dropping in their streets and firing their houses, were loth to quit the place to which were linked all their associations and all their interests. The night was one long horror: cannon roaring through the fire-flecked darkness, shells whistling through the air and crashing into the houses, the rumbling of the waggons carrying in the wounded, the groaning of the poor creatures torn by bullet or shattered by shell. We spent the whole of it in the hospital, for the claims of common humanity had converted Villiers and myself into nurses, and in company with a most resolute, tender, and composed Russian lady, we did our best to help the surgeons. It was a dread experience, even to one who had seen much war.

The hospital and its vicinity were littered with broken and mangled human beings. Through the long terrible night, Baron Mundy, Mr. Mackellar, and their young comrades toiled on unremittingly, amputating, extracting, probing, bandaging. No sooner was a batch of wounded attended to and cases affording a chance of life disposed of, than fresh cargoes were in waiting, now from the other side of the river, now from the other scene of action in front of the entrenchments on the heights. Several hundreds of cases were hurriedly seen to during the night by the English ambulance surgeons alone; but the proportion of wounded brought in was but small compared with the numbers of poor wretches left to the ruthlessness of the Turks during the sudden retreats of the Servian soldiery. The Russian ambulance was doing its work of humanity as assiduously as were our own countrymen, and a few Servian surgeons were behaving with courage and assiduity, in marked contrast to too many who were good for nothing in any sense. Although daylight was certain to bring an exacerbation of the long struggle, there was surely no human being in Alexinatz that night who was not glad when the young rays of the morning sun came glinting through the lurid pall of smoke that overhung the town.

To this fearful night succeeded a bloody day. The Turks had been massing all night behind cover, around the fringes of the bare slopes in front of the entrenchment line, and, after a preliminary artillery duel, their gallant infantry darted forward to attempt the storm of their strong position. It was a bold undertaking, fought out with stubborn valour, for the effort was renewed over and over again.

There was little variety in the method of the Turkish assaults. Let a sketch of one which I find in my note-book serve for a description of them all. The short jotting was made while I watched. "The Turks, in loose order, jump out of the lateral hollow and come on at the double, under cover of a shower of shells. The Servian guns open with shrapnel, and a Gatling mitrailleuse rains bullets on the charging Turks. At five hundred yards the Servian infantry behind the breastworks open fire. The Turk reply, and still keep pressing forward, falling fast as they come. They make a rush, headed by a gallant leader. A hundred yards more, and the forwardest of them are on the lip of the ditch. The leader rolls into it, shot, and his voice rings no more above the din of the strife. His followers waver, stagger, then turn and run. The assault has been repulsed."

These efforts lasted till sundown, when the slopes leading up to the entrenched line were strewn with Turkish dead. In the early evening, Tchernaieff, rightly believing that the Turks were discouraged, took the offensive, and attacked them on both banks of the Morava. There was desperate fighting all night; but when morning dawned it was apparent that the Turks were slowly and sullenly falling back from every point. Tchernaieff, striking them hard as they went, sent them "reeling up the valley" till they had recrossed their own frontier. No longer for a time did the people of Alexinatz hear the cannon thunder, or start at the near rattle of the musketry fire.

VII

The same afternoon I started for Belgrade, eager to regain communications with my newspaper. Political complications had arisen there, the interest of which detained me in the Servian capital—with the less reluctance that all seemed quiet for the time in the upper Morava valley. Villiers I had left in Alexinatz, with the tryst that I was to rejoin him there as soon as circumstances would permit; and I was sure that were there signs of trouble in the air, I should promptly hear from him by telegraph. At length I was free to quit Belgrade, and started on my return journey to Alexinatz early in the morning of Friday, Sept. 2, travelling right through. As I was nearing Tchupria in the small hours of the following morning, a carriage dashed past me, travelling at great speed. Tchupria I found, although it was three o'clock, already awake and agitated. On every lip were the words, "Alexinatz has fallen!" "How have you heard?" I asked of the landlady of the inn. "It was told us by the English lords who drove through about half an hour ago. They were almost the last to escape from the place!"

Here was news indeed! Who were the English lords? What had happened to Villiers? How had it fared with our courageous comrades, the English surgeons? I pressed on, to the chorus of "Alexinatz is fallen," through Paratschin, and on to Raschan, a village only a few miles short of Deligrad. As I drew rein at Raschan, there caught my eye the figure of a man slumbering on the broad shelf outside the window of a butcher's shop. It was Mackellar. As he rubbed his eye, he told me the news in scraps. On the previous day the Turks had come sweeping into the Morava valley, on the opposite bank from Alexinatz, had driven the Servians in on their bridge-head, and had actually touched the river between Alexinatz and Deligrad. He and his mates had been in the field all day, had got cut off from Alexinatz, and had swum the river and got to Raschan here somehow, after an uncommonly unpleasant night. Mackellar knew nothing as to the fate of Alexinatz, but feared that at the best it was surrounded. On an adjoining slab, Mr. (now Sir William) MacCormac was reposing, and in a house close by were the other surgeons. Mr. MacCormac could tell more of Alexinatz than Mackellar had been able to do. He had been there with Colonel Loyd-Lindsay in the interests of the British Red Cross Society, and had been in the field among the wounded until nightfall. After dark the Turkish musketry fire had drawn closer and closer in on the place; the news spread that the bridge had been carried, and then there came the clamour that the Turks were actually fighting their way into the town. It had seemed wise to get away from the place when as yet there was the possibility of leaving it; and Colonel Lindsay and he had therefore started with a couple of companions. Colonel Lindsay had pressed on to Belgrade—it was his carriage I had passed near Tchupria: he (Mr. MacCormac) had halted in Raschan to ascertain the fate of the other surgeons, and in the hope that there might be opportunities for him to be of service in organising assistance to the wounded.

All this was interesting enough; but there were two matters as to which I could learn nothing specifically—what had befallen Alexinatz, and how Villiers and my servant were faring in all this turmoil and confusion. Villiers had been left by MacCormac finishing his dinner in the hotel; Colonel Lindsay had offered to take him out, but he had declined the offer somewhat curtly, and gone on with his dinner. When I heard this, my anxiety for the young man was sensibly alleviated. I knew Villiers to be cool without being rash, and I drew the inference that he had not regarded the plight of Alexinatz as quite so desperate as it had appeared to the "English lords." So I pursued my way to Deligrad, where I found the troops holding that position, on the alert, but in no state of unwonted excitement. And on the roadside at Deligrad I found my servant guarding a waggon which contained the collective baggage of Villiers, the surgeons, and myself. Andreas had been sent out of Alexinatz by Villiers about midnight with the baggage, as a precautionary measure; when Andreas had left Villiers, that composed young man was going to bed. Up till then Alexinatz had not fallen into the hands of the Turks. The fighting had died out; but Tchernaieff had given orders that all the civilian inhabitants were to evacuate the place at daylight.

Andreas made me some coffee—it was still early morning—and then I started forward on the Alexinatz road. Presently I met the long column of civilian inhabitants, who had quitted the place by the General's order. It was at once a mournful and a laughable procession. Here a weeping woman, with two children on her back, was trying to drive a little flock of miscellaneous live stock—goats, a cow, three pigs, and about a dozen geese; there a man was wheeling his bed-ridden wife in a wheelbarrow.

A long convoy of piled-up waggons crawled along the dusty road. From the apex of one of these poor "Belle Hélène" hailed me sadly; her sergeant was dead, and she had no future worth caring for. The current of Alexinatz emigration lasted for several miles; and close on its rear came tramping a long column of Servian soldiers, at the head of which rode General Tchernaieff and his staff. Neither scare nor hurry was apparent; no flankers lined the peaceful-seeming march; no roar of cannon or rattle of musketry broke the monotone of the tramp of feet and hum of voices. What did it all mean? Well, one problem was solved; there was Villiers, with a cigarette between his lips, as he strode along on foot chatting with Tchernaieff's aide-de-camp. The sententious young man seemed rather bewildered by the eager warmth of my greeting. Why this quite uncalled-for emotion? I had made the tryst with him that we should rendezvous in Alexinatz. Well, for his part, he had been loth to break troth, and had only come away when he saw no prospect of procuring food. No single civilian was left in all Alexinatz; you could not even buy a piece of bread; and he respectfully submitted that, with all imaginable anxiety to keep faith, he could not see his way to living on air.

As he talked, Tchernaieff pulled on one side and informed me of the military situation. The Turks had meddled no more with Alexinatz since their previous discomfiture. Their new scheme was to mask it, and press past it northward down the left bank of the Morava. This had involved driving in what force he had been maintaining in the valley on the left bank; and it was their doing of this that had brought about the battle of the previous day. It was necessary for him, with part of the troops that had been holding Alexinatz, to retire on Deligrad, there and thereabouts to oppose the new line of the Turkish advance; but he had left to garrison the Alexinatz lines General Popovitz with 5000 men. Alexinatz had not fallen, nor although its situation was obviously precarious—hence the evacuation of the civilian population he had thought himself bound to enforce—was there any prospect of its immediate abandonment.

VIII

And so the General rode on. It seemed to me that the best way to give evidence that the story of the fall of Alexinatz was untrue was to go there, and despatch telegrams from the place, of whose fall assured tidings had been disseminated far and wide. So Villiers and I took the road by which he had travelled, and plodded our way into empty Alexinatz. It presented an aspect of strange weird loneliness. Not even the cats had been left behind. Popovitz was living in a shed away at the bridge-head, and his soldiers were disposed along the line of the entrenched position in the reverse slope of the upland curtain. No creature was in all that place, whose normal population was close on 10,000 souls. All the doors had been left open. We strolled into the "Crown," to find the kitchen hearth cold, and what had been our bedroom stripped stark of furniture. Then we went down to the "Greek King," and gazed on the deserted counter at which "La Belle Hélène" had been wont to preside. On a trestle in a corner of the hospital, where the surgeons had been slaving a fortnight previously, there lay a dead man, her sweetheart. He had died, no doubt, during the night in the midst of the bustle of evacuation, and the heedless Servian orderlies had not troubled to see to the poor fellow's interment. We were idle, we two, so we carried him out into the garden, and hid him in a shallow grave under the blossoming standard roses. This done, we tramped along the silent streets out to where, at the bridge-head, honest Popovitz had his rough quarters. As we went, Villiers told me the story of the previous day.

The fighting had been very hard, and there had been a time when he had believed the Turks were bent on crossing the Morava, and taking the place in reverse, on the side where it was unprotected. But even had they persevered in this intention, he had realised that there would still remain open the line of retreat out to the east in the direction of Banja, and that it would be quite time for him to go when he saw the troops commencing their evacuation. As the evening drew in, it had been clear to him that the Turks were gaining no ground. He had previously listened to a good deal of heavy firing around Alexinatz, and had learnt to form an estimate of its distance, so when the clamour arose that the bridge had been taken, and when scared breathless men — who ought to have kept their heads better — had panted out that the Turks were "at the bottom of the street," he had gone out and listened, and had made up his mind that the firing was as yet a good two miles away at the least. And then he had come in and gone on with his dinner, as became a sensible man, and when he had been pressed to come away with the departing people of his nationality, had been unable to recognise the urgent necessity of the hurried retreat.

Popovitz was very civil, and allowed me to despatch a telegram; but could not ask us to luncheon, for the very good reason that he had no luncheon for himself. So we left him, and returned into the silent town. Up at the head of the main street there was, we bethought ourselves, a pretty cottage inhabited by an old Tâtar, who, in the days when the quickest route between Western Europe and Constantinople was through Belgrade, Alexinatz, Nisch, Sophia, and Adrianople, used to accompany the King's messengers, who had to ride without a halt, save to change from one horse to another, that long rough journey. He was an interesting man, this old Tâtar, with his tales in a broken composite of many languages, of the long winter gallops through the snow-wreaths with Heneage or Johnson, when the wolves would chase the emissary of Britannic majesty, and the Albanian robbers would strive to make prize of him. We had been wont to sit with him in his garden-bower, and listen to his polyglot yarns of the old rough days when he, now bent and shrivelled, thought nothing of riding 800 miles at a stretch. We bethought ourselves now of the old fellow's cottage, as likely to furnish the most comfortable quarters; and since there was more of the Turk than the Serv in the old Tâtar, it was possible that he might not have cared to clear out with the other inhabitants. We found him at home, sitting quietly in his own leafy porch under the great hanging bunches of grapes; he was too old, he said, to go travelling now, and had resolved to stay and take his chance. Stay he did later, when Popovitz went and left Alexinatz to him and the Turks; and badly enough did he fare at the hands of the latter. The Bashi-Bazouks promptly killed the poor old fellow.

Well, he was as kind to us as his means permitted of. He had neither meat nor wine, but he made us coffee, and gave us bread and grapes, and he gave us sleeping-quarters as well; but when I remember the insect-horrors of that night, I shudder still. Next morning, recognising that empty Alexinatz was extremely stupid, and that probably there would be some fighting soon away in the Krusevatz direction, we paid our farewell respects to Popovitz, took leave of the friendly old Tâtar—the "last man" of Alexinatz, and started back to Deligrad on as hot a walk as ever I remember. We had to make a detour to avoid a handful of Circassians who had crossed the Morava on a foray, and found great amusement at a wayside tavern in the boasting of some Servian militia, who claimed that they had done doughty battle with the Tcherkesses, and driven them back across the river. When I ventured to point out that the barrels of their pieces were clean, they lost their tempers, and threatened to shoot us—a menace which we could afford to smile at, since the old muskets had lost their locks. We never went back to Alexinatz again, but stout Popovitz held the place till the Servian strength was shattered on the heights of Djunis in the end of October; and he then evacuated it only by order of Tchernaieff. Had he been left there one day more, it would have remained with the Servians under the terms of the armistice; but before that came into effect the Turks had occupied Alexinatz, and it was Fazli Pasha's headquarters during the following winter. When the peace was signed, and its people came back to what had been their homes, they found the place a wreck. The Turks had made firewood of everything that would burn.

AN OUTPOST ADVENTURE

The war correspondent who accompanied the Russian Army which crossed the Danube in the summer of 1877, and who had the good fortune to be a welcome person, found his path of duty made exceedingly easy for him. And whether he was a welcome person or not depended almost entirely on himself. His newspaper might be held in obloquy, but the authorities ignored the hostility of the paper with something that closely resembled magnanimity, and the correspondent was not held responsible for the tone of his journal, but only for the matter in it which he himself contributed. It is rather a mild way of putting it to say that the *Standard*, for instance, was not friendly to Russia throughout the period in question; but Mr. Boyle, its representative, was quite frankly accepted, and has testified to the courtesy and comradeship of the Russian officers. He had to go, and everybody ought to rejoice that this fate befell him, because it was the occasion of his brilliant and amusing book, *The Diary of an Expelled Correspondent*; the *teterrima causa* assigned was a passage in one of his letters. The *Daily Telegraph* could not have struck the reader as being more bitter against the Russians than was its contemporary of Shoe Lane; but the gentleman designated to represent it when he presented himself at Kischeneff was refused his legitimation. This, however, was for reasons purely personal to the candidate, against whom there was some ill-will in the Russian headquarters, and not, as I understood, because of the tone of the journal by which he was accredited.

His distinguishing badge once strapped round his upper arm—he had repudiated with a shriek of horror the dreadful brass plate such as street-corner messengers now wear that was first served out to him—the well-seen correspondent stood, or moved, chartered to do pretty much anything he pleased. It may seem a paradox; but the Russians are simply the most democratic people in Europe, and for a Russian to be *borné* would be a contradiction in terms. Every officer was the correspondent's comrade. Prince Schahofskoy, the ill-conditioned general who made such a mess of the July Plevna attack, was the only exception I ever knew. If the samovar was in service, the officer shared his tea with the correspondent; in the middle of a battle, if the officer had a couple of sandwiches he would offer one of them to the correspondent. From the highest to the lowest, in regard to military information, the Russians were incredibly frank; the correspondent never required to ask questions as to situation, dispositions, or intentions—information in regard to those matters was volunteered to him. The only secret they ever had—and I must own they kept it well—was in regard to the point at which the crossing of the Danube was to be made. Skobeleff "had not the faintest idea," although a couple of hours previously he had been reconnoitring the approaches. Prince Tzeretleff "really had not the remotest conception." Still, even in regard to the crossing of the Danube, the friendly Russians were not inexorable. I could not be told the locality of the crossing, but I should be escorted betimes to the headquarters of the general commanding the division which was to take the lead in the operations. It was rather an amusing experience. The guide sent to escort me was in the uniform of a private soldier—a tall handsome man, riding a fine gray horse. He spoke English fluently and without a trace of accent. As we rode along together and talked, the tone of this private soldier's conversation bewildered me. He knew his Europe as if it had been his native parish. He had what Americans call "the inside track" in regard to English affairs, social, political, and financial. He spoke of country-houses of which he had been the guest, and commented on the merits of a piece of statuary in the drawing-room at Sandringham. At last I asked his name. He was of one of Russia's oldest princely families, and belonged to the diplomatic corps, but when the war began had volunteered for military service, and, not being qualified to be an officer, had fallen into line as a private soldier. As we rode along I asked him where we were bound for, not imagining that a destination to which we were actually travelling could be any longer a secret. But he looked upon it still in this light, no doubt in accordance with his instructions, and of course I had no more to say for the time being. By and by we reached a point whence radiated four cross-roads. It became obvious to me that my guide was himself at fault. I took no heed while he led me first along one road a little way, then along another, each time returning puzzled to the cross-roads. At last he had to confess, "It seems to me that I've lost my way." "Sorry I cannot be of any service," was my remark, "since I do not know where it is you want to go to. I have been all over this region and know where each of these roads leads." My prince-private-soldier-diplomatist burst into a laugh, and then mentioned our destination. "Then this way," said I, "about an hour's ride."

After the crossing of the Danube in the last days of June the Russian army spread out into the adjacent Bulgarian country like a fan. Krüdener went west to subdue Nicopolis, and later to come to grief at Plevna. Gourko rode away over the Balkans, through the Hankioj Pass, on that adventurous expedition which sanguine people expected to end at Adrianople. The Twelfth Corps forged away slowly in the easterly direction, toward the Danubian fortress of Rustchuk, the key-point of the Turkish quadrilateral in Bulgaria, and its advance I accompanied over the low rolling country, towards the Jantra, and later athwart the more broken terrain between the Jantra and the Lom. It was a sort of holiday stroll for Driesen's cavalry division, which leisurely pioneered the way for the force that later came to be known as "the Army of the Cesarewitch." We were received with offerings of corn, oil, and wine by the Conscript Fathers of Biela, and tarried in that pleasant *rus in urbe* for a couple of days. Then after a while we dawdled on, past the copses of Monastir and the grain-clad slopes of Obertenik, until well on into July we pitched camp on a long swell falling down to the Danube at Pirgos, with Rustchuk away in front of us, some ten miles off. We were far enough forward, pending the coming up of supports; so we threw out pickets to the front and flanks, and made ourselves as comfortable as might be in the bright sunshine tempered by cool breezes blowing down from the Balkans.

Baron Driesen was an active man, and made work for himself. He was always leading reconnaissances into the country along and across the Lom, in the course of which he had the occasional amusement of a skirmish. I used to accompany him on those expeditions, just to keep myself and my horses in exercise; they were quite unimportant from my professional point of view, and a dozen of them would not have been worth the cost of a five-line telegram. My comrade Villiers preferred to go sketching in the glens with dear old General Arnoldi, one of the brigade commanders, the simplest, quaintest, most lovable of old gentlemen, and I should think the worst cavalry brigade commander to be found even in the Russian Army. The other brigade chief, Staël von Holstein, read and wrote all day in the shade under the wide fly of his pretty striped tent, coming over to us in the evening to smoke a cigarette, drink a tumbler of tea, and relieve our *ennui* with his pleasant gossip about men, women, and things.

It was not my affair, but I confess I did not greatly relish the position we occupied. The division, with its batteries of horse artillery, was out here all by itself, with no infantry within several miles, both its flanks bare, overlapped by the Turks on its right, its left utterly in the air, and its line of retreat by no means safe. But while the Russians treated those conditions with a fine indifference, the Turks did not display any enterprise. A few weeks later they woke up, it is true; and then the Russians had to fall back out of the unsafe angle, with considerable losses, and not without confusion; but by that time I was elsewhere, and in watching the abortive efforts to drive Osman Pasha out of Plevna had ceased to feel a vivid interest in the fortunes of the Army of the Lom.

I must go a little more into detail as to the position of Driesen's cavalry division in those July days of 1877, and as to the country in its vicinity, because I wish to describe a risky little experience that happened to me then, to follow the narrative of which this minuteness is requisite.

I have already mentioned that our camp was on a long swell running inland at about right angles from the Danube. Before us, as we looked out from the front of the camp in the direction of Rustchuk, there ran parallel to our position a long valley—deep, but with smooth bottom and sides—on which were fields of grain that had been cut and set up into stooks. Over against us, on the farther side of this valley, rose a ridge very similar in formation to our own, but having its crest clothed with woods, and on its slope facing us were clumps of trees interspersed among the corn-fields. The valley between the two ridges was for the time neutral ground. The Turks held the wooded ridge confronting us, and our fore-post line ran along in our front about half-way down the slope of our ridge as it trended down into the intervening valley.

One bright warm afternoon our friends the enemy brought forward a couple of batteries of field-guns, and from a position in front of the wood which crested their ridge opened fire against our camp. The range was a long one, but the Turks had Krupp guns, and their shells came lobbing across the valley and occasionally pitched among the tents. The Russians, who have a great propensity to lazy idleness when the weather is warm, apparently could not be bothered to reply to this fire for quite a while; but at length, about four o'clock, I saw their gunners busy among the field-guns that were ranged in position along the front of the camp.

Just then I met Baron Driesen, who told me that he had remained quiet thus long because of a little scheme he had adopted to surprise and perhaps to cut off the Turkish guns opposite us there. Some two hours earlier, when he first noticed the guns being brought up into position, he had sent off Holstein with the light cavalry regiment of his brigade—the "Gray Hussars" we used to call them, from the colour of their horses—away to our right, with orders, if practicable, to cross the valley higher up out of sight of the Turks, and, getting on to the slope of their ridge, work northward through the clumps of trees, till, if they had the luck to get so far, within charging distance of the left flank of the Turkish batteries, when the Russian troopers were to do their best to capture the guns.

I am an old cavalry-man, and was naturally always eager to be with the mounted arm on any duty assigned to it; and I rather made a grievance of it to the Baron that he had not let me know of the despatch of Holstein and his Grays, that I might have gone along with them. Driesen was the best-tempered man in the world. "Why," said he, "standing here, you've got the whole panorama under your eye, and if they have the luck to get up and do anything you can see their work a great deal better, and, what is more, a great deal more safely, than if you were over there with them, blinded by dust and smoke." But, nevertheless, I was only half-content.

The Russian guns opened presently, and then there was an hour or two of reprisal at long bowls, and nothing else. The Russians lost a horse or two, and one unfortunate fellow was cut in two back in the camp, but the futile powder-burning was getting very tedious. All at once, however, I noticed some horsemen showing little glimpses of themselves out of a long clump of trees a few hundred yards below, and on the left of the Turkish batteries.

"Look, Baron!" cried I, "there are Holstein's cavalry fellows, sure enough. They've worked round beautifully—quite artistically—and now they are gathering in that clump, getting ready for their dash at the guns!"

Driesen was not an enthusiastic man, and he rather drawled in his speech. "You may be right," he said, "but I, for my part, have a shrewd suspicion these horsemen are Turkish Tcherkesses, prowling about there just to cover that left flank of the batteries which I gave Holstein as his objective."

"Why," I exclaimed, "look at the gray horses. There can be no mistake!"

"*Mon Dieu!*" retorted the Baron, "can't a Turkish Tcherkess ride a gray horse as well as a Russian Hussar?"

"Well," said I—for Driesen's apathy made me the more stubborn in my own opinion—"I'm positive they are our fellows; and I am going across the valley to watch closely how they make their rush."

"Don't be a fool!" said the Baron genially. "Even if they are our fellows, you are much better here; and if you cross, and they are not, why then——" and he shrugged his broad shoulders.

But I was obstinate; Driesen was sufficiently conversant with our language to quote the proverb about "a wilful man"; and so away I rode to the front out beyond the Russian guns, down the slope, and through the outpost line, crouching behind the corn-stooks about half-way down. I cantered briskly across the bottom of the valley, which I found to be a deeper trough than I had imagined; and then at a slower pace began to ascend the slope of the Turkish ridge, heading for the clump of trees about which I had seen the horsemen.

I had got nearly half-way up. I could hear the shrill scream of the shells speeding from ridge to ridge high over my head, as I plodded on upward, leaning well forward over my saddle, with a grip of my horse's mane in one hand. Just as I entered a corn-field, crack, crack, whizz, whizz, came a couple of bullets close by me from behind a corn-stook just in front of me. I halted involuntarily dazed with surprise, and took a hurried survey of the situation. It was not difficult to comprehend it at a glance. Moving in an easy careless way I had ridden right up against the Turkish outpost line, which, just as was the Russian line on the opposite side of the valley, was drawn athwart the slope behind the cut grain. So close was I that I could actually see the Paynim rascals grinning at my attitude of scare.

Shot followed shot, and each one served to quicken my realisation of the fact that it was extremely injudicious to remain there longer than was quite convenient. So I wheeled sharply in my tracks and galloped headlong down the steep slope, stretched along my horse's neck. I did not wait to exchange any civilities of leave-taking with the humorous gentlemen squatting behind the corn-stooks.

In a twinkling, long before I had reached the bottom, the Russian outpost line had opened fire on the Turkish outliers who were persecuting me, and this friendly act drew off from me the attention of the latter. Quite a general, although desultory, musketry skirmish ensued, the bullets of both sides whistling over my head, down in the bottom of the valley as I was by this time. But though I had ceased to be a target I did not feel in the least comfortable. I could not get home among the Russians while they kept up this abominable shooting of theirs—that was too clear—unless I was prepared to take an equal risk to that from which I had just been mercifully preserved. If you are shot it makes no perceptible difference to you whether it is friend or foe who performs the deed. The Turkish side, again, was renewing its inhospitable demonstrations; and it was not at all nice to remain quiescent down in the bottom of the valley, since every now and then a malignant Turk, disregarding his natural enemies the Russians over against him up there, would take a shot by way of variety at the inoffensive neutral prowling down below in the middle distance.

In my perplexity I resolved to follow up the trough of the valley till I should reach a section of the Russian front where quietude might be reigning, and where, therefore, I would have the chance to get back inside the friendly lines and out of my embarrassing predicament.

But as I moved along I carried strife and the fire along with me. The Russians, out in front of whom I had originally ridden down into the valley, had known at least that I had come from their camp, and had let me alone as being a friend. But as I moved out of their ken I found myself the pariah of both sides, the Ishmaelite against whom was every man's hand. Neither side had any good feeling toward me, and both took occasional shots at me, which came a great deal too near to be pleasant. Then, having fired at me, nothing would content them but that they should set about firing at each other, and so I was like a fox with a firebrand tied to its tail, spreading conflagration whithersoever I went. By and by I came on a bend in the valley, and this gave me hope; but as I moved along I thought I should never get to where the two hostile outpost lines ceased to confront each other. And then all of a sudden the valley began to disappear altogether and merge into the uplands, a change in the ground which bade fair to deprive me of what little cover the valley had been affording.

Suddenly, from an adjacent clump on the Turkish side of the shallowing valley, three horsemen came dashing down on me at a gallop. The alternatives were so clear that he who ran might read, and I was moving at a walk. Either the Turks would make a prisoner of me (if, indeed, they did not kill me on the spot), or I must, if I would make an effort to escape this fate, take my chance of the Russian fire as I galloped for the shelter of the Russian outpost line.

"Of two evils choose the less," says the wise proverb. I had made up my mind, much more quickly than I can write the words down, to ride in upon the Russians; and so I gave my horse the spur and fled from my Turkish pursuers. It was pretty clear that the Russians had no sort of comprehension of the situation, but they judged that the simplest course, pending an explanation, was to try to kill somebody; so they opened fire with zeal.

For me it was like charging a square. I actually all but rode over a man who was confronting me kneeling, with his (presumably empty) rifle held like a pike; and when I was pulled up abruptly inside the Russian straggling line by a strong jerk on my horse's bit that threw him back on his haunches, I found myself surrounded by the *chevaux de frise* of bayonet-points projecting from rifles held by angry, vociferating, and unintelligible persons of Sclavonic extraction.

I never knew very much practicable Russian, and at that time three words were the sum of my acquaintance with that euphonious tongue. None of the three was at all applicable to the conditions of the moment, but I emitted them all in succession, making the best of my scanty stock-in-trade. They availed me nothing. Neither the officer nor any of his men knew a word of English, French, or German. In vain I looked for the Polish Jew who forms an occasional item in most Russian regiments, and who has always a smattering of abominable low German. Failing to make my captors understand anything concerning me, I was dismounted with considerable vigour, and promptly taken prisoner, one armed man on either side of me, and a third in a strategic position in the rear. As for my Turkish pursuers, two of them had turned when within a few yards of the Russian post; the third left his horse dead on the ground and himself limped back wounded.

For the only time save one, while I was with the Russian Army, did I now produce my formal "pass" — my captors refused to give any heed to the badge on my arm, and probably had no conception what it meant. Now the "pass" consisted of a photograph of the correspondent, with a dab of red wax on his chest, on which was impressed the headquarter seal, while on the back were written certain cabalistic figures, which, I had been given to understand, instructed all and sundry to whom "these presents" might come to recognise the bearer and assist him by all means in their power. It happened that I had removed my beard since the photograph was taken which constituted my authentication; my captors failed to recognise any resemblance between my shaven countenance and the hairy face of the photograph, and there was thus an added element of suspicion. At length it was resolved to send me up to the camp, to be dealt with there by superior authority.

A sergeant and two men shortly marched me off in the direction of the headquarters, while a third led my horse. It was a long tramp, and I was not allowed to choose my own pace. At length, on the plateau before the camp, the divisional flag was seen. The artillery firing was over, and Baron Driesen and his staff were standing behind the still hot guns.

My appearance was greeted with a simultaneous roar of laughter, in which I tried to join, I confess rather ruefully.

"Well," said Drieson drily, "can you believe now that Turkish Tcherkesses can ride gray horses as well as can Russian Hussars?"

But as we walked back together to drink tea in his tent, there was genuine feeling in the quiet heartiness with which he congratulated me on my escape from this outpost adventure.

THE DIVINE FIGURE FROM THE NORTH

The Romanoffs have always been a soldierly race. Peter the Great did a good deal of miscellaneous fighting in Finland and elsewhere, and commanded at the battle of Pultowa. Alexander I. marched across Europe to participate on French soil in the desperate fighting of Napoleon's most brilliant campaign in the early months of 1814. Nicolas, lad as he was in years, was already a veteran in war when Mortier and Marmont threw up the sponge on the heights of Montmartre, and the Imperial father and son rode along the Champs Elysées at the head of the triumphal entry into Paris of the allied armies. Alexander II. crossed the Danube in 1877, with the march of invasion of Turkey, that ended only at the gates of Constantinople. Peter commanded in fact as well as in name; he was perhaps a better shipwright than a general. Alexander I. was at least the nominal head of the Russian contingent in the great composite host of which Schwarzenberg was actually the Commander-in-Chief. But, in a strict military sense, Alexander II. had no definite position of any kind in the field. Head of the armies of Russia as he was, in virtue of his position as Czar, he was nevertheless not the Commander-in-Chief, even nominally, of the great hosts which his behest had drawn from the enthusiastic masses of his devoted subjects. That onerous duty and dignity he had assigned to his brother, the Grand Duke Nicolas. The Emperor, in a military sense, made the campaign simply as an august spectator, for whom as monarch and as Russian the operations presented an engrossing interest, and whose presence in the field further inspired the nation with added fervour. Solomon's adage that in the multitude of counsellors there is wisdom does not apply to war. "Councils of war never fight" has passed into a proverb; if the proverb did not hold as regards the Russo-Turkish war, it must be owned that the battles directed by the councils were not always judicious. The American historian of that war, commenting on the lack of unity in the command of the Russo-Roumanian armies which attempted unsuccessfully to carry Osman's lines around Plevna, in September 1877, thus alludes to the military effects of the Emperor's presence: "Finally, the Emperor was present, with the Minister of War and a large staff. The Emperor came merely as a spectator, to encourage his troops by his presence, and in the hope of witnessing their victory. But the Emperor of Russia is regarded by every Russian soldier, from the highest to the lowest grade, with a feeling which it is difficult to explain in other countries; *at all* times his will is law, and his wish a command, and it is not possible for him to be a mere spectator. He took no part, however, in the command, although every report and order was instantly communicated to him, until after the assault of the 11th and 12th of September."

Alexander's life on campaign was a life of extreme simplicity, of great seclusion, always of deep concern, and at times of intense anguish. He was not strictly in the field until he had crossed the Danube; but, for more than a fortnight before doing so, he lived a sort of campaign life in a little country-house a few rods to the westward of the miserable Roumanian village of Simnitza, overhanging the bed of the great river. He himself had accommodation here under a roof, but most of his numerous *entourage* dwelt in tents among the trees of the little park, and in the adjoining paddocks. He sat at meals with the suite in a great marquee on the lawn; but the repasts served there partook rather too much of the Duke Humphrey sort of fare to accord with the tastes of the dainty aristocrats who, in their various capacities, or in no capacity at all, were in attendance on their sovereign; and they were lavish patrons, occasionally neglecting to pay their bills, of the temporary restaurant which Brofft, the Bucharest hotel-keeper, had set up close to the gate of the boyard's château in which the Emperor quartered. Under the canvas roof of the hostelry where Müller, Herr Brofft's head man, served dubious champagne at twelve roubles a bottle, members of the Imperial family and the nobles and generals of the suite made very merry, no matter how things were going on the farther side of the river. But the Emperor himself was scarcely seen outside the gates of his own habitation, save to visit the hospitals in which lay the wounded of the crossing, or to drive to a point commanding some long stretch of the great river and the undulating Bulgarian region beyond its swift brown current. He always travelled on wheels. I do not remember to have seen him oftener than twice on horseback during the whole campaign. The Russians, indeed, are not an equestrian people— that is, they are not addicted to riding because of a love for the saddle. A Russian, if he has the choice, will always sooner drive than ride; and even on campaign it was nothing uncommon to see a general at the head of his division on the march, snugly ensconced in a comfortable carriage.

The day after Dragomiroff had carried the passage of the Danube opposite Simnitza, the Czar crossed the river for the purpose of visiting Sistova, the Bulgarian town on the Turkish side, and of thanking in person the gallant division which had so valiantly fought its way across the great river, and carried the heights on the other side. There was no formal review; the troops were already too widely dispersed for that. Yolchine's brigade, the one which had crossed first, had got under arms as the Emperor came up from the river's brink; and Generals Dragomiroff and Yolchine stood in front of it, along with the young General Skobeleff, who had shown brilliant valour and all his rare gift of leadership in the action of the previous day. The troops replied to the Emperor's greeting in accents which were eloquent of an emotion of absolute adoration; the simple private men gazed on their Czar with entranced eyes of childlike love and awe.

His aspect on that day, when as yet anxiety and ill-health had not broken him down, was singularly imposing. It was Charles Brackenbury who applied to him the term which I have placed at the head of this article; but he did not invent it. It was the exact translation of the phrase in which the Bulgarians of Sistova hailed the potentate who on that afternoon, when first his foot touched their soil, shone before their eyes as the more than mortal being who was to be their Saviour, their Redeemer from the rule of the heathen. At that moment they would have worshipped him. They cooled in their adoration presently, and before the campaign was over there were among them those who openly said that since they were seemingly to be a subject race, they preferred to be subject to the Turk rather than to the Russian.

The glamour of the hour stirred to idealisation the stolid, self-centred Bulgarians; but the most indifferent spectator could not but realise the nobility of Alexander's presence, as he returned the greeting of his victorious soldiers. A man not far off sixty, he then looked exceptionally young for his age; the long dark moustache showed hardly a streak of gray, and the majestic figure was as straight as a pine. He looked a very king of men, as with soldierly gait he strode up to Dragomiroff, shook him cordially by the hand, and arrested his attempt at obeisance by clasping him in a hearty embrace. Tough old Yolchine was similarly honoured, but the Czar turned away from young Skobeleff with a frown, for that brilliant officer had returned from Central Asia under a cloud of baseless accusation, and the opportunity for vindication had not yet been permitted.

Gourko dashed across the Balkans on that promising but abortive raid of his, and the advance-guard of the "Army of the Lom," to the command of which the Czarewitch was appointed, pushed slowly eastward till it came within sight of the earthworks which the Turks were throwing up as an outer circle of defence to the fortress of Rustchuk. The Emperor and his suite had meantime crossed the Danube, and, following in the track of the eastward advance, had taken up quarters in a great farmyard near the village of Pavlo, a position fairly central for receiving intelligence from both lines of advance, and also within easy reach of the bridge across the river at Simnitza. Some ten days later the Imperial headquarters moved farther eastward, into the little town of Biela, in the direct rear of the Czarewitch's command. At Biela the headquarters were for several weeks in the enclosed yard of a dismantled Turkish house, which the Bulgarians had quitted when its occupants fled. A high wattled fence surrounded this yard, in which grew a few willow-trees that afforded some shade. The bureaux were in the battered Turkish house. The Emperor lived in two officer's tents, communicating with each other by a canvas-screened alley, up in a corner of the yard under the willow-trees. In the centre of the yard was the large dining marquee in which the Emperor joined at meals the officers of his suite, and such of the foreign military attachés as were not in the headquarters of the Commander-in-Chief. He was wont to breakfast alone in his own tent, where he worked all the morning with Milutin the Minister of War, Ignatieff the Diplomatist, Adlerberg the Chamberlain of the Palace and the Emperor's foster-brother, and other high officials who solicited interviews. It must be remembered that from his camp far away in Bulgaria, the Emperor was administering the affairs of a huge empire whose capital was many hundred miles distant.

At noon luncheon was served in the great marquee, and all the suite were wont to gather in the yard for conversation a short time in advance. The Emperor came out from his own private tent, shaking hands with the nearest members of the suite, greeting always the foreign attachés, as he passed into the marquee. His seat was in the centre of the right-hand side of the table, usually with General Suwaroff on one side of him and General Milutin on the other, the foreign attachés sitting opposite. The greatest simplicity prevailed in the fare served at the Imperial table; three courses were the rule at dinner, and champagne was given only on exceptional occasions. When the time for coffee came, the Emperor gave the signal for smoking, and immediately the marquee was filled with a cloud of cigarette smoke. He was wont to talk freely at table, directing most of his conversation to the foreign officers opposite to him, and occasionally, especially when addressing Colonel Wellesley, the British representative, his tone was that of grave badinage.

No elaborate precautions were to outward seeming taken for the Emperor's safety, living here as he was in the midst of a curiously-mixed population of wretched Bulgarians and prowling Turks—for all the Turks had not fled from Biela. His only escort consisted of a handful of the Cossacks of the Imperial guard on duty at the entrance of the yard in which he lived. He drove out every day, attended by an escort of a dozen of these; and he would make the round on foot of the hospitals in the environs of the little town, accompanied by a single companion, a Cossack following a little distance behind. He spent many an hour in talking with the poor ailing fellows in the wretched hospitals, to whom his kindly presence did more good than all the efforts of the surgeons. Once during a drive his eye fell upon a miserable company of Turkish fugitives, among whom were many women and children, lurking in a wood. He at once alighted and went among them, and by assurances of protection he succeeded in prevailing on them to return to their homes in Biela, where he had them supplied with rations until they were able to do something for themselves.

After the disaster met with by Krüdener and Shahofskoy in front of Plevna on the 30th of July, and Gourko's enforced retirement to the northern side of the Balkans, the Imperial headquarters were moved westward to a village called Gorni Studen, about equidistant from Plevna, Sistova, and Tirnova. Biela had become poisonous by reason of an utter disregard of all sanitary precautions, and the Emperor had been ailing from low fever, rheumatism, and asthma, the last his chronic ailment. At Gorni Studen he abandoned tent-life, and only occasionally came to the general table in the mess marquee. A dismantled Turkish house was fitted up for him after a fashion, and his bedroom was a tiny chamber with mud walls and a mud floor. It was in the balcony of this house where I had an interview with him in August, when I had ridden in from the Shipka with the unexpected good news that Radetski was holding his own stoutly in the St. Nicholas position among the Shipka rocks, against the fierce assaults of Mehemet Ali's Turks.

I had a difficulty in recognising him, so changed was he from the early days at Simnitza. He had shrunken visibly, he stooped, his head had gone down between his shoulders, and his voice was broken and tremulous. He was gaunt, worn, and haggard, his nervous system seemed quite shattered. There was a hunted expression in his eye, and he gasped for breath in the spasms of the asthma that afflicted him. I left him with the vivid apprehension that he was not to break the spell that was said to condemn every Romanoff to the grave before the age of sixty.

The spell of course was nonsense, yet it is the fact that Czar Alexander's father, and the four male Romanoffs of the generation preceding Nicolas, the sons of the mentally affected Emperor Paul, died before the attainment of this age, and of disease affecting the brain. Alexander I., who was Napoleon's enemy, his friend, and then again his bitter and successful enemy, died at the age of forty-eight in a deep, brooding melancholy, which Metternich described as a "weariness of life." His elder brother, the Grand Duke Constantine, had the good sense to know that his mental condition rendered him unfit to rule. If he had been a private person, he would probably have spent most of his life in an asylum. He died in his fifty-second year of congestion of the brain. The Grand Duke Michael ended his life by falling from his horse in a fit at the age of forty-eight, and had shown before his death so much morbid irritability that his physician did not hesitate to treat him as insane. If the Western Powers had temporised for a year with the imperious Nicolas, his death would have occurred, and there would have been no Crimean War. And it is the fact that the professional assurance had been communicated to the English Government so early as 1853, that Nicolas had at most only two years to live; he died four months before the two years were up. A well-known English physician, Dr. A. B. Granville, had detected in Nicolas the symptoms of the hereditary disease of his family, from which he predicted his death within the term mentioned. He communicated his prognosis to Lord Palmerston, as a strong argument for the maintenance of a temporising policy until death should have delivered Russia and Europe from a Czar whose mental balance was disturbed. The authenticity of this letter, which was published in the *Times* in 1855, was vouched for to Count Vitzthum on the day of its publication by Lord Palmerston himself, who added that the English Government could be guided only by facts, and could not allow their policy to be influenced by the opinion of a physician. Alexander outlived the fated period by three years, and then it was by a violent death that he perished; but his younger brother, the late Grand Duke Nicolas, died recently before completing his sixtieth year.

As epilepsy is the domestic curse of the Hapsburgs, so hypochondria is the family malady of the Romanoffs. Alexander was a prey to it in the Gorni Studen hovel. But it had not full sway over him. There was something wonderfully pathetic in the eagerness with which he grasped at the expressed belief of an unprofessional neutral like myself, in the face of the apprehensions to the contrary of all about him, that Radetski would be able to make good the tenure of his position on the top of the Shipka.

The Czar was present in the field during the six days' struggle around Plevna, in the September of the war. The sappers had constructed for him on a little eminence, out of the usual line of hostile fire, a sort of look-out place from which was visible a great sweep of the scene of action. Behind it was a marquee in which was a long table continually spread with food and wine, where the suite supported nature jovially while men were dying hard by in their thousands. As for the Czar himself, after the first two days he neither ate nor drank. Anxiety visibly devoured him. He could not be restrained from leaving the observatory and going around among the gunners. I watched him on the little balcony of the look-out place, late on the afternoon of the fifth day of the struggle—it was his fête-day, save the mark!—as he stood there in the sullen autumn weather, gazing out with haggard straining eyes at the efforts to storm the great Grivitza redoubt. Assault after assault had been delivered; assault after assault had failed; now the final desperate struggle was being made, the forlorn hope of the day. The Turkish fire crushed down his Russians as they battled their way up the slope, slippery already with Roumanian blood: the pale face on the balcony quivered, and the tall figure winced and cowered. As he stood there bearing his cross in solitary anguish, he was a spectacle of majestic misery that could never be forgotten.

After Plevna had fallen in December, the Emperor returned to St. Petersburg, there to be greeted with a reception the like of which for pure enthusiasm I have never witnessed. From the railway station he drove straight to the Kasan Cathedral, in accordance with the custom which prescribes to Russian Emperors that in setting out for or returning from any enterprise, they shall kiss the glittering image of the Holy Virgin of Kasan which the Cathedral enshrines. Its interior was a wonderful spectacle. People had spent the night sleeping on the marble floor, that they might be sure of a place in the morning. There had been no respect of persons in the admissions. The mujik in his skins stood next the soldier-noble whose bosom glittered with decorations. The peasant woman and the princess knelt together at the same shrine. At the tinkle of a bell the great doors were thrown wide open and on the surge of cold air was borne a great throbbing volume of sounds, the roar of the cheering of vast multitudes, the booming of artillery, the clash of the pealing joy-bells. In stately procession the Emperor reached the altar, bent his head, and his lips touched the sacred image. When he turned to leave the building, the wildest confusion of enthusiasm laid hold of the throng. His people closed in about the Czar till he had no power to move. The great struggle was but to touch him, and the chaos of policemen, officers, shrieking women, and enthusiastic peasants swayed and heaved to and fro; the Emperor in the centre, pale, his lips trembling with emotion, just as I had seen him when his troops were cheering him on the battlefield; struggling for the bare possibility to stand or move forward, for he was lifted by the pressure clean off his feet, and whirled about helplessly. At length, extricated by a wedge of officers, he reached his carriage, only to experience almost as wonderful an ovation when he reached the raised portico of the Winter Palace. As for the Czarevna, the lady who is now Empress of Russia, her experiences at the Winter Palace were unique. As her carriage, following that of the Emperor, approached the terrace, the populace utilised it as a point whence to see and cheer the Emperor. Men scrambled on to the horses, the box, the roof, the wheels; progress became utterly impossible. A group of cadets and students, who lined the base of the terrace, were equal to the occasion. They dragged open the carriage door by dint of immense exertion: they lifted out the bright little lady, who clearly was greatly enjoying the fun, and they passed her from hand to hand above their heads, till the Emperor caught her, lifted her over the balustrades, and set her down by his side on the terrace.

The fall of Plevna, and the welcome of his capital, had restored the Czar to apparent health and spirits. I watched him as he moved around the great salon of the Winter Palace, greeting his guests at the home-coming reception. He strode the inlaid floor a very emperor, upright of figure, proud of gait, arrayed in a brilliant uniform, and covered with decorations. A glittering court and suite thronged about the stately man with enthusiastically respectful homage; the dazzling splendour of the Winter Palace formed the setting of the sumptuous picture; and as I gazed on the magnificent scene, I could hardly realise that the central figure of it, in the pomp of his Imperial state, was of a verity the self-same man in whose presence I had stood in the squalid Bulgarian hovel, the same worn, anxious, shabby, wistful man who, with spasmodic utterance and the expression in his eyes as of a hunted deer, had asked me breathless questions as to the episodes and issue of the fighting.

In many respects the monarch whom the Nihilists slew was a grand man. He was absolutely free from that corruption which is the blackest curse of Russia, and whose taint is among the nearest relatives of the Great White Czar. He had the purest aspirations to do his loyal duty toward the huge empire over which he ruled, and never did he spare himself in toilsome work. He took few pleasures; the melancholy of his position made sombre his features, and darkened for him all the brightness of life. For he had the bitterest consciousness of the abuses that were alienating the subjects who had been wont in their hearts, as on their lips, to couple the names of "God and the Czar." He knew how the great nation writhed and groaned; and he, absolute despot though he was, writhed and groaned no less in the realisation of his impotency to ameliorate the evils. For although he was honest and sincerely well intentioned, there was a fatal weakness in the nature of Alexander II. True, he began his reign with an assertion of masterfulness; but then, unworthy favourites gained his ear; his family compassed him about; the whole huge *vis inertiæ* of immemorial rottenness and obstructive officialism lay doggedly athwart the hard path of reform. Alexander's aspirations were powerless to pierce the dense, solid obstacle; and the consciousness of his impotency, with the no less disquieting consciousness that it behoved him to cleanse the Augean stable of the State, embittered his whole later life.

A YARN OF THE "PRESIDENT" FRIGATE

Concerning the history of the subjoined curious narrative, the original manuscript of which, written in now faded ink on the rough dingy paper of sixty years ago, was placed in my hands in the course of a recent visit to America, only a few words are necessary. The narrative is addressed to "Mrs. Rodgers and sister," and bears to have been written at the request of the former lady, after its author's return from sea on the termination of his service as surgeon of the *President* frigate, the famous fighting cruiser of the American Republic in the war with England of 1812–14. Commodore Rodgers, who commanded the *President* during the war, and who was the husband of the lady for whom the account was written, gave to Dr. Turk's narrative his endorsement of its perfect accuracy. Of the authenticity of the document there can be no possibility of doubt.

Narrative

"Although the events now for the first time recorded occurred ten years since, they are still fresh in my recollection, and have made so strong an impression on my mind that time can never obliterate them. They partake so much of the marvellous that I would not dare to commit them to paper were there not so many living witnesses to the truth of the facts narrated, some of them of the greatest respectability, even sanctioned by Commodore Rodgers. The story is considered by all who have heard it too interesting to be lost; I therefore proceed to the task while those are in existence who can confirm it. Living in an enlightened age and country, when bigotry and superstition have nearly lost their influence over the minds of men, particularly among the citizens of this republic, where knowledge is so universally diffused, I have often been deterred from relating circumstances so wonderful as to stagger the belief of the most credulous. But facts are stubborn things, and the weight of testimony in this case cannot be resisted. Unable for want of time and room to enter so far into particulars as I should wish, I will give, to the best of my recollection, the most prominent and striking occurrences, in the order in which they took place, without comment or embellishment.

"Some time in the latter part of December 1813, a man by the name of William Kemble, aged about twenty-three (a seaman on board of the U.S. Frigate *President*, commanded by Commodore John Rodgers, on a cruise, then near the Western Islands), was brought to me from one of the tops, in which he was stationed, having burst a vessel in his lungs, being at the time in great danger of instant death, the blood gushing with great violence from his mouth and nostrils. With much difficulty I succeeded in stopping the discharge, and he was put upon the use of remedies suited to his case. I visited him often, and had the best of opportunity of becoming acquainted with his temper, habits, and intellectual attainments; and under all circumstances, during his illness, found his language and behaviour such as stamped him the rough, profane, and illiterate sailor. It is my belief, although I cannot positively assert it, that he could not either read or write. It is certain that his conversation never differed in the least from that of the most ignorant and abandoned of his associates, constantly mixed with oaths and the lowest vulgarity. Had he possessed talents, or learning, he must have betrayed it to me during his long confinement.

"In the early part of January (1814), a vessel bore down upon us, with every appearance of being an English frigate. All hands were called to quarters, and after a short and animated address by the Commodore to the crew, all prepared to do their duty. Before I descended to the cockpit, well knowing Kemble's spirit and how anxious he would be to partake in the glory of the victory (defeat never entered our thoughts), I thought it best to visit him. After stating to him the peculiar situation he was in, and the great danger he would be exposed to by the least emotion, I entreated him and ordered him not to stir during the action, which he promised to observe. We were soon obliged to fire. At the sound of the first gun he could restrain himself no longer, but, regardless of my admonitions and of his own danger, he rushed upon deck and flew to his gun, laying hold to help run her out. A fresh and tremendous discharge from his lungs was the consequence, and he was brought down to me again in a most deplorable state. I apprehended immediate death, but by the application of the proper remedies, I succeeded once more in stopping the hæmorrhage, by which he was reduced to a state of the most extreme debility. Being near the equator, and suffering much from heat, his hammock was slung on the gun deck between the ports, affording the best circulation of air. He continued for some time free from hæmorrhage, but was under the constant use of medicine, and was confined to a particular diet. This made him fretful, and he would frequently charge my mates with starving him, at the same time damning them in the true sailor fashion. After some time, the crew being again called to quarters at night, he was necessarily removed below to the sick berth (commonly called bay). This was followed by another discharge of blood from his lungs, which was renewed at intervals until his death.

"On January 17, in the afternoon, Dr. Birchmore, my first mate, came to me on deck, and reported Kemble to be dead. I directed him to see that his messmates did what was usual on such occasions preparatory to committing his remains to the deep. About two hours after this, Dr. Birchmore again called on me. He said that Kemble had come to life, and was holding forth to the sailors in a strange way. I directly went down, where I witnessed one of the most remarkable and unaccountable transactions that perhaps had ever fallen to the lot of man to behold. Kemble had awakened as it were from sleep, raised himself up, and called for his messmates in particular, and those men who were not on duty, to attend to his words. He told them he had experienced death, but was allowed a short space of time to return and give them, as well as the officers, some directions for their future conduct in life. In this situation I found him, surrounded by the crew, all mute with astonishment, and paying the most serious attention to every word that escaped from his lips. The oldest men were in tears, not a dry eye was to be seen or a whisper heard; all was as solemn and as silent as the grave. His whole body was as cold as death could make it. There was no pulsation perceptible at the wrists, the temples, or the chest. His voice was clear and powerful, his eyes uncommonly brilliant and animated. After a short and pertinent address to the medical gentlemen, he told me in a peremptory manner to bring Commodore Rodgers to him, as he had something to say to him before he finally left us. The Commodore consented to go with me, when a scene was presented, truly novel and indescribable, and calculated to fill with awe the stoutest heart. The sick bay (or berth) in which he lay is entirely set apart to the use of those who are confined to their beds by illness. Supported by the surgeons, surrounded by his weeping and astonished comrades, a crowd of spectators looking through the lattice-work which enclosed the room, a common japanned lamp throwing out a sickly light, and a candle held opposite his face by an attendant, such was the situation of things when our worthy Commander made his appearance; and well does he remember the effect produced by so uncommon a spectacle, especially when followed by the utterance of these words from the mouth of one long supposed to have been dead: 'Commodore Rodgers, I have sent for you, sir; being commissioned by a higher power to address you for a short time, and to deliver the message entrusted to me when I was permitted to revisit the earth. Once I trembled in your presence, and was eager to obey your commands; but now I am your superior, being no longer an inhabitant of the earth. I have seen the glories of the world of spirits. I am not permitted to make known what I have beheld; indeed, were I not forbidden, language would be inadequate to the task; 'tis enough for you and the crew to know that I have been sent back to earth to re-animate for a few hours my lifeless body, commissioned by God to perform the work I am now engaged in.' He then, in language so chaste and appropriate as would not have disgraced the lips or the pen of a divine, took a hasty view of the moral and religious duties incumbent on the commander of a ship of war. He reviewed the vices prevalent on ship-board, pointed out the relative duties of officers and men, and concluded by urging the necessity of reformation and repentance. He did not, as was feared by our brave commander, attempt to prove the sinfulness of fighting and wars, but, on the contrary, warmly recommended to the men the performance of their duty to their country with courage and fidelity. His speeches occupied about three-quarters of an hour, and if the whole could have been taken down at the time, they would have made a considerable pamphlet, which would no doubt have been in great demand. Dr. Birchmore, now at Boston, heard all the addresses, I only the last.

When he finished with the Commodore, his head dropped upon his breast, his eyes closed, and he appeared to have passed through a second death. No pulsation nor the least degree of warmth could be perceived during the time that he was speaking. I ordered him to be laid aside, and left him. I was soon sent for into the cabin, where the Commodore required from me an explanation of the case on rational and philosophical principles. This I endeavoured to give. I but in part succeeded. It would swell this narrative too much to repeat all I said in endeavouring to elucidate the subject. At best it proved a lame attempt, for when asked how this man, without education, reading, or mixing in other society than that of common sailors, should acquire the command of the purest language, properly arranged, and delivered clearly, distinctly, with much animation and great effect?—to this question I gave no reply, as it was, and ever will remain, inexplicable, without admitting supernatural agency. The days of miracles are past, and I know I shall be laughed at by many for dwelling on, or even repeating, this story. But never, since I arrived at the years of discretion, has anything taken a stronger hold upon my mind, and that man must have been made of strange materials who could have been an indifferent spectator. Was he divinely illuminated? was he inspired? or was the whole the effect of natural causes? These are questions which must have arisen in the minds of many, and which must be left for the learned of two professions to answer.

"I retired to bed, deeply reflecting upon the past, unable to sleep, when about nine o'clock P.M., many hours after Kemble had been laid by, I was called out of bed to visit a man taken suddenly ill in his hammock, hanging near Kemble's apartment. It was an hour when all but the watch on deck had turned in; general silence reigned, and all the lights below put out, with the exception of a single lamp in the sick apartment, where lay the remains of Kemble. I had bled the sick man—he was relieved. I entered the sick-room before I retired to replace something, and was turning round to leave it, being alone, when suddenly I was almost petrified upon beholding Kemble sitting up in his berth, with his eyes (which had regained their former brilliancy and intelligence) fixed intently upon mine. I became, for a moment, speechless and motionless. Thinks I to myself, what have I done, or left undone, in this man's case, that should cause him thus to stare at me, at this late hour, and I alone? I waited a long time in painful suspense, dreading some horrid disclosure, when I was relieved by his commanding me to fetch him some water. With what alacrity I obeyed can easily be imagined. I gave him a tin mug containing water, which he put to his mouth, drank off the contents, and returned to me; then laid himself quietly down for the last time. His situation was precisely the same in every respect as before described. The time was now expired which, he had said, was given him to remain in the body. The next day by noon, all hands attended as usual to hear the funeral service read, and see his remains consigned to a watery grave. It was an unusually solemn period. Seamen are naturally superstitious, and on this occasion their minds had been wrought upon in a singular manner. Decorum is always observed by sailors at such times; but now they were all affected to tears, and when the body was slid from the plank into the sea, every one rushed instinctively to the ship's side to take a last look. The usual weights had been attached to the feet, yet, as if in compliance with his comrades' anxiety to see more of him, the body rose perpendicularly from the water breast-high two or three times. This incident added greatly to the astonishment already created in the minds of the men. I beg leave to remark that it was not thought proper to keep the body longer in the warm latitude we were in.

"I have now given a short and very imperfect sketch of the important events attending the last illness and death of William Kemble. It is submitted to the ladies in this state, begging they will excuse haste and inaccuracy. The change produced upon the crew was for a time very remarkable. It appeared as if they would never smile or swear again. The effect wore off by degrees, except when the subject was renewed.

W. Turk."

Apart altogether from the weirdness of it, worthy Dr. Turk's simply-told story is full of interest, by reason of the side-light it throws on the nautical character of his time. No maker of phrases is the honest naval surgeon. A fight the good man curtly accepts as in the day's work; and as all "prepare to do their duty," he "descends into the cockpit" to do his, in the serene assurance of victory, since "defeat never entered our thoughts," and the mere reference thereto is contemptuously relegated to a parenthesis. So matter-of-fact is he, so doggedly does he stick to the topic he has in hand, that he has not a word to spare to describe the fight, or to tell of its issue. That is outside his task. He has stayed on deck, indeed, to hear the Commodore's "short and animated address," and then his place is in the cockpit, with his instruments out, his coat off, and his shirt-sleeves turned up, waiting for what contributions the effort to attain the "glory of the victory" may send down the ladder to him.

But as he goes he thinks of his patient. Quite an ordinary sea-dog, this patient, clearly, in the surgeon's estimation. "The rough, profane, illiterate sailor" of the period—proved by his conversation to be "ignorant and abandoned"; destitute utterly of talents and learning. No word of approval for this waif from out the "tops" has the laconic surgeon; yet, although seemingly because it was so commonplace an attribute that he does not care to go out of his way to apply the term, he has discerned in him the spirit of heroism. So he condemns William Kemble to death, should he stir; and further, he bethinks himself of the force of discipline, and so adds to his representations as a surgeon his order as an officer. William Kemble, as well he might, has promised obedience; but the "sound of the first gun" overcomes at once the assurance of death and the bonds of discipline. Little good can "the glory of the victory" work for this "rough, profane, and illiterate sailor." It is the fighting impulse in him, the ardour of the fray, as Kinglake has it, that conquers death and discipline, whistles down the wind "my admonitions and his own danger." And so, by and by, after he has survived to characteristically damn the surgeon's mates "in true sailor fashion" for starving him, William Kemble removed to the "sick berth, commonly called bay," finds that there is no more fight left in him, and Dr. Birchmore comes on deck and reports him dead.

The present writer considers himself specially fortunate in that no commodore requires from him an explanation "on rational and philosophical principles" of the question, which worthy Dr. Turk leaves "for the learned of two professions to answer." Certain theories might be diffidently put forward, and Kemble, spite of Dr. Turk's adverse diagnosis, might have been a gentleman before his conversation sank to the level of "that of the most ignorant and abandoned of his associates," while the dramatic instincts belonging to others of his name may have kindled in him in the interval of a syncope that simulated actual dissolution. Dr. Turk, with naïve frankness, confesses that his effort to elucidate the subject was but "a lame attempt"; and why need one who is not of the "learned of two professions" wantonly risk a like judgment?

FIRE-DISCIPLINE

The compound word which I have taken as the title for this paper is the non-technical expression for that conduct of the soldier under the stress of actual battle which is expected from him as the crowning result of assiduous moral and professional training. It is fire-discipline that is the grand test of true soldierhood, not dapper marching on the parade, not smartness in picking up dressing, not ramrod-like setting up, polished buttons, and spotless accoutrements. These all have their value, not, however, as results, but as contributories; they are among the means that help to the all-important end, that when the bullets are humming and the shells are crashing the soldier shall be a composed, alert, disciplined unit of a mighty whole whose purpose is victory. The soldier of the great Frederick's era was a machine. Moltke's man is trained with this distinction between his predecessor and himself, that he shall be a machine endowed with, and expected to exercise, the faculty of intelligence. But his intelligence must help toward, not interfere with, that discipline which must be to him a second nature.

In certain criticisms that have appeared in our newspapers from time to time on the German military manœuvres, severe strictures have been pronounced on the freedom with which the soldiers were allowed, and indeed occasionally forced, to expose themselves to the enemy's fire. There were allegations of resultant "annihilation" if the sham foe had been a real one, and contrasts were instituted between the German "recklessness" of cover and the carefulness with which in our own drills the duty of availing himself of cover is impressed on the British soldier. That a live man, whose life has been protected by his carefulness of cover, is a more useful weapon of war than is a dead man whose life has been sacrificed by his neglect of cover, would seem a matter beyond controversy. And yet there are conditions in which a dead soldier may be of incalculably greater value than a living soldier. The Germans recognise the force of this apparent paradox. Our critics of their manœuvres do not. The latter seem to regard a battle as an affair the ruling principle of which is, that the participants should have for their single aim the non-exposure to hostile fire of their more or less valuable persons. The Germans, on the other hand, in their practical, blunt way, have asked themselves, what is the business aim of a battle—to save men's skins, or to win it, and so have done with it? and they have answered the question in every battle they have fought since that terrible massacre of their Guards on the smooth glacis of St. Privat, thus: This battle has got to be won. We will not squander men's lives needlessly as we did then, but we will not put its issue in jeopardy by over-assiduous cover-seeking. Striking and dodging are not easily compatible, and it is by hard striking that the battle is to be finally won.

The ideal soldier—well, what is the need of describing him, seeing that, because of fallen human nature, he is all but an impossibility? But as the marauding "Yank" philosophically remarked to General Sherman, "You can't expect all the cardinal virtues, uncle, for thirteen dollars a month!" No, but you can get a good many of the simpler martial virtues for less money. There is not much subtlety about the ordinary run of martial virtues. My own belief, founded on some experience of divers nationalities in war-time, is that most men are naturally cowards. I have the fullest belief in the force of the colonel's retort on his major. "Colonel," said the major, in a hot fire, "you are afraid; I see you tremble!" "Yes, sir," replied the colonel, "and if you were as afraid as I am, you would run away!" I do think three out of four men would run away if they dared. There are doubtless some men whom nature has constituted so obtuse as not to know fear, and who therefore deserve no credit for their courage; and there are others with nerves so strong as to crush down the rising "funk." The madness of blood does get into men's heads, no doubt. I have the firmest conviction that in cold blood the mass of us would prefer the air quiet rather than whistling with bullets. Most men are like the colonel of the dialogue—they display bravery because in the presence of their comrades and of the danger they are too great cowards to evince poltroonery. Thus the average man made a capital soldier in the old shoulder-to-shoulder days. British yokels, British jail-birds, German handicraftsmen, German bauers, French peasants, and French artisans, were all pretty much alike made creditable "cannon-fodder." They would all march into fire and brave its sting, each man's right and left comrade reacting on him and his rear file supporting at once and blocking him. Once in the fire the national idiosyncrasies developed themselves. The "funk" zone, so to speak, had been traversed, and the Briton marched on steadfastly, the German advanced with resolute step, the Russian stood still doggedly, and the Frenchman spurted into a run with a yell. When the blood began to flow and the struck men went down, the passion of the battle became the all-absorbing question. And so, whether by greater or less steadfastness, by greater or less dash, the battle was won or lost. Till the culminating-point, no man ever was thrown wholly upon his own individuality, or ever lost the consciousness of public opinion as represented by his comrades.

"Shoulder-to-shoulder" is long dead, and its influences have mostly died with it, but in the present days of the "swarm attack" human nature remains unchanged. The soldier of to-day has to wrestle with or respond to his own individuality; public opinion no longer touches him on each of his elbows. He is tried by a much higher test than in the old close-formation days. And I know, because I have seen, that he often fails in the higher *moral* which his wider scope of individuality exacts of him if he is to be efficient. Herein lies the weak point of the loose order of fighting. Cover is enforced, and while physical contact is lost, the moral touch is impaired. The officer gives the forward signal, but the consequences of not obeying it do not come home with so swift vividness to the reluctant individual man. He is behind cover, having obeyed the imperative instructions of his drill master. How dear is that cover! he thinks, and what a fiendish air-torture that is into which he must uprear himself! So he lies still, at least awhile, and his own particular wave goes on and leaves him behind. He may join the next, or he may continue to lie still. It is a great temptation; human nature is weak, and life is sweet.

I have seen six nations essay the attack in loose order, and there is no doubt in my mind that the German soldier is the most conscientious in carrying it out. His qualifications for it are unique. He was a man of some character when he came to the army. In the home circle out of which he stepped into the ranks he was no black sheep; he has a local public opinion to live up to; his comrades around him are of his neighbourhood, and will speak of him there either to his credit or the reverse. He is a sober fellow, who knows nothing of dissipation; his nerves have their tone unimpaired by any excesses; he has a man's education, yet something of the simplicity of a child; he glows with a belief in the Fatherland; his military instruction has been moral as well as mechanical. In fine, he is a soldier-citizen and a citizen-soldier. But nevertheless he is human—very human indeed; and his first experience of the advance in loose order under fire is a severe strain upon him. He has never yet seen death plying his shafts all around him. He still thrills with a shudder as he thinks of real warm blood. He has not learned to be indifferent when he hears that dull thud that tells where a bullet has found its billet.

The German military authorities understand their people, and they know the process which men undergo in being inured to war. Therefore it is that they do not enforce resort to "cover" with so much solicitude as I have noticed our officers do. They know that in every company there are men who will "lie" if allowed too great independence of individual action; and "cover at all risks" impairs every link in the chain of supervision. Again, they know that it is good for soldiers to die a little occasionally. The dead, of course, are "out of it"; but their death does not discourage, but hardens their comrades. It seems brutal to write in this tone, but is not war all brutal? And it is the solid truth. It may be written down as an axiom that fire-discipline unaccompanied with casualties is weak. I remember standing with a German general before Metz watching a skirmish. The German battalion engaged happened to consist chiefly of young soldiers, and they were not very steady. The old General shrugged his shoulders and observed, "Dey vant to be a little shooted; dey vill do better next time." All young soldiers want to be a "little shooted"; and it is only by exposing them somewhat, instead of coddling them for ever behind cover, as if cover, not victory, were the aim of the day's work, that this experience can befall them. All soldiers are the better of being "blooded"; they never attain purposeful coolness till they have acquired a personal familiarity with blood and death.

After the experience of St. Privat, which stimulated the Germans to the un-precedented feat of fundamentally altering their fighting tactics in the very middle of a campaign, no man would be foolish enough or homicidal enough to advo-cate a return to close-formation in these days of swift-shooting firearms. As little would one argue in favour of frequent war for the mere object of inuring sol-diers to fire-discipline. But the later tactics unquestionably tell against the efficien-cy of young soldiers in their first experience of battle, when contrasted with the old. Most of Wellington's men at Waterloo were green troops, yet they stood up manfully under the brunt of that long terrible day, and after the long endurance there was heart left in them for the final advance in line. They were thus steadfast because such training as they possessed had habituated them to no other prospect than the prospect, when they should be summoned to the real business, of standing squarely up and looking in the face an equally upstanding enemy. Now all our preliminary training is directed to forbidding men standing up at all, and inculcating upon them, with emphatic language, the paramount duty of dodging and sneaking. They must be good men indeed whom a course of such tuition will not demoralise. That it does demoralise, our recent military history goes clearly to show. Our catastrophe at Isandlwana was due partly to the error of employing loose formation against great masses of bold men, whom a biting fire would deter no whit from advancing; but resulted in the end, from the scared inability to redeem this error by a rapid, purposeful resort to close-formation in square or squares. Once the loose fringe of men dodging for cover was impinged on, all was over save the massacre. The test of fire-discipline failed whenever the strain on it became severe. The men had worked up to their skirmishing lessons to the best of their ability; when masterful men brushed aside the result of those lessons, there was no moral stamina to fall back upon, no consuetude of resource to be as a second nature. A resolute square formed round an ammunition-waggon might have made a defence that would have lasted at least until Lord Chelmsford came back from his straggling excursion; but no man who saw how the dead lay on that ghastly field could persuade himself into the belief that there had been any vigorous attempt at a rally. The only fragment of good that came out of the Isandlwana catastrophe was the resolution, in any and every subsequent encounter, to show the Zulus a solid front; and the retrospect of Isandlwana infused a melancholy into the success of Ulundi, where the most furious onslaughts recoiled from the firm face of the British square.

The Majuba Hill affair was simply a worse copy of Isandlwana. There was no methodised fire-discipline. It has been urged as the lesson of Majuba Hill that the British soldier should have more careful instruction in marksmanship. Probably enough, that would do him good—it could not do him harm; but it was not because he was a bad marksman that Majuba Hill was so discreditable a reverse. It was because he is so much a creature of cover and of dodging that he went all abroad when he saw a real live enemy standing up in front of him at point-blank range. It may be contended that there were fire-seasoned soldiers who participated in this unfortunate business. Yes; but these, with no strong *moral* to begin with, because of their early training in assiduous "cover" tactics, had suffered in what *moral* they might have possessed because of previous reverses. One regiment was represented on that hill-top which had not participated in those reverses, and was indeed fresh from successes in Afghanistan. But Afghan fighting is not a very good school in which to acquire prompt, serene self-command when, in old Havelock's phrase, the colour of the enemy's moustaches is visible. It was but rarely that the Afghan did not play the dodging game. He mostly does not care to look his enemy full in the face, and he tries all he knows to prevent his enemy from having the opportunity of looking him in the face. When the adventurous Boer breasted the crest of the Majuba he and the British soldier confronted each other at close quarters. It was no time for long-range shooting, it was simply the time for fire-discipline of the readiest practical order to make its effect felt. I imagine Briton and Boer staring one at the other in a perturbed moment of mutual disquietude. Who should the sooner pull himself together and take action on returning presence of mind? The Boer had the better nerve; to use the American expression, he was quicker on the draw. And then, for lack of fire-discipline, for want of training to be cool, and to keep their heads within close view of a hostile muzzle, the British went to pieces in uncontrollable scare, and the sad issue was swift to be consummated.

The influence of the "get to cover" tactics has made itself apparent, if we care to read between the lines, in numberless pettier instances during our recent little wars. The indiscriminate bolt of a picket may seem a small thing, and it will happen now and then in all armies, but when it occurs frequently it is the surest evidence of a feeble *moral*. It has happened too often of late in British armies, and I trace its prevalence, which I do not regard as too strong a word, to the lack of fire-discipline brought about by the "cover at any price" training. A man of tufts and hillocks, and bushes and molehills, from the day he is dismissed the manual exercise, a being who has never been let realise in peace-time the possibility that in war-time he may find himself uncovered in the face of an enemy; when that crisis impends suddenly, or seems to do so, the young soldier shrinks and breaks. He is unfamiliarised in advance with his obligation to die serenely at his post. He does not make a bolt of it because he is a coward, or rather a greater than average coward, but simply because his training has not furnished him with a reserve of purposeful presence of mind. Men who remember Ginghilovo, "Fort Funk," and the nights on the white Umvaloosi, cannot but own to the force of this reasoning. Several experiences of the Eastern Soudan expeditions go to strengthen it; and if the conduct of the desert column seems to weaken it, there is the answer that the desert column consisted wholly of picked men.

Tel-el-Kebir furnished an incidental illustration of our shortcoming in fire-discipline, which, as I contend, has its main cause in the effects of too stringent urgency to cover. Lord Wolseley showed that discernment which is one of his most valuable characteristics, in refraining from submitting his soldiers to the strain of a "swarm attack" up to the Egyptian position in fair daylight; and in choosing instead, as a minor risk, a night advance, spite of all its contingencies of hazard, with the hoped-for culmination of a surprise at daybreak. The issue proved his wisdom; and a phase of that combat, described with soldierly frankness by Sir Edward Hamley, must have given the commanding general a thrill of relief that he had conserved the spirit of his troops for the final dash, without exposing them to a previous ordeal of fire. That dash, made while yet the gloom of the dying night lay on the sand, General Hamley tells us, was 150 yards long, and it cost the brigade that carried it out 200 casualties ere the Egyptian entrenchment was crowned. It was done with the first impulse; no check was let stop the onward impetus of the *élan*; fire-discipline was not called into exercise at all. The whole of Hamley's first line pressed on into the interior of the enemy's position. The second line followed, but Hamley, with a wise prescience, "stopped the parts of it that were nearest to him as they came up, wishing to keep a support in hand which should be more readily available than such as the brigade in rear could supply." It was well he did this thing; but for his doing of it, the shadow of a far other issue to Tel-el-Kebir lies athwart the following quotation. "The light was increasing every moment;

our own men had begun to shoot immediately after entering the entrenched position, and aim could now be taken. The fight was at its hottest, and how it might end was still doubtful, for many of our advanced troops had recoiled even to the edge of the entrenchment" (beyond which they had penetrated 200 or 300 yards into the interior); "but there I was able to stop them, and reinforcing them with a small body I had kept in hand (who had remained, I think, in the ditch) I sent in all together, and henceforth they maintained their ground." They recoiled, and they recoiled by reason of their weakness in fire-discipline. It is a fair query— How severe was the strain? As regards its duration, but a few moments' fighting sufficed to bring about the recoil; that is made clear by the circumstance that the supporting brigade, following close as it did, yet was not up in time to redress the dangerous situation. In regard to its severity, General Hamley permits himself to use language of the most vivid character. "A hotter fire it is impossible to imagine." The brigade was "enclosed in a triangle of fire." "The enemy's breechloaders were good, his ammunition abundant, and the air was a hurricane of bullets, through which shells from the valley tore their way." "The whole area was swept by a storm of bullets." Stronger words could not have been used by an enthusiastic war correspondent gushing his level best about his first skirmish; General Hamley's expressions are fuller-volumed than those used by the compilers of the German staff chronicle in describing that Titanic paroxysm the climax of Gravelotte. What stupendous damage, then, did this hottest of all hot fires, this hurricane of bullets, effect? The casualties of the whole division reached a total of 258 killed and wounded. Of these, "nearly 200," General Hamley distinctly states, occurred exclusively in the first brigade in the rush up to the entrenchment. If we assume that the second brigade had no losses at all, and that the whole balance of casualties occurred to the first brigade when in "the triangle of fire," the fall of some 60 men out of 2800 was hardly a loss to justify the "recoil even to the edge of the entrenchment" of troops possessed even of a moderate amount of fire-discipline. General Hamley explains that but for the darkness and the too high aim of the enemy, "the losses would have been tremendous." In other words, if an actual loss of 2 per cent, and the turmoil of the hottest fire imaginable, yet fortunately aimed over their heads, caused the troops "to recoil even to the edge of the entrenchment," the "tremendous losses" that a better-aimed fire would have produced, it seems pretty evident, would have caused them to "recoil" so much farther that Tel-el-Kebir would have been a defeat instead of a victory. The Egyptians did not shoot straight because they were flurried, that is, were deficient in fire-discipline; our men "recoiled" after a very brief experience of a devilish but comparatively harmless battle-din, because the ardour of the first rush having died out of them, fire-discipline was not strong enough in them to keep them braced to hold the ground the rush had won them. It was fortunate that in Hamley they had a chief who had prescience of their feebleness of constancy, and had taken measures to remedy its evil effects.

During the afternoon and evening of August 18, 1870, six regiments of the Prussian guard corps made repeated and ultimately successful efforts to storm the French position of St. Privat. What that position was like, the following authentic description sets forth. "In front of St. Privat were several parallel walls of knee-high masonry and shelter trenches. Those lines, successively commanding each other, were filled with compact rows of skirmishers, and in their rear upon the commanding height lay like a natural bastion, and girt by an almost continuous wall, the town-like village, the stone houses of which were occupied up to the roofs." There was no shelter on the three-quarters of a mile of smooth natural glacis, over which the regiments moved steadfastly to the attack; every fold of it was searched by the dominant musketry fire. They tried and failed, but they kept on trying till they succeeded. And what did the success cost them? The six regiments (each three battalions strong) numbered roughly 18,000 men; of these, 6000 had gone down before Canrobert quitted his grip of the "town-like village." One-third of their whole number! It was the cost of this sacrifice that caused the Germans to adopt the unprecedented step of altering their attacking tactics in the middle of a campaign. But the change was made, not because the troops had proved unequal to the task set them, but because the cost of the accomplishment of that task, in the face of the Chassepot fire, had been so terrible. Now I am not concerned to exalt the horn of the Prussian fighting men at the cost of the British soldier. I will assume, and there is full evidence in favour of the assumption, that the British soldier of the pre-dodging era could take his punishment and come through it victoriously, as stoutly as any German that ever digested *Erbswürst* and smelt of sour rye-bread. Of the 10,000 British fellows whom Wellington sent at Badajos, 3000 were down before the torn old rag waved over the place. Ligonier's column was 14,000 strong when the Duke of Cumberland gave it the word to make that astounding march through the chance gap, a bare 900 paces wide, between the cannon before the village of Vezon and those in the Redoubt d'Eu, right into and behind the heart of the French centre on the bloody day of Fontenoy. There is some doubt whether those quixotic courtesies passed between Lord Charles Hay and the Count d'Auteroche, but there is no doubt whatever that when the column, thwarted of the reward of valour by deficiency of support, had sturdily marched back through the appalling cross-fire in the cramped hollow-way, and had methodically fronted into its old position, it was found that at least 4000 out of the 14,000 had been shot down. Carlyle, indeed, makes the loss much heavier. Yet a notabler example of the British soldier's gluttony for punishment is furnished in the statistics of the Inkermann losses. The total force that kept Mount Inkermann against the Russians amounted to 7464 officers and men. Of these, when the long fierce day was done, no fewer than 2487 had fallen, just one-third of the whole number. The manner in which our soldiers successfully contended against fearful odds in this battle is a phenomenal example of fire-discipline of the grand old dogged type. It is but one, however, of the many proofs that the world has no stauncher fighting-man than is the British soldier intrinsically.

But I think it would be difficult to convince the mind of an impartial man that the British soldiers who, at Tel-el-Kebir, "recoiled even to the edge of the entrenchment" under the stress of a "hurricane of bullets" fired high and of a loss of 2 per cent, could have borne up and conquered under such a strain of sustained and terrible punishment as that through which the Prussian Guard struggled to the goal of victory at St. Privat. And if not, why not? There was a larger proportion of veterans among the Prussians at St. Privat than in the Highland Brigade at Tel-el-

Kebir, and that gave a certain advantage, doubtless, to the former. Some would lean on the superior "citizenhood" of the Prussian over the British soldier; but our Highland regiments are exceptionally respectably recruited. Yet I venture to set down as the main distinction that, while the Prussian soldier of 1870 was a soldier of the "shoulder-to-shoulder" era, the British soldier of 1882 was a creature of the "get-to-cover" period. Then, it may be urged, the Prussian soldier of to-day—creature, nay, creator as he is of this new order of things—is as incapable of repeating St. Privat as the British soldier of to-day is of rivalling that stupendous feat. No. It is true the German is no longer a "shoulder-to-shoulder" man, but he is not drilled with so single an eye to cover-taking (and, I might add, cover-keeping) as is our British Thomas Atkins. He is trained to expect to be "a little shooted" as he goes forward; he has better-experienced non-commissioned officers to supervise the details of that advance than our soldier has; his individuality is more sedulously brought out. In a word, everything with him makes toward the development in him of a higher character of fire-discipline even in his first initiation into bullet-music.

It may be said that the Germans, because of the magnitude of their forces, have not so urgent need to be careful of their men as is requisite in regard to an army of scant numbers and feeble resources. They can afford, it may be said, to be a little wasteful; whereas a weaker military power must practise assiduous economy of its live material. But if the seeming wastefulness contributes to win the battle, and the economy endangers that result, the wastefulness is surely sound wisdom, the economy penny-wise. The object before either army is identical—to win the battle. If an army shall come short of success because of its reluctance to buy success at the price success exacts, the wise course for it is to refrain altogether from serious fighting. It is the old story—that there is no making of omelettes without the breaking of eggs. You may break so many eggs as to spoil the omelette; but the Germans have realised how much easier it is to spoil the omelette by not breaking eggs enough. And so they break their eggs, not lavishly, but with a discreet hand, in which there is no undue chariness. They lay their account with taking a certain amount of loss by exposure in the "swarm-advance" as preferable, for a variety of reasons, to the disadvantages of painful cover-dodging. They can afford to dig a few more graves after the battle is won, if, indeed, taking all things into consideration, that work should be among the results of the day's doings.

Than "annihilation" there is no more favourite word with the critics of manœuvres and sham-fights. In truth it is as hard a thing to "annihilate" a body of troops as it is to kill a scandal. In a literal sense there are very few records of such a catastrophe; if used in a figurative sense to signify a loss so great as to put the force suffering it *hors de combat*, there is amazing testimony to the quantity of "annihilation" good troops have accepted without any such hapless result. Here are four instances taken almost at random. The Confederates, out of 68,000 men engaged at Gettysburg, lost 18,000, but Meade held his hand from interfering with their orderly retreat. Of that battle the climax was the assault of Pickett's division, "the flower of Virginia," against Webb's front on the left of Cemetery Hill. Before the heroic Armistead called for the "cold steel" and carried Gibbon's battery with a rush, the division had met with a variety of experiences during its mile-and-a-half advance over the smooth ground up to the crest. "When it first came into sight it had been plied with solid shot; then half-way across it had been vigorously shelled, and the double canisters had been reserved for its nearer approach. An enfilading fire tore through its ranks; the musketry blazed forth against it with deadly effect." This is the evidence of an eye-witness on the opposite side, who adds, "but it came on magnificently." Yes, it came on to cold steel and clubbed muskets, and after a desperate struggle it went back foiled, to the accompaniments which had marked its advance. But, heavy as were its losses, it was not "annihilated." Pickett's division survived to be once and again a thorn in the Federal side before the final day of fate came to it at Appomatox Court-House. At Mars-la-Tour, Alvensleben's two infantry divisions, numbering certainly not over 18,000 men (for they had already lost heavily at the Spicheren Berg), sacrificed within a few of 7000 during the long summer hours while they stood all but unsupported athwart the course of the French army retreating from Metz. But so far were they from being annihilated, that forty-eight hours later they made their presence acutely felt on the afternoon of Gravelotte. In the July attack on Plevna, of the 28,000 men with whom Krüdener and Schahofskoy went in, they took out under 21,000. One regiment of the latter's command lost 725 killed and 1200 wounded—about 75 per cent of its whole number—yet the Russian retirement was not disorderly; and next day the troops were in resolute cohesion awaiting what might befall them. In the September attack on Plevna, of 74,000 Russo-Roumanian infantry engaged, the losses reached 18,000. Skobeleff commanded 18,000 men, and at the end of his two days' desperate fighting, not 10,000 of these were left standing. But there was no annihilation, either literally or conventionally, if one may use the term. The survivors who had fought on the 11th and 12th September were ready at the word to go in again on the 13th; and how they marched across the Balkans later is one of the marvels of modern military history.

Those examples of stoicism, of fire-discipline strained to a terrible tension, but not breaking under the strain, were exhibited by soldiers who did not carry into practice the tactics of non-exposure. The Russo-Turkish war, it is true, was within the "cover" era, but the Russians in this respect, as in a good many others—such, for instance, as in their lack of a propensity to "recoil"—were behind the times. But with a strange callousness to the effect of breechloading fire against infantry, the Russians were singularly chary of exposing their cavalry to it. Indeed, cavalry may be said to have gone out of fashion with many professors of modern war. With the most tempting opportunities we made the scantiest use of our brigade of regular cavalry in the Zulu war, and the best-known occasion on which the cavalry arm was prominently called into action in Afghanistan was the reverse of a signal success. But although the critics oracularly pronounce that the day of cavalry charges has gone by, and blame the Germans for exposing their cavalry to the breechloader in their manœuvres, the Germans adhere to the conviction that in the teeth of the breechloader a cavalry charge is not only not an impossibility, but an offensive that may still be resorted to with splendid effect. They can point back to an actual experience. I think there is no more effective yet restrained description of fighting in all the range of war literature than the official narrative of Bredow's charge with the 7th Cuirassiers and the 16th Lancers on the afternoon of Mars-la-Tour.

"It was only 2 P.M., the day yet young; no infantry, no reserves, and the nearest support a long way off.... Now was the time to see what a self-sacrificing cavalry could do.... Bredow saw at a glance that the crisis demanded an energetic attack in which the cavalry must charge home, and, if necessary, should and must sacrifice itself. The first French line" (breechloaders and all) "is ridden over; the line of guns is broken through; teams and gunners put to the sword. The second line is powerless to check the vigorous charge of horse. The batteries on the heights farther to rear limber up and seek safety in flight. Eager to engage and thirsting for victory, the Prussian squadrons charge even through the succeeding valley, until, after a career of 3000 paces, they are met on all sides by French cavalry. Bredow sounds the recall. Breathless from the long ride, thinned by enemy's bullets, without reserves, and hemmed in by hostile cavalry, they have to fight their way back. After some hot *mêlées* with the enemy's horsemen, they once more cut their way through the previously overridden lines of artillery and cavalry, and harassed by a thick rain of bullets, and with the foe in rear, the remnant hastens back to Flavigny.... The bold attack had cost the regiments half their strength."

They had gone in under 800 strong; the charge cost them 363 of their number, including sixteen officers. But that charge in effect wrecked France. It arrested the French advance till supports came up to Alvensleben, and to its timely effect is traceable the current of events that ended in the surrender of Metz. It was a second Balaclava charge, and a bloodier one; and there was this distinction, that it had a purpose, and that that purpose was achieved. It succeeded because of the noble valour and constancy of the troopers who made it. Balaclava proved that our troopers possessed those virtues in no feebler degree. Till the millennium comes there will be emergencies when cavalry that will "charge home" and "sacrifice itself" may be employed purposefully; and cavalry should never be allowed to forget that this is its ultimate *raison d'être*. There is the risk that it may do so, if it is kept always skulking around the fringes of operations, and not given any opportunity of being "a little shooted."

A CHRISTMAS DINNER DE PROFUNDIS

I have eaten a good many Christmas dinners in strange places, and have gone without the great feast of our nation in yet stranger. I have lost my Christmas dinner in a wholly unexpected manner, and have achieved that meal by a not less unexpected stroke of good fortune. At noon on Christmas Day, just thirty years ago, the outlook for our Christmas dinner consisted of a scrap of raw rusty pork and a ship-biscuit sodden in sea-water; and the prospect of even that poor fare was precarious, in face of the momentary danger of a watery grave. Four hours later I was the guest at a board groaning with the good cheer appropriate to the "festive season."

Just of age, I had been spending the summer of 1859 in travelling through Canada, and in the late autumn found myself in Quebec, intending to be back in England in time for the Christmastide with my relatives at home. One evening I took stock of my financial resources, and found I had only a very small sum to the fore—barely enough to clear me in Quebec and pay my fare to England either as steerage passenger in a steamer or as cabin passenger in a sailing-vessel.

I had made the passage out very pleasantly in an emigrant sailing-ship. It had been a summer voyage, and I did not reflect that on the Atlantic summer does not last the year round. My pride rather revolted at a steerage passage, and I determined on the cabin of a sailing-ship. I know now, but I did not know then, that the sailing-ship trading between the United Kingdom and Quebec is of the genus "timber-drogher," species ancient tub, good for no other trade, and good for this only, because, no matter how leaky the timber-laden ship may be, owing to the buoyancy of her cargo she cannot sink, and (unless the working of her cargo break her up) the worst fate that can befall her is that she becomes water-logged.

Of course there are bad timber ships and worse timber ships, but I had left myself no selection. I had dallied on in the pleasantness of Quebec until the close of navigation was imminent, and Hobson's choice offered in the shape of the last lingering drogher. Her brokers advertised a cabin passage at a low fare; I engaged it without taking the trouble to look at the ship, and on the morning named for sailing went on board. My arrival occasioned the profoundest surprise. The skipper had received no intimation to expect a cabin passenger, and there were no appliances aboard for his accommodation. I took possession of an empty bunk, into which by way of mattress I threw the horsehair cushion of the cabin locker. My bedclothes consisted of my travelling rug and a rough old boat-cloak I had brought from England.

We were on salt tack from the second day out, and I could not have believed that there was a ship that sailed so badly found as was this battered, rotten, dilapidated *Emma Morrison*—that was the jade's name. I should have been more savage at the egregious swindle, but that I was too sorry to leave Quebec to have thought to spare for material concerns. By and by that sentiment became less poignant, and was soon supplanted by utter disgust at my surroundings. The skipper of the *Emma Morrison* was a sullen gloomy dog—a fellow of that breed which has all the evil attributes of the Scot and the Irishman, and none of the virtues of either. He hardly made a pretext of being civil to me. He helped readily but gloomily to drink the few bottles of Canadian whisky I had brought aboard, and, when that supply was finished, produced a single flask of the most atrocious gin that ever was concocted in the vilest illicit still of the Lower Town of Quebec, and swore it constituted his entire alcoholic supply for the voyage.

Even in fine weather the loathsome old tub leaked like a sieve: she had about half a foot of freeboard, and the water came through her gaping top-sides and un-caulked deck, so that the cabin and my berth were alike a chronic swamp. The junk we ate was green with decay and mould; the ship-biscuits were peripatetic because of the weevils that inhabited them; the butter was rancid with a rancidness indescribable; and the pea-soup was swarthy with the filth of vermin. With a fair wind—and as far as the Traverse we carried a fair wind—the rotten old hooker—rotten from truck to keel, for her sole suit of canvas was as rotten as the ragged remains of her copper-sheathing—had a maximum speed of five knots per hour. As she rolled lumberingly through the short seas of the Upper Gulf, the green water topped her low bulwarks, and, swashing down on to the deck, lifted heavily the great undressed pine-trunks which, lashed to stanchions, formed her deck load. As those rose they strained the deck till they all but tore it from the beams, and as they dropped when the water receded they fell with a crash that all but stove in deck and beams together. With all her defects and abominations, there was one redeeming feature in the *Emma Morrison*. Her mate—she had but one—was a stanch, frank, stalwart seaman; the boatswain was a tough old man-o'-war's man; and the crew—scant in numbers, for she was atrociously undermanned—were as fine a set of fellows as ever set foot in ratline. How they obeyed the ill-conditioned skipper; how they endured the foul discomfort of the fo'k'sle and the wretched rations; how, hour after hour and day after day, they dragged loyally at the Sisyphean toil of the pumps; how they bore freezing cold, exposure, sleeplessness, and general misery I shall never forget.

Off Anticosta we had our first gale. It was a good honest blow, that a staunch craft would have welcomed; but the rotten old *Emma Morrison* could not look it in the face. It left her sails in ribbons, her top-hamper anyhow, her hold full of water, in which her ill-stowed cargo of timber swashed about with gruesome thuds on her ribs and knees. When the gale blew itself out we were out somewhere on the western edge of the banks of Newfoundland, and dead helpless. All hands went to the pumps save the captain, the mate, and a couple of old seamen, who betook themselves assiduously to sail-mending. My work was at the wheel. With the foresail on her, the only whole sail extant, she had just steerage way; and I stood, twelve hours a day, day after day, at the old jade's wheel. It was bitter work, for by this time it was the middle of December, and the spray froze where it lighted.

Before the sails were half repaired we encountered another spell of heavy weather, which reduced us to tatters again, and the ship was drifting about as wind and wave listed. Her masts and spars were a confused mass of wreckage. A green sea had swept the flush deck, carrying off galley (with the unfortunate cook inside) and long-boat, leaving standing only the wretched pigeon-hole of a topgallant fo'k'sle and the stumpy little companion-house abaft the mizzen. The bulwarks were shattered piecemeal; the tree-trunks constituting the deck load had worked their grapplings loose, and rose and fell with the wash of the cross seas. Two of the best men had been washed under the massive trunks, which had settled down on them and crushed the life out of them. Two more poor fellows had suffered broken limbs, and were lying helpless on the fo'k'sle exposed to the seas that continually broke over the bows. The ship was full of water, and pumping was useless. She lay like a log on the heaving face of the winter sea; helpless, yet safe from the fate of foundering unless the timber cargo working inside her should burst her open. The only dry spot aft was the top of the little companion-house, which belonged to the skipper and myself; the crew had the raised deck of the topgallant fo'k'sle and the upper bunks in its interior. One of these constituted our larder; its contents, some pieces of salt pork and beef, dragged out of the harness cask, and a bag of sodden biscuit rescued from the lazarette ere the water rose into the 'tween-decks. A water-cask had been trundled into the fo'k'sle before the great wave swept the deck. About five feet of water stood in the cabin, under which lay my portmanteau, and every belonging save the rough sea-worn suit I stood upright in. Altogether it was not easy to imagine a grimmer present or a darker future. And it was Christmas morning!

About 11 A.M. the remnant of the crew that were alive and could move came splashing along the main deck aft to the companion-house to propose launching the one boat left and abandoning the ship. The mate was in the maintop, where he had lashed himself and gone to sleep. The skipper had waded down into the cabin, as he said, to fish up from his desk the ship's papers. I followed him to tell him of the errand of the crew. Wading across the cabin I could see into his state-room. There sat the fellow on his submerged bunk, up to the waist in water, with a black bottle raised to the ruffianly lips of him. He had lied when he denied having any store of spirits, and had been swigging on the sly, while his men had been toiling and suffering day and night in misery without a drop of the spirit that would have revived their sinking energies.

Enraged beyond the power of self-restraint by the caitiff's selfishness, I gripped him by the throat with one hand as I wrenched the bottle from him with the other. He fell a-snivelling maudlin tears. I swore I'd drown him if he did not deliver up for the common good what of his spirit-supply remained. He fished up three bottles from out the blankets in the inundated bunk. That ran to just a glass apiece for all hands except him, leaving another glass apiece for "next time." While he yet snivelled, the mainbrace was promptly spliced on deck.

The mate and myself persuaded the crew to hold by the ship yet a little longer. By the morrow the sea might have gone down, or we might sight a ship; the *Emma*

Morrison promised to hold together, after her fashion, a bit longer, and she was, after all, preferable to a frail boat in heavy weather.

About one o'clock the mate, who had gone back to his uncomfortable but dry dormitory in the maintop, suddenly shouted "Sail ho!" The poor fellows came tumbling out of the fo'k'sle with eager eyes; a bit too diffident of fortune to cheer just yet, but with the bright light of hope in their faces. Yes; there she was, presently visible from the fo'k'sle, and the abominable old *Emma Morrison* right in her fairway. And now with a hearty cheer we finished to the last drop the skipper's grog. Our flag of distress had been flying for days, but the chaos aloft was more eloquent than any upside-down Union Jack. With what majesty came the succouring ship, borne by the strong wind of favour, the white seas dashing from her gallant stem, her great wet sides rising higher and higher as she neared us! Up alongside she ranged, scarce a pistol-shot distant, a full-rigged clipper: "One of the flying Yankees," said the mate, with, as it seemed, a touch of envy in his voice. "Get ready smart; going to send for you right away!" came her commander's cheery shout across the sullen water. As she came up into the wind and lay to, she showed us her dandy stern, and sure enough on it in gold letters was the legend, "Moses Taylor, of New York." Her boat put off; her second mate jumped aboard us with a friendly peremptory "Hurry up!" in five minutes more we had quitted the *Emma Morrison* for ever, her skipper skulking off her hang-dog fashion, yet the last man. We had agreed, for the good name of the old country among foreigners, to keep counsel regarding the selfish sneak, but he never held up his head more during the time he and I were in the same ship.

A ship like a picture, a deck trim and clean as a new pin, a hearty skipper with a nasal twang, his comely wife, his winsome daughter, and a smart, full-powered crew welcomed us forlorn and dilapidated derelicts on board the *Moses Taylor*. Circumstances prevented us from dressing for the Christmas dinner to which we—skipper, mate, and passenger—were presently bidden; but there were modified comfort and restored self-respect in the long unaccustomed wash in fresh water; and the hosts were more gracious than if we had been dressed more *comme il faut*. To this day I remember that first slice of roast turkey, that first slice of plum-pudding. But closer in my memory remain the cheery accents of the genial American skipper, the glow of kindness in the sonsy face of his wife, and the smile of mixed fun and compassion in the bright eyes of their pretty daughter. And there hung a spray of mistletoe in the cabin doorway of the *Moses Taylor*.

ABSIT OMEN!

CHAPTER I

Edmund L'Estrange was a man who, because of his daring, his skill in devising, his self-possession, in no matter what situation, the influence he could exercise over his fellow-men, would probably have made a distinguished figure in the world if he pursued an honest and loyal career. Circumstances in a measure, and probably a natural bent toward plotting and duplicity, had made him what he was—a prominent man among the dark and dangerous conspirators who live, and who are ready to die, in the devilish cause of anarchy, and of whose machinations the communities of civilisation may well be more apprehensive than of the most widespread and prolonged war, or any other phase of unquietude with which the future of the world may be pregnant.

Among his ancestors was that Sir Roger L'Estrange who was the earliest of all the vast tribe of British journalists, and whom Macaulay somewhat intolerantly denounced as a "scurrilous pamphleteer." According to the doctrine of evolution, Sir Roger's descendant should have been a broad-acred, narrow-minded, and pretentious squire, chief owner of a lucrative, dictatorial, but somewhat obsolete journal, a trimmer in politics, and ready to accept a peerage at the hands of any party caring to concede the dignity. But Edmund L'Estrange was an emphatic traversal of the Darwinian theory. In vigour, resource, and personal courage he harked back to the original L'Estrange who came over with the Conqueror, and who was the progenitor of a long line of gallant warriors. Wellington's regiments in the Peninsula were fuller of L'Estranges than of Napiers. Guy L'Estrange's stand with the 31st at Albuera contributed as much to the winning of that bloody battle as did the famous manœuvre which gained for Hardinge his earliest gleam of fame. Another L'Estrange escaped from the rock-dungeon of Bitche to fight at Orthez and Toulouse, and to meet a soldier's death on the field of Waterloo.

Edmund L'Estrange's branch of the family had been long settled in Ireland. It was staunchly loyalist. His grandfather, as colonel of an Irish militia regiment, had been active in the quelling of the Rebellion of '98, and had smitten his malcontent fellow-countrymen hip and thigh. His father was a conscientious absentee. Edmund, a younger son, had spent his youth on the old L'Estrange demesne in county Clare, and, an Englishman by extraction, had grown up more Irish than the Irish. As a lad of fifteen he had commanded a scratch company of Fenian rapparees, he armed with a shot-gun, his ragged band with pikes. One dark night the dragoons swept on to the moorland where the Fenian drill was in progress. In the stampede fierce old Major Towers, outstripping his squadron, felled young

L'Estrange with a blow of his loaded riding-whip, and then savagely rode over the prostrate lad. Edmund, bruised and half-stunned, rolled into a bog-hag, and fainted. When he recovered he staggered to his feet, softly cursed a little—he was not a violent person—then knelt down and swore eternal enmity against England and against all persons, things, enterprises, and devices that were English. After two years spent in hard study of Continental languages, he sold for money down his succession to his dead mother's property which he was to inherit when of age, and left the country without the ceremony of bidding farewell to his family.

It is for the most part in the poor and proud old families of Scotland wherein generation after generation has been developed that centrifugal force which propels their cadets all over the face of the earth. But this force has been in operation also in many Irish and in some English houses. It had been a characteristic, for instance, of the L'Estranges. Of that race there had been a cadet family in Russia ever since a young L'Estrange had found his way to St. Petersburg along with a Greig, a Barclay, a Ramsay, a Taafe, and a Mackenzie—bent on taking service in the army or the navy of the Empress Catherine—not Carlyle's *infâme Catin du Nord*, but the greater and perhaps more infamous Muscovite sovereign. To General L'Estrange, the chief of the famous Pauloff Grenadiers, his young cousin betook himself and was well received. Tactful, astute, silent, and resourceful, the youngster made his way marvellously. Treskoff the arch-policeman, and Milutin the War Minister, both had uses for this scion of the British Empire who notoriously hated the realm whose fealty he had repudiated. When the Russo-Turkish War began, Ignatieff brought him to Kischeneff and presented him to the Emperor. He and poor Prince Tzeretleff together exploited the Hankioj Pass for Gourko's troopers. He was with Skobeleff before Plevna and before Constantinople. When, baulked of the fair Queen of the Bosphorus, Alexander determined on the Afghan diversion, young L'Estrange was sent post haste to Samarcand, and rode into Cabul as Stolietoff's subaltern. When Stolietoff and his Cossacks scrambled back to the Oxus over the craggy pathway by Bamian and Balkh, L'Estrange remained in Afghanistan. It was he, when the Afghan Major courteously enough blocked the entrance of Neville Chamberlain and his mission into the Khyber Pass, who jeered at that grand old soldier as he wheeled his Arab in front of the *sungah* behind which the Afghan picket lay with fingers on the triggers. He it was, on that gloomy day in the rough valley beyond the Sherpur cantonment, when the jezail-fire staggered the finest Lancer regiment in the British service, from whose rifle sped the bullet that wrought the long agony and final death of the gallant Cleland.

Commissioned always from Russia, L'Estrange was in Joubert's camp when poor Colley climbed the Majuba to his untimely death. Those who held that it was the futile and garrulous Aylward who gave the Boers the plan of campaign which scared Mr. Gladstone into restoring their independence, were strangely mistaken. L'Estrange prescribed the tactics which prevailed at Laing's Neck and the Ingogo, and it was he who lured Colley to his disaster by enjoining the removal of the Boer picket which had been wont to occupy the summit of the Majuba. When Herbert Stewart was brought a prisoner into the Boer camp, L'Estrange insulted the captive man as he was being led away from his interview with the studiously courteous Joubert. With a straight one from the shoulder, learnt in the big dormitory of Winchester College, Stewart promptly grassed the renegade, who, as he rose to his feet, muttered with an evil smile that he would "bide his time."

From the Transvaal restored to independence by Mr. Gladstone, L'Estrange, having made his way to Egypt, stimulated covertly the Nationalist rising in that country; and he it was who was known among our people in the campaign of 1882 as "Arabi's Englishman." He supervised the preparation of the fortified position of Tel-el-Kebir, and was the real leader of the Egyptian soldiery in the fight of Kassassin, which came so near being disastrous to Sir Gerald Graham. The shout of "Retire! Retire!" which caused the temporary retirement of the Highland Brigade from the *mêlée* inside the Egyptian position in the gray morning of the storm of Tel-el-Kebir, and which Sergeant Palmer has persisted in ascribing to a couple of "Glasgow Irishmen" of the Cameron Highlanders, really came from the lips of L'Estrange—a ready-witted ruse on the part of the renegade, which was foiled only by Hamley's soldier-like precaution. From Egypt, under a safe-conduct and recommendation furnished him by Zebehr, he journeyed southward into the Soudan and joined the Mahdi at El Obeid. It was he who mainly planned and conducted the annihilation of Hicks Pasha's ill-fated army. In the climax of the massacre he recognised and was recognised by Edmund O'Donovan, the correspondent of the *Daily News*, whom he had known and admired in his youth-time in Ireland. In an impulse of kindly emotion, he offered to save the life of his brother Irishman. O'Donovan replied with a contemptuous objurgation and a pistol-shot. L'Estrange, wounded in the arm and faint as he was, pulled himself together sufficiently to send a bullet through O'Donovan's head, and so by the hand of a fellow-countryman was ended a life of singular adventure and vicissitude.

Later, L'Estrange went east to Osman Digna. After the Arab stampede from El Teb, he rallied the spearmen who tried to hinder Herbert Stewart's gallop in pursuit. Stewart, well mounted and a fine horseman, rode him down, parrying his spear-thrust with his sabre. L'Estrange lay where he fell for a moment, till Barrow came dashing on at the head of the 19th Hussars, when he sprang up, gave Barrow the spear-wound which ultimately caused his death, and then leaped into the bush. L'Estrange it was who later headed the sudden rush of Arab spearmen up from out the khor into the heart of Davis's square at Tamai, and drove it back in chaotic confusion on the steadfast phalanx of Redvers Buller. His last fight in the Soudan was at Abu Klea. The rush he headed there on the corner manned by the Royal Dragoons was meant by him to open a path for him toward Stewart, for whose blood he had thirsted ever since that knock-down blow in the Boer camp under the Majuba. The rush was baulked, but L'Estrange doggedly maintained his bloodthirsty purpose. When the British column had halted after the fight, he ascended the low elevation commanding the position. He marked down Herbert Stewart through his field-glasses, he judged the distance, and deliberately sighted his rifle accordingly. Then he drew trigger, and as the gallant Stewart first staggered and then dropped on the sand, L'Estrange muttered while he reloaded, "We are quits now—I told him I should 'bide my time'!"

Journeying from Berber to the coast, he was carried by an Arab dhow across the Red Sea, and at Hodeidah embarked on a British India steamer homeward bound from Kurrachee. Among the passengers in this vessel was an Anarchist leader of dubious and probably complex nationality, named Oronzha, who was returning from a secret mission to India, attended by an East Indian whose name was Shere Ali Beg, and who passed for, and acted as, Oronzha's travelling servant, but whose relations with his apparent master L'Estrange soon discerned were too intimate for those of a domestic. Oronzha cautiously made some advances to the European gentleman who had embarked from a port so unwonted for Europeans as Hodeidah; with at least equal caution those advances were reciprocated by L'Estrange. At length Oronzha made a covert gesture, the significance of which, and the response to which, L'Estrange had learned among his varied experiences in Russia. He made the answering signal, and at once Oronzha and L'Estrange met on the common ground of anarchical Socialism. There was much matter for mutual communication. Oronzha expressed his conviction to L'Estrange that profound discontent with the English *raj* existed throughout the population of the Punjaub, and that the head of a Russian column on the Helmund or above the Bamian would be the signal for a universal uprising. He thought it advisable that, in the hope of such an incentive to revolt, Russia should, for the present, be exempted from the active machinations of Socialist propaganda. L'Estrange, in his turn, informed Oronzha that the harvest of Socialism in that empire might be garnered at any period thought fitting, since Nihilism and Socialism were practically synonymous, and since he believed the Russian people, from the very foot of the throne downward, were honeycombed with Nihilism. His old chief Skobeleff and all his dare-devil staff were Nihilists at heart. Ignatieff, at the late Czar's right hand as he was, had a distinct leaning in the same direction. Nay, he had discerned in the course of his confidential intercourse with that monarch that a warp of Nihilism had been interwoven through the curious and complicated mental texture of Alexander himself.

As the *Chybassa* steamed languidly against the scorching wind that swept down the Red Sea, those two men—so diverse in birth and upbringing, yet so near akin in sentiment and hatred of the British power—discussed many problems and contrived many schemes, while the supple and astute Shere Ali Beg, conversant with the suppressed yet seething disaffection of all the great Indian cities from Peshawur to Calcutta, and thoroughly versed in the tortuous and fanatical plottings of that widespread Wahabee organisation which covers the East from the Golden Horn to the eastern coasts of the Bay of Bengal, interpolated occasionally a sentence of gloomy and ferocious import.

Oronzha was an arch-plotter, all the more influential and dangerous that he played the great game through instruments, and consistently kept his own personality in the background. His mission to the Punjaub had been a mere incident in the deep and far-reaching scheme he had been furthering for years. He had been in close although unobtrusive touch with every phase of the widespread Socialism of Europe, but his absence in India had thrown him somewhat in arrear regarding its latest developments. Before the *Chybassa* reached Port Said, he had confided to L'Estrange the commission to visit all the great centres of Continental Socialism, charged to communicate confidentially with the inner conclave at each, and to bring to him in London a report of the general situation. L'Estrange started on his errand, duly fortified with such credentials—a sign, a watchword, an apparently innocent note of introduction—as would insure to him the unreserved confidence of the leaders of the great International organisation which has for its aim the fundamental subversion of the political and social order of things throughout the length and breadth of the Continent.

It might be interesting to narrate in detail the experiences of L'Estrange in the fulfilment of this commission: how from Galatz he visited Lemberg, from Lemberg went on to Warsaw, from Warsaw to Cracow, thence into the chief cities of Hungary, from the Marchfeldt to Vienna, thence into Croatia and Dalmatia, from Trieste to Prague, from Prague through Dresden, Berlin, Hamburg, into the teeming operative and mining regions of Westphalia and the more southern Rhine provinces; from Alsace to Lyons and thereabouts, through Paris into Belgium, and so, after the lapse of some months from his parting with Oronzha at Port Said, to the house in a court in Soho which Oronzha had designated as a rendezvous. Met here by this *dégagé*-seeming man of many subtle plots, he was bidden, as the best method of furthering the cause, to enlist in that crack English cavalry regiment the Scarlet Hussars, then quartered at Hounslow, with instructions covertly and cautiously to aim at subverting the loyalty of the troopers of that regiment, and to labour to instil mutinous tendencies by dwelling on the materialistically pleasant results, to the appreciation of the private soldier grumbling at scant rations and poor pay, of a fine free-and-easy *régime* of lawlessness and unlimited drink.

Chapter II

L'Estrange was quite a success in his new character as a Scarlet Hussar. At first, it is true, he incurred suspicion. When, at his first essay in the riding-school, he rode with "stirrups up," as if he were "demi-corporate with the brave beast"; and when, at his first dismounted drill, he cut the sword exercise with more grace and precision than did the old ranker adjutant himself, his troop sergeant-major promptly set him down as a deserter. That conviction L'Estrange summarily dispelled by confidentially informing the honest old non-com., with the little compliment of a five-pound note, that he had been an officer in the Bengal Cavalry who had come to grief, and that he had enlisted in an assumed name with intent to work up for a commission. Of course the troop sergeant-major divulged this confidence to the regimental, the regimental told it to the adjutant, and soon every officer in the regiment knew it, and L'Estrange's lines fell in pleasant places. Grim old Sabretasche, the chief, dropped him a bluffly curt word of encouragement. Lord Ebor, the captain of his troop, his courteous and kindly nature moving him, spoke to him as an equal, and expressed the hope that before long he might see him "in the blue coat." In four months from the day of his enlistment L'Estrange was full corporal; in four months more he was a lance-sergeant.

While still a private, by taking his comrades separately, and talking cautiously but suggestively, he had won over quite a large number of the young soldiers of the regiment. When the three stripes were on his arm, and he had become a member of the sergeants' mess, it was with great finesse and adroitness that he made his advances among the non-commissioned officers with whom he now lived. With the grand staunch class of old long-service non-commissioned officers L'Estrange would have utterly failed to make way, and would either have been jeered down or reported to superior authority. Of this type, however, there remained in the Scarlet Hussars only two or three veterans, who were all married men, and therefore were not frequenters of the sergeants' mess. The majority of the non-commissioned officers were flashy young short-service men, "jumped-up non-coms." in soldier phrase, dissipated, hungry for more means wherewithal to pursue dissipation, discontented and unconscientious. Most of them lent a more or less greedy ear to the subtle poison covertly instilled by L'Estrange, and the result of his machinations was that before he had been in the regiment a twelve-month the Scarlet Hussars, spite of their fine old reputation for every soldierly virtue, were fast ripening for mischief.

In sundry short conversations, when Sergeant L'Estrange took the order-book daily to his captain's quarters, and after Lord Ebor had read the details of regimental work for the morrow, the former, who had read his officer like a book, from time to time dropped mildly Socialistic seed into his mind, which fell in not unfavourable soil.

Meanwhile Sergeant L'Estrange was indefatigable in his efforts to proselytise among the soldiery of the London garrison outside his own regiment. In this work he had the advantage that his troop had been moved up from Hounslow to Kensington. In the Scarlet Hussars the wearing of "plain clothes" —*i.e.* civilian attire—by the sergeants was winked at, and L'Estrange could thus when occasion required go about the town and visit places unnoticed, where his uniform might have attracted attention. He met with no success in his attempts to sap the loyalty of the Household Cavalry. Because of his winning address, his fine voice in a song, and his bright talk, he had been made free of the non-commissioned officers' mess of the "Blues" on his first visit to Regent's Park Barracks, and he had made himself agreeable with similar result among the Corporals of Horse of the 1st Life Guards in Knightsbridge. But his particular object made no way either in Regent's Park or in Hyde Park. Because Corporal of Horse Jack Vanhomrigh of the "Blues" was a pariah of society, had been detected and denounced as a card-sharper, had tossed in the smoking-room of a club with a brother reprobate for the possession of a notorious woman whom he had married and then lived on till the poor wretch died of consumption, L'Estrange regarded that scion of a noble family as a person likely to listen to his overtures. He reckoned without his host. Vanhomrigh was on his promotion; he had washed and was now comparatively clean; a few more months of straight conduct would see him on his way to a cattle ranche in Alberta. He had been a blackguard, but he was a Briton. So in perfectly outspoken terms he denounced the Scarlet Hussar to the assembled mess, and told L'Estrange in the frankest manner that he ought to be hanged because shooting was too good for him. The mess president warned L'Estrange against ever showing his face in that company again, and the orderly Corporal of Horse, enjoined by the old Regimental Corporal-Major, escorted him silently to the gate, saw him outside, and then "put his name on the gate"—a measure effectually precluding his readmission into Regent's Park Barracks. L'Estrange fared no better with the non-commissioned officers of the regiment quartered at Knightsbridge, which barracks he no more attempted to enter after the severe corporal chastisement inflicted on him by a stalwart Corporal of Horse, whom he had approached, learning that he was in financial difficulties, with seditious proposals pointed by the offer of a ten-pound note. He fared no whit better with the tall troopers of either regiment. In vain did he frequent the public-houses of Knightsbridge and Cumberland Market. The strapping dalesmen were willing enough to drink with him at his expense, while he led the jovial chorus and told tales of foreign travel. But L'Estrange had to rein back sharply on the curb when blunt old Trooper Escrick of Dent, his face gnarled like the scarped brow of Ingleborough, broke in on a pretty little outline he was venturing to sketch of the good times Socialism offered to the soldier. "Mon," quoth honest Escrick, "thou mun be a dom fuil, if nobbut warse. Wi' your bloody community o' goods, as thou call'st it, what would happen my feyther, t'oud statesman? Gang to hell oot of this!" Whereupon Escrick threw the quart-pot (empty) at L'Estrange's head, who abandoned thenceforth the society of the Household Cavalry.

But he had greater success with the infantrymen of the Household troops—a force whose character, as in a measure its physique, has deteriorated since the adoption of the three years' service system. In the slums of Westminster he gradually corrupted men by beer and blandishments, with such success that in no long time the rank-and-file of one whole battalion were tainted with disaffection, and in a fair way to become dangerous. With all this good fortune, and realising with a lurid gratification that at least one battalion of Her Majesty's Household troops was now little other than a plastic instrument in his hands, the astute conspirator was well aware that it still behoved him to work warily and to consolidate the plot by further specific guarantees for success. He remembered the sardonic adage whose author was an acute fellow-countryman of his own—that of three Irish conspirators it might be taken for granted that one was an informer. There were not many Irish soldiers in the ranks of the Household Brigade, but there were many men whose fealty to his propaganda, spite of their professions, he instinctively felt was not to be relied on. So long as these propaganda were of a loose and general character, there was not anything very specific for the informer to reveal. But it would be a very different thing were all or any large proportion of his converts to be initiated formally into the membership of the disloyal and anarchical confederacy which he represented. Yet he could not trust the situation as it stood. All experience taught him how backward to assert itself actively was the most disaffected community which lacked the inspiration and initiative of ready and energetic leaders. Out of the mass of grumbling discontented soldiery L'Estrange set himself to select a number of men of strongest character, of fiercest nature, of greatest recklessness of consequences. This winnowing method he carried out both in the Scarlet Hussars and in the Household Infantry, and having recruited to his behests a band of desperadoes in either corps, he had those "select men" sworn by detachments into memberhood of the Regenerators at the obscure branch lodge whose quarters were in the Natty Coster beerhouse up Skin-the-Rabbit Court off the New Cut.

Of all the Socialistic workers and plotters who were now actively furthering the cause in London, only two men, Sergeant L'Estrange and Shere Ali Beg, the Lascar, were aware that its leading fosterer was Oronzha, the apparently *dégagé* gentleman who, because of the lavish entertainments he was giving so frequently in his sumptuous house in Bruton Street, and by reason of financial good offices judiciously dispensed among influential people, was rapidly making for himself a position in society. L'Estrange naturally regarded as his chief in the work of the dissemination of anarchy in the metropolis of Great Britain the strange and mysterious man whom he had first met on the *Chybassa*, and who had proved himself in intimate touch with the Socialist leaders of the Continent. He visited Bruton Street under cover of night, his errand being to report to Oronzha the measure of success which he had reached in his mission to sap the loyalty of the garrison of London.

To his surprise, he found the enigmatical Oronzha strangely indifferent to the tidings brought him; and, what struck him forcibly as still more strange, quite lukewarm in his tone in regard to the enterprise as a whole.

"Thanks," drawled the swarthy sybarite as he lit a perfumed cigarette; "all that is very interesting, and I'm sure, my dear L'Estrange, you have done wonders—positive wonders. As for the civilian element, it, too, is fairly ripe, and I believe we might give the signal to-morrow. But there are reasons, my dear L'Estrange—I won't explain them—why the *émeute* had better be postponed for a while. Sedition is a commodity that does not spoil by keeping, but rather improves. Don't let your soldier-fellows get lukewarm, but don't allow them to come to full-cock for the present—there's a broken metaphor for you, and an obsolete one to boot! By the way, how about that quixotic Lord Ebor of your regiment? He is your captain, is he not?"

"Yes," replied L'Estrange, restraining his surprise at this abrupt change of subject on Oronzha's part. "Ebor, born aristocrat as he is, I believe would go almost any length with us, when once thoroughly imbued with the idea that he would be furthering the welfare of humanity at large."

"He is the man of all others," said Oronzha musingly, "whom I want to see involved with us up to the hilt. The truth is, L'Estrange," continued Oronzha, springing to his feet and speaking earnestly—"the truth is, d—n him! I want him ruined socially, utterly and beyond recovery—he has thwarted me in a matter very dear to me. Can you help in this?"

"I think I can succeed in compromising him completely with us, if that is what you aim at," replied L'Estrange. "It is a result you must not expect all of a sudden. Ebor is an officer and a gentleman. He is a dreamer, and he has what the Scotch call 'a bee in the bonnet'; but it is a 'far cry' from that to being a traitor. However, I have studied his character, and I believe I see my way."

Oronzha was a shrewd man, but he had formed an erroneous estimate of L'Estrange's character. He reckoned him simply a serviceable tool, whom he could use for his purposes, and drop when he chose. L'Estrange, in reality, with his Irish mother-wit and the added acumen which his Russian experiences had given him, had seen through Oronzha's veil of new-born indifference, and had penetrated the purely personal motive actuating that dark schemer.

"This man," mused L'Estrange, as he walked away from Bruton Street—"this man is now simply playing with Socialism for his own ends. He is not whole-souled in the cause. His real aim—why, I know not, nor do I care—is to bring Lord Ebor to grief. That accomplished, Socialism in London may go hang for him, and the enthusiasts who are working to bring about anarchy he will leave to their fate with a light heart, or indeed will, as like as not, betray them."

He, L'Estrange, had been content for the time to be the instrument of a power-ful man who was sincere in the cause; but he was not the man to be a tool of a wily dissimulator. Two master-motives swayed him—personal ambition and bitter hate against England. As he pondered, he believed that he saw his way to gratify both motives, and that too by a line of action wholly independent of the specious but treacherous Oronzha.

Chapter III

L'Estrange had gained the conviction that the British Army, as a whole, was seething with disaffection, and ready to mutiny in a mass when once the brand of revolt should be waved. He had corrupted his own regiment and a battalion of Household Infantry; he knew that the seeds of taint had been sown in other regiments of the Queen's service. During a week recently spent at Aldershot he had received assurances from men of every regiment in that garrison, cavalry as well as infantry, that discontent and disaffection were general, and that a leader and an example would promptly be followed. So much for the military element. He had taken some pains to learn the state of feeling among the lower classes of London, and had satisfied himself that they were ready to throw themselves into any vehemence of revolutionary enterprise, if only the encouragement and stiffen-ing of vigorous leadership and armed support were imparted. There opened, then, before this methodical yet reckless desperado the vista of wrecking the Monarchy, the Constitution, the military and social system of that England which he hated so venomously, by kindling a rising in a section of its army, and by marching the mu-tinied soldiery to rouse and rally the masses of the metropolis. If the result, as he hoped, should be a universal anarchy, he, its instigator and contriver, might "ride the whirlwind and direct the storm"; if failure should be the issue of his desperate devices, he, to do him the miserable justice of owning him reckless of his own life, was ready to perish under the avalanche whose fall he had provoked.

The season of summer drill at Aldershot had come to a close, and Sir Eve-lyn Wood was dismissing—some with curt but cordial benediction, some with that outspoken objurgation of which he is so great a master—the regiments which were to find winter quarters elsewhere than on the bleak slope of the Hampshire standing camp. Among the departing regiments was that steady old corps the Re-gal Dragoons, who were bound for Norwich and quietude after three years of scouting and flying column business. The Regals carried no "side," and were not addicted to cheap swagger, but the grand old regiment was, in military phrase, "all there when it was wanted." Peterborough had praised it in Spain, Marlborough in the Low Countries and Bavaria, Wellington in the Peninsula and at Waterloo. The serried mass of Russian horsemen felt the brunt of it as the heavy squadrons thundered behind Scarlett and Elliot on the morning of Balaclava. Old Guardlex was its chief, the senior colonel on active service in the British Army, for his promotion had been cruelly slow since, the junior cornet of the Regals, he had ridden over the hills to the upland on which were dropping stray cannon-shot from the Tchernaya fight. His moustache was snow-white and his hair grizzled, but the old soldier's stalwart figure was still straight as a dart, the broad shoulders were carried square, and the strong right arm could make the sabre whistle again in the sword exercise, of his dexterity in which the chief was proud. Colonel Guardlex was very particular in regard to the recruits he accepted for his regiment; but there never was a regiment in the modern British Army which did not contain some bad characters. Probably there were fewer in the Regals than in any other cavalry regiment in the service. This handful of black sheep it was who, when L'Estrange paid his short visit to Aldershot, had deceived him with the assurance that the regiment as a whole was ready to co-operate in any mischief.

At the end of their second day's march from Aldershot to Norwich, the Regals were to be billeted in Wimbledon and Putney. It occurred to some ardent soldier among the high authorities in Pall Mall that, instead of resuming the route on the following morning, the marching regiment and the Scarlet Hussars from Hounslow and the out-quarters might have a lively brigade field-day on and about Wimbledon Common. The orders for this brigade field-day were read out overnight throughout the troops of the Scarlet Hussars at evening stables, as is the wont in cavalry regiments. Since he happened to be orderly sergeant, L'Estrange had the information a trifle earlier. It came upon him like a flash of inspiration that the morrow would give him the opportunity for which he had been on the alert for weeks. The time was desperately short, it was true, and he had many dispositions to arrange; but the difficulties before him would succumb to method and activity. A man in dead earnest could do much between seven o'clock and midnight.

On his way from Kensington to Waterloo, he made a rush into the Wellington Barracks to arrange for simultaneous action on the part of the 6th Battalion of the Welsh Guards—the battalion he knew to be ripe for mutiny. Its order for the morrow was adjutant's drill, to fall in at eleven; the drill would be over about half-past twelve. He settled with the ringleaders of the battalion that it was then it should declare itself, by which time L'Estrange promised that the Scarlet Hussars and the Regals would be close at hand. At Wimbledon the ardent toiler in an evil cause had what he considered a satisfactory ten minutes with the arch-blackguard of the handful of blackguards of the Regals. By ten o'clock he was in Hounslow Barracks. "Lights out" sounded as he finished his round of the troop-rooms, but he had accomplished what of his task lay to him there. Then he spent a balefully busy half-hour in the sergeants' mess, and by midnight he was back in Kensington Barracks. What few words had to be said to the squadron quartered there would keep till morning. His Hounslow allies had undertaken to inspire the little contingent from Hampton Court.

It was about nine o'clock on a lovely morning in early September when the brigade formed up aligning on the Kingston Road, its right flank on the park-wall of "The Highlands," the pleasant residence that used to belong to "Jim" Farquharson of Invercauld, good soldier and good fellow. Each regiment was but three squadrons strong, the Scarlet Hussars because of the usual duty details, the Regals because their fourth squadron was marching by another route. Colonel Guardlex, as the senior officer, took command, and, as his manner was, proceeded to give the brigade a rattling bucketing. Scouts furtively searched to front and flanks, feeling for the foreposts of the extremely imaginary enemy, who in accordance with the "special idea" was assumed to have breakfasted at Esher, and to be now marching on the metropolis with Tarquin's ravishing strides. Reconnaissances in more or less strength scared the game of the Duke of Cambridge and Lord Dunraven on the hither slopes of Combe Hill, and furnished Lord Archy Campbell with inspiration for a letter to the *Times*, indignantly demanding to know why there is not a Highland cavalry regiment armed with claymores and attired in philabeg and plaid. A grand decisive charge on either flank of the imaginary enemy, represented for the nonce by the 1000-yards butt, brought the field-day to a close. Colonel Guardlex, with a ceremonious bow to Colonel Sabretasche, and a compliment on the smartness of the Scarlet Hussars, ceased from his temporary brigadiership, and cantered off to his Regals. Before quitting the common, the two regiments, as is the custom, halted for a little time, during which the troopers, having dismounted, glanced round their horse-equipments, lit their pipes, and gave vent to professional criticism highly spiced with profanity. The halted formation of each regiment was in column of squadrons. The front of the Scarlet Hussars faced south-westward, in the direction of the hamlet of Roehampton, its right close to the position of the stand from which Royalty was wont to distribute the prizes in the days when as yet Wimbledon remained undisestablished.

Colonel Sabretasche and most of his officers had dismounted, and were chatting and smoking in a group on the sward in front of the regiment. Lord Ebor was in command of the third—the rear—squadron, and, as his custom was, he had remained with his command instead of joining his brother officers at the front. His lordship was "making much" of his gallant charger when Sergeant L'Estrange strode up to him, halted at "attention," and spoke thus in a quiet measured tone—

"My Lord, the regiment is about to revolt—in plain language, to mutiny. The whole British Army is with us, and the people as well, determined no longer to endure tyranny and wrong. Lord Ebor, it will be a great and glorious revolution. Take command of us, lead the regiment back to expectant London, and be hailed the deliverer of your native land from oppression."

For one brief moment it seemed as if Ebor faltered. He drew a long breath, he threw back his fine head, a flush mantled the delicate features, and a wistful radiance flashed in his eyes. Then it was as if a shiver ran through him; but an instant saw him himself again—the nobleman and officer—and he quietly said—

"Sergeant L'Estrange, not another word. Go back at once to your troop. I refrain from putting you under arrest on the spot, because I believe you must be crazed. No more of this! Right about face, quick march!"

L'Estrange stood fast.

"Lord Ebor," said he calmly, "if you will not lead us willingly you shall do so by compulsion."

"Sergeant-Major Hope," Ebor called authoritatively, "put Sergeant L'Estrange under arrest, strip his belts, and guard him while I go to the Colonel."

Sergeant-Major Hope shrugged his broad shoulders with a sneer and did not stir. Lord Ebor put foot in stirrup to ride to the Colonel. Then L'Estrange gave the order—

"Mulligan and Coates, grapple Lord Ebor, throw him down, and gag him!"

Ebor at the word faced about, his face blazing with anger and scorn. The two stalwart troopers laid hold of him on either side. He shook them off with a force that hurled them back, and, grasping his sword-hilt, had the weapon half out of the scabbard.

But L'Estrange was "quicker on the draw." Before Lord Ebor's sword was clear of the scabbard, his point was at the other's breast. The innate savagery of the man was ablaze.

"D—n you, you will have it, then!" he hissed from between his set teeth, as with a strong thrust he sent his sword through Lord Ebor's throat, who fell in his tracks, to all appearance dead.

L'Estrange, with a vicious smile, wiped his sword on the heather, returned it to the scabbard, and then, darting through the second squadron, gave the command—

"Fire on the officers!"

While the regiment had been standing dismounted, a certain number of desperadoes in the front rank of the first squadron had quietly drawn their carbines, had loaded, and were waiting for the word. When it came, the stillness of the air was suddenly broken by a straggling volley, and several of the officers fell.

Old Sabretasche was unhurt. The last bullet of the ragged volley had not whistled by him when he was in the saddle, and facing the regiment he had served in since he was a smooth-faced lad, and which he loved and honoured next to his mother.

"Scarlet Hussars!" he shouted in trumpet tones—and yet there was a break in the voice of him—"in God's name, what means this? All true men, do your duty, for the credit of the regiment! Seize these accursed mutineers, who are disgracing——"

Sabretasche never finished the sentence. Before his last word had reached the rear squadron he was lying on his back on the sward dead, with three carbine bullets in him or through him. A cheer, in which there was the undernote of a quaver, rose from the disordered ranks of the corps that had been wont to take especial pride in their title of "Queen Victoria's Own." Under a straggling fire the officers who remained uninjured, followed by some of the senior non-commissioned officers and by a handful of old soldiers, galloped off to join the adjacent Regal Dragoons. ·

Chapter IV

That regiment, for its part, had halted and dismounted on the neck which in the Wimbledon days had been the camping-ground of the "Members" and of the "Victorias." Its formation was identical with that of the Scarlet Hussars—column of squadrons—and its front looked across the undulating plateau in the direction of Colonel Sabretasche's light-bobs. Colonel Guardlex had allowed his troopers but a short halt, and they had already mounted, and were waiting for the command to return to their billets, when the noise of the first shots fired from out the front rank of the Hussars came down on the soft wind. "Slovenly work, sir," the Adjutant of the Regals was remarking to his chief, "getting rid of blank ammunition only now."

Guardlex suddenly started.

"Blank ammunition be — —!" he exclaimed. "You heard the whistle of that bullet—and there's another—and another! By the living God, the blackguards are shooting down their officers! The Scarlet Hussars have mutinied! Steady there, the Regals!" roared the chief, wheeling his horse and facing his own regiment "Squadrons, eyes centre! Officers, see to the dressing!"

Suddenly from near the flank of the right troop of the first squadron shot out a dragoon, bellowing, as he turned in his saddle—

"To h— with the Widow! Down with the officers! Come on, chaps, and join our gallant comrades yonder. On, lads, to liberty and license!"

One or two men moved out half-a-horse's length, and then halted irresolutely. The captain commanding the right troop drew his sword—he was within three horses' length of the mutineer.

"Steady, officers and men!" rang out in the deep voice of the chief. "Captain Hurst, return your sword, sir!"

As he gave these commands, Colonel Guardlex was cantering steadily and coolly towards the right, where stood the mutineer. The man did not quail as the Colonel approached, with that grim smile on his weather-beaten face which habitual defaulters knew so well. Nay, the trooper, a desperado to the backbone, drew his sword and confronted the Colonel, throwing up his guard.

It was all over in two seconds. A riderless horse was galloping away. On the sward lay a sword with a severed hand still grasping its hilt, and close by a dead dragoon with a sword-thrust through his heart. Cool and stern, the chief was back in his place, issuing curt rapid orders to his officers. Captain Francis commanded the right troop, Captain Clements the left troop, of the rear squadron. Captain Francis he ordered to take his troop out by a circuit through the broken ground, and so by the back of the butts, till well in rear of the Scarlet Hussars; Captain Clements to move down the hollow on his left, the "Glenalbyn" of the Wimbledon days, and, with a wide bend round the right flank of the Hussars, reunite with

Francis in their rear and bar the way of retreat—both movements to be executed at a gallop. To each of his majors he gave a troop of the second squadron, with orders to move out to the right and left front, manœuvre for the flanks of the Hussars, and ride in on both obliquely. The first squadron he kept in his own hand, moving it straight forward at a trot until within about five hundred paces of the front of the Hussars. Then he halted, kept the front rank in the saddle, dismounted two men in each three of his rear rank, and ordered them to load their carbines and stand fast, hidden by the mounted men in their front.

All these dispositions were made in less than half the time it has taken the reader to peruse the necessarily rather minute detail of them. Meanwhile curiosity, excitement, and a certain involuntary awe had considerably disorganised the Scarlet Hussars. L'Estrange had quietly taken the command, and his non-commissioned accomplices, now acting as officers, were busily reconstituting their respective commands, for the accomplishment of which a few minutes sufficed. L'Estrange had for the moment been otherwise engaged, and no one else in the Hussars had noticed what, if anything, in the Regals had occurred consequent on the first demonstration of mutiny among the Hussars. But L'Estrange had now time to notice the conduct of the Regals. *They* had not mutinied, that was now certain; and by Heaven, beyond all question, Colonel Guardlex was skilfully preparing to assume the offensive!

Clever fellow as was L'Estrange, his *coup d'œil* was defective. What he thought he saw in progress was an extension of front on the part of the Regals. He promptly conformed by ordering up the second squadron of the Scarlet Hussars in line with the first, keeping the third squadron in rear of his centre as a reserve. Then he resolved on the hardy, if not desperate, expedient of taking the initiative. Should he remain passive, he rapidly argued with himself, the Regals would drive the lighter corps, perhaps indeed shatter it. He realised that up till now his *coup* had been a *coup manqué*; yet all was not lost if only the dashing and nimble Hussars could smite and break the lumbering and clumsy heavies over against him there. So, hardening his heart, he gave the command, "The line will advance! At a trot, march!" he himself galloping out to the front.

L'Estrange had not galloped far, and the squadrons behind him were instinctively preparing to spring from the trot into the gallop, when he noticed for the first time the two troops of the Regals commanded by the majors coming down obliquely, one on either flank of the Hussars. Unconfronted, they would take him *en flagrant délit*, and roll him up. On the spur of the moment he shouted the order, "First and second squadrons, outwards half wheel!" and he himself rode a little farther to the front, halted, and faced round, to watch the effect of the evolution.

Meanwhile Colonel Guardlex had passed his dismounted men through the still mounted front rank of the squadron he had kept in his own hand, had numbered them off—there were thirty of them—and held them with loaded carbines, waiting for his command to fire. "I can plug that beggar out to the front there, sir," said Jack Osborne, the champion marksman of the Regals, in a low tone to the Adjutant; "will you ask the Colonel whether I may fire?" Colonel Guardlex overheard the entreaty. "No, my man," answered the chief; "please God, we'll take that scoundrel alive. Shooting is too good for him!"

But the aspiration was not to be fulfilled. Rough-riding Sergeant Bob Swash was a historic character in the Regal Dragoons while as yet he was in the regiment. He had been born in it, he had served in it for ever so many years, and he meant to die in it. He was as good a man at fifty-five, he swore, as he had been at twenty-five; he had enlisted "for life or until unfit for further service"; he was still eminently fit for service, and he spurned the acceptance of the pension to which he had been entitled for more than a decade. Generation after generation of recruits had been quaintly objurgated by him in every riding-school in the United Kingdom. Old Bob could neither read nor write, else he would not now have been a "simple sergeant," but at fifty-five he was still the best horseman and the best swordsman in the Regal Dragoons. He always went on the line of march with the regiment, riding one of the officers' young horses, to which he taught manners on the journey. He rode about independently, not being tied to any particular position; and it happened that he had been close to the Scarlet Hussars when the mutiny in that regiment burst out. The old man's glance toward his own regiment told him that Colonel Guardlex was alive to the situation, and did not need any information that he could bring, so he continued in the vicinity of the mutinied regiment, watching for a chance at L'Estrange, whom he had discerned to be the arch-mutineer.

That chance he saw, and grasped, when L'Estrange, alone and well out to the front, halted to watch the outward half-wheel of his first and second squadrons. It was but a snap chance, Swash realised, since the reserve squadron of the Hussars was rapidly advancing to fill up the interval which the outward wheel was creating. But if it had been a worse chance old Bob would have taken it. Shooting past the flank of one of the wheeling squadrons, he galloped furiously on L'Estrange with a great shout of execration. L'Estrange had just time to fire a couple of shots from his revolver, one of which wounded but did not disable Swash, when the big man on the big horse struck the smaller man on the lighter horse with terrific impetus and weight. L'Estrange and his horse were hurled to the ground with a crash; the horse staggered to his feet, but L'Estrange lay stone dead—the dragoon's sword-point had pierced his heart. Swash galloped on for a few strides, then swayed in the saddle, and fell to the ground. At the moment of impact, L'Estrange's revolver had sent a bullet through his brain. Old Bob had his wish: he died, as he had been born, in the Regal Dragoons.

The swift sudden death of the man who had been their inspiration and their leader staggered the mutinous Hussars. The squadrons drew rein and lapsed from trot to walk. Colonel Guardlex had his finger on the pulse of events. He gave the word to his marksmen to fire a volley. But he was not bloodthirsty. Ten men only he ordered to take aim; the rest were bidden to fire high. The volley sped: two or three men in each of the three Hussar squadrons went down. The marksmen promptly reloaded, but no more firing was necessary. The Hussar squadrons halted for a moment, then broke up into wild confusion, the troopers crowding independently in toward the centre. All at once the ordered ranks fell into utter chaos. The marksmen of the Regals remounted; Guardlex formed his squadron in rank entire, and galloped in upon the Hussars. The other squadrons of his regiment promptly conformed, and in a few minutes the weltering chaos of Hussars was encircled by a ring of Regal Dragoons.

The stentorian commands of Colonel Guardlex dominated the babel of sounds that pulsated within the silent cordon formed by his staunch troopers. The cowed Hussars sullenly obeyed him as he formed them up, dismounted them, stripped their belts and arms, and took away their horses.

The mutinied regiment remained strictly guarded in a "prison-camp" on Wimbledon Common for several days, and was then conveyed by train to Dartmoor Prison, where the court-martial era set in with stern severity, in spite of the vehement and persistent remonstrances of certain members of Parliament who appeared to regard murderous mutiny as rather laudable than otherwise. The *Gazette* presently promulgated the melancholy intimation that the Scarlet Hussars had been disbanded, and that there was no longer a regiment of that once proud name in the British Army. Colonel Guardlex, having undergone a *pro-formâ* trial by court-martial, was acquitted with honour and credit, and his promotion to major-general was announced in the same *Gazette* in which the Scarlet Hussars were obliterated.

Chapter V

While the Scarlet Hussars were being "rounded up" on Wimbledon Common by the staunch old Regals, another abortive rising was being crushed with equal completeness.

The 6th Welsh Guards was the show battalion of the Household Infantry, and never did it parade in finer form than on the morning after L'Estrange's hurried visit to Wellington Barracks on his way to concert the mutiny of the Scarlet Hussars, the summary frustration of which has just been described. It happened that some German officers were at this time in London, and they were escorted to the Guards' parade-ground in Hyde Park by several of the field-officers of the Brigade, anxious to prove to the Teutonic soldiers that elsewhere than in the German armies could perfection of drill be attained by men enlisted for only three years' service. The Kaiser's warriors were frank and outspoken beyond their reserved wont as, under the surveillance of the smart and peremptory adjutant, the battalion marched passed in divers formations. This ceremony finished, Captain Falconer marched it across the Row to the more open ground northward. After an hour's sharp drill, the battalion was halted about three hundred yards to the east of the low elevation on which stand the police-station and the guardhouse. Its halted formation was in open column of companies, the front of the column directly facing the interval between the two buildings just named.

During the brief "stand at ease"—the hour was just noon—there was to be seen riding to and fro in the interval between the front of the battalion and the rise crowned by the police-station and the guardhouse a keen-eyed elderly gentleman, who, although in civilian attire, could not be mistaken for any other than a soldier. The men in the ranks recognised him at a glance as the General commanding the

Home District; and a Cockney lance-corporal remarked, "Hif hold Phil don't cut his lucky, we'll give him 'what for' by and by!"

"Hold Phil" evinced no symptoms of an intention to "cut his lucky." He quietly beckoned the adjutant to him, said a few words, and then glanced sharply toward where, in the interval between the two buildings on the ridge, there stood an officer in the uniform of the Horse Artillery. Then he nodded to the adjutant of the battalion.

That officer in a loud voice gave the consecutive commands—

"Attention!"

"Shoulder arms!"

"The battalion will return to barracks!"

Save for the colour-sergeants and sergeants, the battalion remained at the "stand at ease," and a jeering laugh ran along the ranks.

"Once again, Captain Falconer," said the General with a composure in which there was something ominous.

Captain Falconer called the battalion to "Attention!" a second time. This time he was hooted, and a man pointed his rifle at him, but the weapon was struck up by a sergeant. The battalion broke out into oaths and shouts.

The General bade Captain Falconer order the non-commissioned officers to fall out to the flanks; and then he raised aloft his right arm and shouted, "Major Hippesley!"

Major Hippesley was the horse-gunner on the ridge. That officer did not so much as turn his head, but the command he gave carried half-way across the Park, so loud was it. And the sense of the command was as truculent as was Hippesley's tone—

"By hand, run out the guns! Action front!"

With a bicker and a rush there shot from out the police-station yard gun after gun, whirled by stalwart artillerymen, till in a few seconds six pieces filled the interval between the police-station and the guardhouse, their sullen mouths pointed straight down on the dense mass of guardsmen.

Major Hippesley glanced at the General, and saw that his right arm was again in the air. At this signal, he bellowed—

"With case, load!"

A tremor agitated the ranks of the Foot Guard battalion. And at the moment from the right and from the left came through the still air the muffled noise of the hoof-beat on the sward of many horses galloping furiously. From Cumberland Gate and from Victoria Gate the Blues were racing on the battalion's right flank; from Knightsbridge the Life Guards were heading at a straining gallop towards its left. Clearly there was to be no paltering. The swords of the massive troopers were out and flashing in the sunshine. Destruction and death lay panting in the dark cruel throats of the cannon up there, where the gunners stood ready for the word to fire. And there was no ruth in the stern face of the gray chief out on the left front clear of the line of fire, grimly waiting for the "psychological moment."

The battalion was writhing and heaving, a prey to the emotions of terror, fury, and the sense of having been betrayed. On it, thus agitated, fell like a sedative the General's calm, firm command—

"Battalion, pile arms!"

The battalion confessed its mutiny abortive in its prompt obedience to the order. Escorted by cavalry and artillery, the disarmed guardsmen were marched straight into the great inner yards of Millbank Prison, where they remained encamped until their fate was decreed. A brief Act temporarily permitting the use of the lash was passed in a single day almost without opposition. It followed that, when the battalion sailed for Aden, with out-stations at Perim and Socotra, it left few prisoners behind, but took with it many men who were unable to wear their knapsacks during the journey by river from Millbank to the Albert Docks. It is needless to add that the revelations of an informer had enabled the General to make the dispositions which were so quietly effectual; they would have taken a wider range but that the informer was not cognisant of the arrangement for a simultaneous rising between the Scarlet Hussars and the Guards battalion.

A FORGOTTEN REBELLION

The following Reuter's telegram was published in the morning papers of the 12th February 1889: "Melbourne, February 11th. The death is announced of Mr. Peter Lalor, formerly Speaker of the Victorian Legislative Assembly."

Some nine years ago, during the course of a visit to the Antipodes, I happened to spend some time in Her Majesty's and Lord Normanby's (the Vice-King of Victoria for the time being) loyal and prosperous city of Melbourne. One afternoon I strolled into the public gallery of the hall in the big pile at the head of Collins Street West, on the floor of which are held the momentous deliberations of that august assembly, the Lower House of the Victorian Legislature. Aloft on the daïs in his chair of state I beheld the Speaker of the Victorian Commons, a short, plump, one-armed gentleman in court dress; swarthy of feature, lips full, chin indicative of some power, with a bright, moist eye, and a countenance whose general expression was of unctuous contentment and sly humour. In answer to my question, my neighbour on the bench of the gallery informed me that the gentleman whom I was regarding with interest was the Hon. Peter Lalor, an Irishman of course—that his name betokened—a man held in high repute by his fellow-colonists, a scholar, an eloquent orator, and possessed of great political influence, which he always exerted in the furtherance of steady moderation and sound legislation. It occurred to me to inquire of my neighbour if he knew how Mr. Lalor came to be short of an arm, the reply to which question was that he believed he had lost it in some trouble on the gold-fields in the early days, the true story of which my informant had "never rightly learned." Subsequently I frequently met Mr. Lalor, and conceived for him a great liking. We used to meet at a little evening club off Bourke Street, and the worthy Speaker, as often as not still in the old-fashioned single-breasted coat of the court dress which he had worn in the chair of the Legislative Assembly, smoked his pipe, drank his stiff nobbler of Irish whisky, sang his song, and told stories always droll and often very interesting, chiefly of his experiences on the gold-fields in the early "surface-diggings" days. But he never alluded to the way in which he had lost his arm, and it grew upon me in a gradual sort of way that the topic was one which he would prefer should not be introduced.

It is the strange truth that this douce elderly gentleman, this high functionary of the Colonial Legislature, was, in the year of grace 1854, the commander-in-chief of an armed force in a state of declared rebellion and fighting under an insurrectionary flag against an attack made upon it by regular troops in the service of Queen Victoria. It was in the far from bloodless combat of the "Eureka Stockade" that he had lost his arm—the loss caused by a hostile bullet; and but that, wounded as he was, he escaped and lay hidden while recovering from the amputation, he would have stood in the dock where many of his comrades did stand, undergoing his trial on the charge of high treason, as they actually underwent theirs.

I do not believe that in all the world, the United States of America not excepted, any community has ever progressed with a swiftness and expansion so phenomenal as has the colony which Her Gracious Majesty permitted to take her own name when she granted it a separate existence in November 1850. It had been but fifteen years earlier that the first settlers—the brothers Henty, one of whom died only a few years ago—came across Bass Straits from Van Diemen's Land in their little *Thistle*. In 1837 the town of Melbourne was laid out, and one hundred allotments were then sold on what are now the principal streets. The aggregate sum which the hundred allotments fetched was £3410. Two summers ago the same allotments were carefully valued by experts, and it was calculated that, exclusive of the buildings erected on them, they could now be sold for nineteen and a half million pounds. This stupendous increment has accrued in half a century, but in effect the appreciation has almost wholly occurred during the last thirty-five years. Before 1851, when the gold discoveries were made, Victoria prospered in an easy gentle fashion. Its scanty population, outside its two petty towns, were wholly engaged in stock-raising; almost its sole exports were wool, hides, and tallow. The gold-find upset as by a whirlwind the lazy, primitive social system of the bucolic era. From all the ends of the earth, gentle and simple, honest man and knave, hurried swarming and jostling to the new El Dorado. Mr. Ruxton, one of the Colonial historians, omits to particularise the reputable elements of the immigration deluge, but in his caricatured Macaulay-ese, he zealously catalogues the detrimental and dangerous accessions. "From California," he writes, "came wild men, the waifs of societies which had submitted to or practised lynch law. The social festers of France, Italy, and Germany shed exfoliations upon Australia. The rebellious element of Ireland was there. The disappointed crew who thought to frighten the British Isles from their propriety in 1848 were represented in some strength. The convict element of Australia completed the vile ingredients." And yet it was wonderful how small was the actual crime of a serious character, when the utter disintegration of restraining institutions is taken into consideration. In January 1852, when daily shiploads of gold-mad immigrants were being thrown into Melbourne, only two of the city constables remained at their duty. The chief constable himself had to go on a beat. In the country the rural police to a man had forsaken their functions and made haste to the diggings. In the first rush the capital was all but depopulated of its manhood; there remained behind but the women and children, who had to shift for themselves. An advance of 50 per cent of salary did not avail to retain at their desks the officials in the public offices. Servants had gone. Gentlemen and ladies had to carry water from the river for household purposes, for the water-cart supply had been arrested by the departure of the carters. It was said that poor Mr. Latrobe himself, the amiable but weak Lieutenant-Governor, had to black his own boots and groom his own horse. In the wholesale absence of workmen no contract could be insisted on. The squatters shuddered, too, as the shearing season approached, knowing that all the shearers were digging or cradling in Forest Creek, or on Mount Alexander. It was then that Mr. Childers, who at the time was an immigration agent, made his famous bull:

"Wages of wool-pressers, 7s. to 8s. a day; none to be had." To such an extent did prices rise that there was the danger lest Government could not afford to supply food to prisoners in gaol. A contractor for gaol necessaries claimed and got 166 per cent over his prices of the year before, and, notwithstanding this stupendous increase, had to default. In April 1852 fifty ships were lying useless in Hobson's Bay, deserted by their crews. Carriage from Melbourne to Castlemaine was at one time £100 per ton.

Diggers who had "struck it rich" came down to Melbourne for a spree, and it was a caution how they made the money fly. The barber I employed used to tell me how the lucky diggers would chuck him a sovereign for a shave, and scorn the idea of change. A rough fellow called a cab in Bourke Street and wanted to engage it for the day; the cabman replied that the charge would be seven pounds, which he supposed was more than the digger would care to pay. "What is the price of the outfit as it stands, yourself included?" demanded the latter, and forthwith bought the said "outfit" for £150. When a digger and the lady he proposed temporarily to marry went into the draper's shop, the only question asked was whether the tradesman had no goods dearer than those he had shown. Ten-pound notes were quite extensively used as pipe-lights.

The additional expenditure entailed on the Colonial Government by the immense increase to the Colony's population, by the enhanced cost of administration, and by the added charges for the maintenance of order, it was perfectly fair should be met by a tribute levied in some manner on the gold the quest for and the yield of which had occasioned the necessity. An export duty would have met the case with the minimum of expense in collection and of friction, but Latrobe and his advisers preferred the expedient of exacting from each individual miner a monthly fee for the license permitting him to dig.

While the gold-field population was small, the license system, although from the beginning hated as an oppressive exaction, did not excite active hostility. Every digger was bound to produce his license on demand; but the officer or trooper charged with the inquisition did not need to put it in force oftener than once a month in a community pretty well every member of which he knew by sight. But with the swarms of new-comers the facility for evasion and the difficulty of detection were alike increased. In the throng of thousands, the demand for production of the license might be repeated frequently, and give not wholly unreasonable umbrage to the busy digger. It naturally angered a man digging against time at the bottom of a hole, to have to scramble out and show his license; it angered him worse to be peremptorily sent for it to his tent if he had omitted to bring it along with him. And if the license could not be produced at all, the defaulter was summarily haled away to be dealt with according to the bye-laws. Men were to be seen standing chained in "the camp," as the Gold Commissioner's quarters were called, waiting for their punishment.

The license fee at first was £1:10s. a month. As expenses increased Mr. Latrobe notified its increase to double that amount. Neither sum hurt the lucky digger who was down among the nuggets; but the smaller tariff was a strain on the unsuccessful man, with food at famine prices and every necessary costing wellnigh its weight in gold. The doubled impost was declared a tyranny to be resisted; the lower one an injustice only tolerated on sufferance. Violent meetings were held at Forest Creek and elsewhere, at which the new tax was vigorously denounced; and poor Mr. Latrobe cancelled the order for it before it had come into effect. He could not help himself; had he been prepared to go to extremities, he had inadequate strength, with a handful of soldiers at his disposal, to enforce the enactment. But, spite of his temporising, a bitter feeling grew between the miners and the gold-field officials. The Commissioner at Forest Creek burned the tent of a camp trader, on a perjured charge of illicit spirit-selling brought by an informer. Then followed an excited public meeting, and the gold-field was placarded with notices: "Down with the troopers! Shoot them! Down with oppression! Diggers, avenge your wrongs! Cry 'no quarter,' and show no mercy!"

The informer was convicted of perjury and the authorities compensated the burnt-out trader, but the ill-feeling was not mitigated. A deputation of miners waited on the Governor to report the irritation engendered by collection of the license fees by "armed men, many of whom were of notoriously bad character"; to complain of the chaining to trees and logs of non-possessors of licenses, and their being sentenced to hard labour on the roads; and to demand the reduction of the fee to 10s. a month. Mr. Latrobe simply told the deputation he would consider the petition; and the deputation went out from his presence to attend a public meeting of Melbourne citizens convened by the Mayor. There some of the delegates spoke with threatening frankness. "What they wanted, they would have; if peacefully, well: if not, a hundred thousand diggers would march like a ring of fire upon Melbourne, and take and act as they listed." Under threat Mr. Latrobe yielded, and announced that for the month of September no compulsory means would be adopted for the enforcement of the license fee; at the same time inconsistently sending to Forest Creek a detachment of regular soldiers which had reached him.

In the beginning of 1854, not before it was time, the weak and vacillating Latrobe was succeeded as Governor of Victoria by the more peremptory Hotham, who was not long in office before he issued a circular ordering the gold-fields police to make a strenuous and systematic search after unlicensed miners, and soon after concentrated several hundred regular soldiers at Ballarat, the centre of a densely thronged gold-field, where an incident had exasperated the chronic irritation of the diggers caused by the rigorous enforcement of the license inquisition. In a Ballarat slum a digger was killed in a scuffle by a fellow named Bentley, an ex-convict who kept a low public-house. The police magistrate before whom Bentley was brought promptly dismissed the charge. He was proved to be habitually corrupt, and there was no doubt that he had been bribed by Bentley's friends. The miners, enraged by the immunity from punishment of the murderer of one of themselves, gathered in masses round Bentley's public-house, and sacked and burned it in spite of the efforts of the police to hinder them. Hotham dealt out what he considered even justice all round. He dismissed from office the corrupt magistrate; he had Bentley tried and convicted of manslaughter; and he sent to gaol for considerable terms the ringleaders of the mob who had burnt that fellow's house. The jurymen who reluctantly found them guilty added the rider, that they would have been spared their painful duty "if those entrusted with the government of Ballarat had done their duty."

The conviction of their comrades infuriated the miners, and thenceforward their attitude was that of virtual rebellion. A "Ballarat Reform League" was promptly formed, whose avowed platform it was "to resist, and if necessary to remove, the irresponsible power which tyrannised over them." The League was not yet indeed eager for an "immediate separation from the parent country ... but if Queen Victoria continues to act upon the ill advice of dishonest Ministers ... the League will endeavour to supersede the royal prerogative, by asserting that of the people, which is the most royal of all prerogatives." The leading spirits of the League were of curiously diverse nationalities. Vern was a Hanoverian, Raffaello an Italian, Joseph a negro from the United States, Lalor—Peter Lalor, my friend of the Speaker's chair, the court suit, and the one arm—was of course an Irishman, H. Holyoake (socialist), Hayes, Humfrays, and others were Englishmen. Delegates were despatched to the other gold-fields to bring in accessions of disaffected diggers. Holyoake went to Sandhurst; Black and Kennedy to Creswick. With drawn sword in hand, Black led into Ballarat the Creswick contingent, marching to their chant of the "Marseillaise."

On 29th November more than 12,000 miners gathered in mass meeting on "Bakery Hill," just outside Ballarat. An insurrectionary flag was unfurled, and one of the leaders who advised "moral force" was hooted down as a trimmer. Peter Lalor, at that time in the enjoyment of both his arms, made himself conspicuous at this meeting, which ended with shots of defiance and a bonfire of the obnoxious licenses. But the miners, although they had pretty well by this time drawn the sword, had not yet thrown away the scabbard. Governor Hotham was a resolute man, and had the full courage of his opinions. He had concentrated at Ballarat about 450 regular soldiers and armed police, the command of which force he had given to Captain Thomas of the 40th Regiment, with instructions "to use force when legally called upon to do so, without regard to the consequences which might ensue." As his retort to the "Bakery Hill" manifesto, he sent instructions that the license inquisitions should be more diligently enforced than ever. If he were convinced that the trouble must be brought to the definite issue of bloodshed as the inevitable prelude to the tranquillity of the defeated, he probably acted wisely in this; and doubtless he had calculated the risk that might attend this policy of forcing the game. One of the Gold-Field Commissioners, duly escorted by police, went out from the camp on the 30th, on the hunt after unlicensed miners. He and his police were vigorously stoned; more police came on the ground led by a specially resolute Commissioner. He ordered the diggers to disperse; they would not; so he read the Riot Act, and sent for the soldiers. Shots were fired—it is not said that anybody was wounded by them; but a policeman had his head cut open. The mob dispersed, and the Commissioner triumphed in making sundry miners show their licenses.

It was then that war was declared, at a mass meeting held on the "Bakery Hill" on the afternoon of the 30th. Who was to command? Peter Lalor, fired by enthusiasm—sarcastic persons have hinted at whisky—volunteered for the duty, and was nominated Commander-in-Chief by acclamation. Hundreds swore to follow and obey him. Drilling was immediately commenced. Lalor was said to have recommended pikes to those who had no firearms. The words attributed to him were that the pikes would "pierce the tyrants' hearts." He set himself systematically to requisition horses, arms, food, and drink, designating himself in the receipts he gave as "Commander-in-Chief of the Diggers under arms."

After the 30th there was no more digging for a time on any gold-field in the vicinity of Ballarat. A reinforcement of soldiers for Thomas was reported on the way from Melbourne, and patriots were sent into the roads to notify its approach so that it might be intercepted. Arms and ammunition were taken wherever found, and a thousand armed men paraded Ballarat in full sight of the camp, robbing stores, forcibly enrolling recruits, and seizing arms. It was reported that the camp—the enclosure in which were quartered the authorities, the soldiers, and the police—was to be assailed in force, and on the night of 1st December dropping shots were actually fired into it. Captain Thomas forbade reprisals. Like Brer Rabbit he "lay low." The world wondered why the Thiers Government in Versailles delayed so long to give the word to the troops to go at the Communards in Paris. The delay was at the suggestion of Bismarck. "Keep the trap open," he said in effect, "till all the anarchical ruffianhood of Europe shall have gathered inside it; the time to close it is when the influx of scoundrels ceases. Once in we have them to a man; nobody can get out—the German cordon prevents that." Captain Thomas, in a small way, reasoned on the Bismarckian lines. He refrained from attacking while as yet the miners were straggling all over the place, and waited calmly, spite of provocation and appeals to do otherwise, until they should have concentrated themselves into a mass.

Lalor, however, was not drifting around Ballarat; he was seriously attending to his duty as rebel "Commander-in-Chief." The summit of Eureka Hill, about a mile and a half from the town, was rather a commanding position, and there he was engaged in the construction of a hasty fortification with entrenchments and other obstacles, such as ropes, slabs, stakes, and overturned carts. This construction is known in the history of the Colony as the "Eureka Stockade." Captain Thomas did not allow the rebel chief much time in which to elaborate his defences. He kept his own counsel rigorously until after midnight of 2d December; at half-past two on the morning of the 3d he led out to the assault of the "Eureka Stockade" a force consisting of 100 mounted men, part soldiers, part police, 152 infantry soldiers of the line, and 24 foot police; all told, 276 men exclusive of officers. Approaching the stockade he sent the horsemen round to threaten the rebel position in flank and rear, while his infantry moved on the front of the entrenchment. The defenders were on the alert. At 150 yards distance a sharp fire, without previous challenge, rattled among the soldiers. Thomas ordered his bugler to sound "Commence firing," sent the skirmishers forward rapidly, caught them up with the supports, and rushed the defences with the words "Come on, Fortieth!" The entrenchment was carried with wild hurrahs, "and a body of men with pikes was immolated under the eye of the commander before the bugle to cease firing recalled the soldiers from the work to which they had been provoked. The rebel flag was hauled down with cheers, all found within the entrenchment were captured, and some of the many fugitives were intercepted by the cavalry."

The insurrection was at an end. About thirty diggers had been killed on the spot, several subsequently died of wounds, and 125 were taken prisoners. Of the attacking force an officer and a soldier were killed, and thirteen men were wounded, some mortally. The military were promptly reinforced from Melbourne, and martial law was proclaimed, but resistance had been quite stamped out with the fall of the "Stockade." A commission of inquiry was sent to the gold-fields without delay, and its report recommended a general amnesty (to include the prisoners awaiting trial) and the modified abolition of the license fee. Nevertheless some of the Eureka "insurgents" were arraigned on the charge of high treason, but in every case the Melbourne juries brought in a verdict of acquittal, and therefore no steps were taken to apprehend their comrades who had escaped and were in hiding. The amnesty was complete, although never formally proclaimed. Peter Lalor, for whose apprehension a reward of £200 had been offered, affably emerged from the concealment into which he had been so fortunate as to escape from the stockade. While lying perdu, one of his arms, which had been smashed by a bullet in the brief action, had been skilfully amputated, and Peter had made a satisfactory recovery. During his retirement he wrote a defence of his conduct, and claimed that, as hour after hour of the eventful night passed without an attack, the greater number of the 1500 defenders who were in the stockade until midnight had gone away to bed, so that when the attack was made there actually remained in the enclosure only about 120 men. He expressed the frankest regret that "we were unable to inflict on the real authors of the outbreak the punishment they so richly deserved." A year after he emerged from hiding, the one-armed ex-rebel was returned to Parliament by a mining constituency. Thus he ranged himself, and five-and-twenty years later was sitting in a court dress in the chair of the Legislative Assembly of the Colony.

MY CAMPAIGN IN PALL MALL

For better or for worse, the war correspondent, as regards a British army in the field, has been stamped out. The journalist who now accompanies an army is a war reporter. He dances in the fetters of the censorship, whose power over him is absolute: it may not only detain or withhold his work, but at discretion may alter it so that he may be made to say the direct reverse of what he wrote. If the position has its humiliations, it also has its compensations. The censorship which makes a slave of the war reporter, *ipso facto* relieves him of all the responsibility for the words he writes. His waking hours are unclouded by forebodings of aspersions on his veracity, emanating from officials chafing under inconvenient interpellations. His slumbers are disturbed by no dream-vision of a bad quarter of an hour with the chief of staff, when the paper containing that outspoken telegram of his arrives in camp. The authorities in Pall Mall, by the institution of the rules and the censorship, have indeed scotched the war journalist, but have not succeeded in killing him. Lord Wolseley in the early editions of the *Soldier's Pocket-book* described the war correspondent of the unreformed era as "the curse of modern armies"; that somewhat strenuous expression he retains in the latest edition as still applicable to the reporter who works under the yoke of the regulations set forth in its pages. I may humbly venture to remark, having given the matter considerable attention, that from the military point of view I entirely concur in Lord Wolseley's objections to the presence of journalistic persons with an army in the field against a civilised enemy. Were I a general, and had I an independent command in war offered me, I should accept it only on condition that I should have the charter to shoot every war correspondent found within fifty miles of my headquarters. The most careful correspondent cannot write a sentence—a sentence which the strictest censor, if he is to pass anything at all, cannot refrain from sanctioning—that may not give a hint to the astute intelligence-officials of the other side. This fact I realised at the beginning of my career, and my conviction of its truth grew till the end of it. What then? It is not a question for the newspapers, which dread a war because of the huge expense it entails without adequate compensation. It is a question solely for the public, whose servants the general and the war journalists alike are. If the public deliberately prefers news to victories—for that is the issue in a nutshell as regards a European war—then on the head of the public be it.

The war correspondent of the era that ended with the introduction of the handcuffs had a chequered lot. His fetterless condition gave him many advantages and some opportunities. He could stir the nation by his revelations of mal-administration. Uncompelled to specified and conventional methods of communication, he might win some fleeting fame by sending to his countrymen the earliest tidings of a victory achieved by their army, at the cost of some toil and danger incurred by the courier-correspondent. On the other side of the account was this unpleasantness, that if he were not a toady and a sycophant, but an independent man, he could hardly escape being regarded as an Ishmaelite, against whom in the very nature of things was the great heavy hand of officialdom. He had constantly to confront that kind of contemptuous contradiction which is equivalent to impugnment of the veracity of the person contradicted. Of late years it is true, for weighty reasons, there has been discernible in the tone of official contradictions a droll infusion of funk in the insolence. The insolence was, of course, in the very essence of the official nature; the funk came from a nervous foreboding of refutation begotten of experience. That experience did not deter, because the average official shudders, as if it were sheer revolution, at a departure from the old arrogant use and wont; but it had a tendency to engender disquietude in the bureaucratic breast.

A man must either be well endowed with philosophy, or, to quote a historic witness, must be "on very good terms with himself," who is not galled by a contumelious aspersion of untruthfulness thrown on him from high places and circulated throughout the length and breadth of the land. He may have his vindication to his hand, but it rarely has the vogue of the calumny. In some memorable instances, however, this has been the case. Before the Crimean war was over, England had come to recognise that it was the pen of William Howard Russell which had saved her army from extinction. Lord Beaconsfield, when he tried the *de haut en bas* method of whistling truth down the wind, and sneered at MacGahan's revelations of Turkish barbarities in Bulgaria as "coffee-house babble," found himself conclusively confuted by Mr. Walter Baring's intensification of the unofficial disclosures. But in the game between him and the correspondent the official plays with cogged dice. Let me give an instance. That portion of the public who believed Lord Wolseley accepted his denial of the truth of the assertions made by Dr. Russell regarding the excesses of our troops in the Transvaal between the close of the Zulu war and the beginning of the Boer war. Those most conversant with the circumstances were aware that the statements made by Russell were substantially accurate, but Lord Wolseley roundly pronounced them utterly destitute of foundation. Now it happened that Russell—strange omission on the part of a journalist of his experience—had neglected to fortify himself with evidence which he should be able to adduce if challenged. A man of high spirit and implicit veracity, the imputation cast on him roused him to just indignation, and he was bent on making good his words. But the effort was futile; Landrost after Landrost testified with complaisant unanimity to the immaculateness of the British soldier. Russell had to grin and bear the situation; but he spoke his mind on the subject in the direct manner which is his characteristic.

I recall a little experience of my own, which ended for me, perhaps because I am a Scot whereas he is an Irishman, more successfully than did Russell's Transvaal controversy. When the brigade of British troops landed in Cyprus, with which he took possession of that island in 1878, Lord Wolseley sent it to encamp on the ridge of Chiflik Pasha, a few miles inland from Larnaca. There sickness soon set in among the soldiers with great severity. The disorder was that insidious complaint known as "Cyprus fever," which has long since disappeared from Cyprus itself, but which still harbours in the constitution of most of those who were of the expedition of original occupation. Accompanying that expedition in a journalistic capacity, for a fortnight or so previous to August 15 I had been telegraphing to the *Daily News* increasingly serious details regarding the ill-health of the troops. On that day I wired: "In all about 25 per cent of the whole force are fever-stricken; about two-thirds of the medical staff are also down." On the following afternoon a question was put in the House of Commons on the subject to the Secretary for War. Colonel Stanley replied by quoting a telegram from Lord Wolseley stating that "only about six per cent of the troops were in hospital"; which was literally true, since the hospitals could hold no more, and, being literally true, was quite smart, although utterly misleading. Of course the minister inculcated belief in the official version; and equally, of course, he had his airy little gibe at the non-official person. It was not until August 26, being then at Malta on my way home, that I saw a newspaper containing the question and answer in Parliament. Then I straightway telegraphed to my journal repeating my previous statements in detail, giving as my authorities for them the respective medical officers of the brigade, and adding: "Assertion and counter-assertion are childish in a matter wherein the documents furnish exact and detailed information. The Secretary for War will find that the official returns sent in to the Principal Medical Officer on the evening of the day in question amply bear out my statements." Yet officialism had the best of it after all. Parliament had risen before the telegram I have quoted reached England, and so no Parliamentary friend had the opportunity of enforcing the minister's admission of the accuracy of my statement by moving for the production of the returns.

In one curious instance a set was made at a war correspondent, not by officialism, but by the many-headed itself. He was with the force that was confronting Arabi in the Kafre Dowr position outside Alexandria during the interval between the bombardment of that city and the arrival in Egypt of Lord Wolseley's reinforcements. One afternoon his paper brought out a "special edition" on the strength of a telegram from him to the effect that one of the pickets of our force had run in on its supports. Whether or not the telegram was "written up" in Fleet Street, is a question which need not be dwelt on, in the face of the fact that the correspondent did not deny that he had sent intelligence of the misbehaviour of the picket. It was passing strange, the gust of popular indignation against this penman—in this particular matter at least a quite inoffensive although in a professional sense silly person. The angry nation would not have it at any price that a picket of British soldiers could act as described. The correspondent was denounced far and wide as the vilest of calumniators. *Punch* pandered to the undignified and perverse clamour in some doggerel jingle; the correspondent's journal temporised in the face of the storm, and cashiered its representative. Yet his act was in no way blameworthy; it was simply officious and superfluous. Such a trifle as the casual bolt of a picket was an incident which a correspondent who had ever seen war—and this man had made a previous campaign—should have ignored as not worth chronicling. In war such petty fallings away from the ideal are happening all the time. They occur in every army I have ever known, and I have watched the conduct in the field of the armies of eight European nations. There is infinitely less steady valour in the soldiery of any nationality than the civilian who idealises it imagines. I never was in a battle, with the single exception of Ulundi, in the course of which I did not witness a stampede. The Germans are grand fighting men, and at Gravelotte they had the glow in them of three victories in a fortnight; yet in the afternoon of that day there was a sudden panic in Steinmetz's army—one half of it at least was on the run; and I saw old Wilhelm borne back in the *débâcle*, resisting vehemently, belabouring the runaways with the flat of his sword, and abusing them with fine racy German oaths shouted at the top of his voice. Nevertheless the Germans won the battle of Gravelotte. Our own fellows have never been in the habit of evincing inability to hold their own against no matter what foe. But for all that they are not uniformly heroes, and it is folly to believe that they are. I am not the man, an old soldier myself, to run down the British soldier; but the cheap froth of the cockalorum civilian disgusts me. I who write say that I have known British pickets, like the pickets of other nations, run in discreditably once and again. For instance, on the evening before Ginghilovo, when a picket of one of our crack regiments bolted back into the position headed by its sergeant, leaving its officer the sole defender of the abandoned ground. For instance, on the night but one before Ulundi, when a picket of Wood's most seasoned regiment, a regiment that had distinguished itself grandly at Kambula, scuttled into the laager in uncontrollable scare. It was in each case a momentary panic. No doubt the first-named picket behaved quite well in the fight next day. As for Wood's fellows, he gave them five-and-twenty apiece; they got their tunics on their sore backs in time for Ulundi, were as good as the best there, and, in virtue of the flogging and the victory together, regained their good name. I knew personally of this little accident in Wood's force; but it never occurred to me to report it. It was not that I shunned doing so, but simply because the thing was not worth while. My comrade, with his experience, should have taken the same view of the petty mischance he happened to witness in Egypt; but it was sheer truculence to hound him down because he looked at events microscopically.

I am anxious to quote a correspondence which seems to me to illustrate, not a little vividly, the tergiversations and tortuosities of officialdom in its relations with the war correspondent; but it is impossible to make the letters intelligible without an amount of egotism which is eminently distasteful to me. The desire, however, to make public the correspondence outweighs the repugnance to being egotistic, and accordingly I proceed.

After the decisive victory of Ulundi gained over the Zulus on July 4, 1879, I quitted the same evening the laager in which Lord Chelmsford's army was encamped, and, after a continuous ride of about seventeen hours, reached the telegraph-wire at Landmann's Drift with the earliest news. Thence I telegraphed to Sir Bartle Frere at Cape Town, and to Sir Garnet Wolseley, then on his way to Port Durnford on the Zululand coast, a brief summary of the action and the result. Both those officials telegraphed me thanks in reply. Sir Garnet's expression of his "sincere thanks for the most welcome news" was naturally most grateful to me, as he was the Commander-in-Chief of all the forces then in the field. No further intelligence than that which I had wired him reached Sir Bartle Frere before the departure of the mail, and it was my message to him which was read in both Houses of Parliament as the only intelligence which up to date had reached the home authorities. The question of a member, whether some recognition was not due to the bringer, under somewhat arduous circumstances, of tidings so welcome was negatived by Sir Stafford Northcote with the remark that the bearer was a newspaper correspondent who had toiled and adventured in the interest of his journal. As it happened, this was a mistake. When on the evening of the fight, in accordance with previous arrangement, I took to Lord Chelmsford's headquarter the packet containing my short description of the day's work, I had not the remotest idea that half an hour later I should be galloping through the lonely bush on my way to the telegraph-office on the far-distant Natal frontier. There was no hurry to catch the mail, and there was then no telegraphic communication between South Africa and England. My colleagues who remained in camp and sent away their matter at their leisure next day, were in easy time for the outgoing mail from Cape Town. I rode out of the Umvaloosi laager that night because I have a quick temper and a disgust for military ineptitude. When Lord Chelmsford told me that he did not intend to despatch his courier until next morning, the assigned reason being the absence of some petty details, it was in the angry impulse of the moment that I passionately exclaimed, "Then, sir, I will start myself at once!" I knew with what anxiety Wolseley was waiting for news, and what immediate influence on his plans the tidings of the day's work would have; and I realised, too, the spirit that actuated the delay in their despatch. I was sorry for myself the moment I had spoken, for I needed no one to tell me the risks in front of me. I got through safely; the same night, not five hundred yards off the faint track along which I groped, Lieutenant Scott Douglas and Corporal Cotter were slaughtered with unmentionable barbarity. It should be said that when Sir Stafford Northcote was shown that it was not "in the interest of my paper" that I had ridden from Ulundi to Landmann's Drift, he acknowledged the error with the manly frankness which was but one of the fine features of a noble character.

I had sworn to my hurt, but unless I ate dirt there could be no withdrawal. When, before starting, I went to Sir Evelyn Wood to ask for his home messages, he would have detained me, but that in a word I told him how I must go; he understood, bade me Godspeed, and let me go. There was no sentiment about his limb of an aide-de-camp—"the boy," as we called him. As I turned from Wood's tent "the boy" shouted an offer to bet me five pounds I would not get through. "Done!" I cried. "Ah!" quoth "the boy," with a regard for his pound of flesh beyond his years, "you must put the money down, for I don't in the least expect to see you back again." So I posted my fiver and rode away into the dense all but trackless bush, just as the great red sun touched the westward ridge overhanging the Umvaloosi gorge.

I had "got through" and been back in England some time, when it occurred to me to claim the Zulu medal. A war medal is not a decoration in the sense that the Albert medal, or the "C.I.E." or the "D.S.O.," or that proud symbol the "C.M.G.," is a decoration. The medal for a campaign once granted, a military person of whatever rank is entitled to it as a right who has been inside hostile territory in the course of the campaign; he need not have been under fire, or indeed within miles of a battle. In the Zulu business many got the medal who had never crossed the Natal frontier, and the whole wing of a regiment received the Ashantee medal that never disembarked at all. I found copious precedents in favour of civilians being the recipients of war medals. William Howard Russell has the Crimean and Indian medals. A British Museum *employé* who accompanied the expedition to pick up specimens for that institution received the Abyssinian medal. The Victoria Cross was given to four civilians for gallant acts in the Indian Mutiny, and the Mutiny medal to all civilians who were under fire. It was worn by a lady lately dead, who was born in the Lucknow Residency during the siege, and earned it by that achievement. I did not presume to claim the Zulu medal in virtue of having made the campaign as a correspondent, but because of a specific service for which I had received the thanks of the local commander-in-chief. True, a claim I had put in for the Afghan medal had been rejected on the specified ground that "the Secretary of State is of opinion that the service on the performance of which that claim is based was not of a character which would entitle you to the medal." But then that "service" was merely the having been mentioned in his despatch by the commanding General for saving life in action—a ground surely not to be mentioned in the same day with the acknowledgment of a superior General's gratitude. So my claim went in to the War Office based on the ride from Ulundi to the telegraph-office, and the results thereof set forth above. The not unexpected reply came back, that, "As it would appear that no application was made for your services on the occasion referred to in your letter, Mr. Childers regrets his inability to comply with your request."

I felt for Mr. Childers: it is always unpleasant to the humane man that for any reason he should cause regret to a fellow-mortal; and I believed by a further representation I could dispel his regret and enable him to rejoice in the ability of compliance. That representation was as follows. The letter (April 2, 1881) was sent from America:—

> I respectfully beg to repeat the claim, on the ground of another service to which your previous objection does not apply. On reaching Landmann's Drift, and having handed to General Marshall (in command there) the despatches which had been entrusted to me by Lord Chelmsford, he, expressing his belief that no direct communication between Lord Chelmsford and Sir Garnet Wolseley at Port Durnford could be opened up for some time, and his conviction that details as to the disposition of the troops in Zululand and of the recent action could not fail to be of consequence to the latter, requested me, as a matter of public service, to continue with all speed my journey to Port Durnford and place my knowledge of affairs within the enemy's country at Sir Garnet's disposal. In furtherance of this project General Marshall handed me a special authorisation to claim means of speedy transit along the route I should have to take. In fulfilment of this request I rode about 150 miles to Pieter Maritzburg without rest, and suffering

from a contusion sustained in the Ulundi action; and thence journeyed on with all speed to Port Durnford, reaching that place in advance of any other messenger from the column in the interior. Sir Garnet Wolseley availed himself of the information I brought, and did me the honour to thank me for the service done as being materially in the public interest.

Sir Garnet Wolseley and General Marshall confirmed the above statements in so far as they concerned each.

* * * * *

The reply to the above representation bore date June 2, 1881, and was as follows:—

> I am to inform you that Lord Chelmsford reports that he did not make any use of your services on the occasion specified by you, and on reference to General Marshall, it appears that he did not receive any despatches by you from Lord Chelmsford. Under these circumstances, and as the fact of your having ridden from Landmann's Drift to Port Durnford would not justify the grant of the decoration under existing regulations, Mr. Childers is unable to alter the decision already conveyed to you.

When Mr. Edmund Yates was resuming his seat, after having listened to the censure with which Lord Coleridge accompanied the sentence awarded him in a well-remembered action, I heard him murmur, I believe unconsciously, "That's a snorter!" A similar view of this communication suggested itself to me. It was a lesson never to write an important letter at a distance from one's diaries. While feeling sure of the ability to justify in effect the averment that I had carried despatches from Lord Chelmsford, there was a clear mistake in the statement that I had handed these to General Marshall. I had met him on my way to the telegraph-office, and had shown him the packet I carried; it was addressed to the telegraph-master, and to him I delivered it. My reply to the "snorter" was as follows:—

> I would have accepted without troubling you further your disinclination to alter your previous adverse decision, but for one circumstance. Your letter conveys a grave charge against my personal veracity, a matter of infinitely greater importance to me than the receipt or non-receipt of a medal. Writing as I did from America without access to memoranda, I erred in naming General Marshall as the recipient of the official enclosure carried by me from Ulundi. I have the honour to enclose a detailed statement of the actual events which occurred in Lord Chelmsford's headquarter, with the request that you submit the same to Lord Chelmsford and Colonel North Crealock, his lordship's military secretary; satisfied as I am that the result of such submission will be to alter the terms of Lord Chelmsford's report as conveyed in your letter.

STATEMENT ENCLOSED.

In the course of the day of the fight at Ulundi, it had been intimated to the newspaper correspondents that if they desired to forward communications to Landmann's Drift, their packets should be sent into headquarters to catch the outgoing courier the same evening. About 6 P.M. I carried my parcel to Lord Chelmsford's headquarter in the laager. I found his lordship with Colonel North Crealock, his military secretary, seated at a table under an awning. I tendered my packet, when his lordship stated that he had altered his intention as to the despatch of Mr. Dawnay that evening, because of the absence of some details from Colonel Buller's command. On hearing this I said, "Then, my lord, I shall start at once myself!" A few remarks having passed, I asked, addressing Lord Chelmsford, "Can I take anything down for you, sir?" Colonel Crealock, who had been writing hard during the brief interview, then struck in—"If you will wait five minutes, Forbes, till I have finished, I will give you this packet for Landmann's Drift." While I waited, Colonel Crealock, having finished writing, enclosed sundry papers in a large yellow "O.H.M.S." envelope, addressed it to the "Telegraph-clerk in charge, Landmann's Drift," adding the endorsement "J. North Crealock, Military Secretary," and handed the packet to me. This packet, entrusted to me by Lord Chelmsford's military secretary in his lordship's actual presence and sight, I duly conveyed to Landmann's Drift, and handed it to the official in the telegraph-office there.

The reply from the War Office to this communication was as follows:—

Colonel Crealock corroborates that portion of your statement to the effect that you conveyed an envelope for him on the occasion alluded to from Ulundi to the telegraph office at Landmann's Drift, but at the same time he emphatically denies that the envelope contained any document of a public nature, and moreover states that he explained to you that the Hon. Guy Dawnay had already been directed to take charge of the despatches when concluded. He also reports that the few words contained in the telegram to Mrs. Crealock which was enclosed in the envelope, were of such a nature as to preclude the possibility of the Director of Telegraphs supposing the message was despatched in the public service, and that he was subsequently charged with the cost of it.

Assuming that the contents of Colonel Crealock's letter were of a private character, I was none the less for that journey an official courier. What was inside the envelope was immaterial; the outside was rigorously official. The F.O. bag carried by a Queen's messenger is every whit as official when its contents are old lace and ball slippers as when they consist of despatches on whose terms hang peace or war. Again, I knew that Colonel Crealock's alleged statement must be untrue that his enclosure consisted of a "few words" and no "document of a public character." I had carried down nothing save his packet and my own written description of the battle. The telegraph official permitted me, as soon as I arrived, to despatch the few lines which reached Sir Garnet Wolseley and Sir Bartle Frere. He then was occupied for several hours in telegraphing the contents of Colonel Crealock's envelope, which, as he explained, had precedence as being official matter; and it was not until after the "many hundred words" (those were his words) to which his matter extended had been sent off, that my descriptive message was put on the wires.

It is not easy to imagine that a man can honestly confuse between a short domestic telegram and a public message many hundred words long. Be this as it may, there was no difficulty in finding unchallengeable evidence of the untruthfulness of the statements attributed to Colonel Crealock in the above letter. At Aldershot I found the R.E. officer who had been in charge of the field telegraph office at Landmann's Drift when I arrived there on July 5, and the operator who had despatched the contents of the official envelope of which I was the bearer from Ulundi. The records had been mutilated, so that documentary evidence was lacking; but the parole evidence of the officer and of the operator given in the former's hearing and mine, was conclusive. I begged Lieutenant Jones to put into writing his recollection of the circumstances, and the following is his letter:—

> I perfectly well remember seeing you arrive at Landmann's Drift on the afternoon of July 5, 1879. You brought with you, to my certain recollection, a mass of written matter, of what description I cannot quite remember, but I am sure that, whatever it was, it took precedence of your own telegram to your paper, which proves that it was what we call "service messages"—that is, on military service. This the telegrapher at Landmann's Drift also remembers well, as also the telegrapher at the transmitting station at Quagga's Kraal. The entire bulk of the messages you brought amounted to nearly 4000 words, of which not more than 1200 were your own press message, which did not go till late in the night. I regret to say the abstract books are lost or destroyed, so that I cannot quote from that evidence. My memory, however, is so clear that I am quite certain to the extent I have mentioned.

> (Signed) FRANCIS G. BOND,
Lieut. R.E.

A copy of Mr. Bond's communication I promptly forwarded to the War Office, making the following observations in the covering letter:—

> 1. I handed Mr. Bond no other matter than the official envelope I received from Colonel Crealock in Lord Chelmsford's presence, and my own press message.

> 2. I knew nothing of the contents of the said official envelope, save that they were bulky. The envelope was endorsed "J. North Crealock, Military Secretary," which, with the "O.H.M.S.," gave it, I submit, an official character, and constituted the missive a

despatch, and not a private communication, as Colonel Crealock alleges it to have been.

3. Colonel Crealock's assertion that the envelope entrusted to me contained merely a telegram to his wife is utterly incompatible with the facts detailed in Mr. Bond's letter, and confirmed by the personal testimony of the operators. Mr. Bond and they agree that the "service messages" handed in by me amounted to 2800 words, and that they had the official precedence which would not have been granted to a private telegram addressed by an officer to his wife.

4. I have never claimed to have carried the despatch describing the engagement. My standpoint is simply, as already set forth, that I carried a service despatch entrusted to me by Lord Chelmsford's military secretary, in the presence, with the cognisance, and so with the tacit sanction of Lord Chelmsford himself. Apart from the word "Immediate," which was written on the envelope, the inference is that this despatch, whatever it was, was of urgent importance, seeing that it was given to me setting out immediately, and not reserved for Mr. Dawnay's later departure.

To this letter, which, along with its enclosure, may perhaps be regarded as of an inconvenient tenor, I have never received any reply whatsoever.

While waiting for what never came, it occurred to me to strengthen the case by asking the sapper of the R.E. telegraph train who had been the operator at Landmann's Drift, to put into writing the verbal testimony he had given to his officer and myself. In reply to the letter in which this request was made, there came to me this interesting and pregnant communication:—

> Mr. Forbes,—Your letter received. Don't you think you'd better write to me again and state something more definite as to what you are prepared to "part" for the negotiation?
>
> I'm willing to give you my recollections to as great an extent as you desire (between you and I), but you must cross the palm.— Yours,
>
> Harry Howard.

The man was utterly brazen. I wrote to him that if he chose to send me the statement I had asked for, I should accept his doing so as an evidence that he was ashamed of the letter just quoted, and would regard it as never written. "Should I not hear from you," I continued, "I shall be forced to assume that you experience no shame for having written so base a letter, and it will be my duty to forward that letter to your commanding officer." Howard's reply came by return:—

> Mr. Forbes,—You can button up your coat and take my letter round to the nearest *General's* quarters.
>
> The letter you desire you can have if you like.—Yours,

HARRY HOWARD.

He must have either been quite reckless, or what is known as a "barrack-room lawyer." I let him be, as I was not sure that there is any military law under which he could have been punished. A comfortable man, Mr. Harry Howard, to be entrusted with the despatch of an all-important message at the critical moment of a campaign, while a spy who had "crossed the palm" was waiting round the corner!

It was presently disclosed that this correspondence on the official side was from the first simply what the Germans expressively call "a blow on the water." It began with a foregone conclusion. An influential friend conversant with the circumstances wrote to the authorities representing with a certain vigour that he considered the treatment I had met with to have been ungracious and unfair. He was told in reply that, "As the Secretary of State for War considers that civilians who attach themselves to an army ought not be deemed eligible for war medals, the adverse decision with regard to Mr. Forbes must remain untouched."

This is explicit, and therefore it would not have been in accordance with official tradition to have simply intimated the *à priori* resolution to me when I sent in my claim.

THE END.

Lector House believes that a society develops through a two-fold approach of continuous learning and adaptation, which is derived from the study of classic literary works spread across the historic timeline of literature records. Therefore, we aim at reviving, repairing and redeveloping all those inaccessible or damaged but historically as well as culturally important literature across subjects so that the future generations may have an opportunity to study and learn from past works to embark upon a journey of creating a better future.

This book is a result of an effort made by Lector House towards making a contribution to the preservation and repair of original ancient works which might hold historical significance to the approach of continuous learning across subjects.

HAPPY READING & LEARNING!

LECTOR HOUSE LLP
E-MAIL: lectorpublishing@gmail.com